12454

MOUNTAINEERING IN SCOTLAND

ROCK

W. H. Murray on Buachaille Etive Mor

W. H. MURRAY

MOUNTAINEERING
IN
SCOTLAND

Illustrated with
32 pages of photographs
and 5 pages of
maps and diagrams

LONDON
J. M. DENT & SONS LTD.

Made in Great Britain
by
The Temple Press · Letchworth · Herts.
First published 1947

THERE is a region of heart's desire
  free for the hand that wills;
land of the shadow and haunted spire,
land of the silvery glacier fire,
land of the cloud and the starry choir,
  magical land of hills;
loud with the crying of winds and streams,
thronged with the fancies and fears of dreams.

There are perils of knightly zest
  fit for the warrior's craft;
pitiless giants with rock-bound crest,
mystical wells for the midnight rest,
ice-crowned castles and halls, to test
  steel with the ashen shaft;
realms to be won by the well-swung blow,
rest to be earned from the yielding foe.

Frosted cities of timeless sleep
  wait for the errant knight;
kingly forest and frowning steep,
spirits of mist and of fathomless deep,
snow-winged dragons of fear that keep
  watch o'er each virgin height;
treasure of dawn and a crown of stars
his who can shatter the frozen bars.

All that the wanderer's heart can crave,
  life lived thrice for its lending,
hermit's vigil in dreamlit cave,
gleams of the vision that Merlin gave,
comrades till death, and a wind-swept grave,
  joy of the journey's ending:—
Ye who have climbed to the great white veil,
heard ye the chant?   Saw ye the Grail?

(From the Collected Poems of Geoffrey
Winthrop Young.)

Acknowledgments

Many people have helped me to produce this book, but I want especially to thank the following:

The members of the Junior Mountaineering Club of Scotland, who taught me to climb.

Mr. Edward R. Zenthon, for drawing all maps and diagrams.

Mr. Geoffrey Winthrop Young, for permission to use by way of introduction four stanzas from *Knight Errantry* (Collected Poems).

The Editor of the *Scottish Mountaineering Club Journal*, for permission to reproduce in Chapters VII, XVII, XX, and XXII, matter which he had previously published.

The Editor of *Open Air in Scotland*, for permission to reproduce in Chapters XIII and XIV matter which he had previously published.

All the photographers, whose names are given elsewhe.e, for their generosity and readiness in helping me.

Mr. E. F. Bozman and the Editorial Department of Messrs. J. M. Dent & Sons Ltd., for giving me invaluable advice, which had the result of improving my book.

W. H. MURRAY.

Contents

Illustrations

Photographs

MAPS AND DIAGRAMS

The maps on pages 113, 151, and 211 are based upon the Ordnance Map with the sanction of the Controller of H.M.S.O.

The Routes

WALL AND SLAB CLIMBS

SUMMER   Cioch Direct .   .   . The Cuillin
            Rubicon Wall .   .   . Ben Nevis
            Slav Route   .   .   . Ben Nevis

WINTER Agag's Groove   .   .   { The Rannoch Wall of Buachaille Etive Mor

RIDGES

SUMMER   B C Rib .   .   .   . Cir Mhor
            East Ridge of Sgurr Dubh . The Cuillin
            Tough-Brown Ridge   . Lochnagar

WINTER Crowberry Ridge   .   . Buachaille Etive Mor
            Observatory Ridge .   . Ben Nevis
            Tower Ridge .   .   . Ben Nevis

BUTTRESSES

SUMMER   Church Door Buttress . Bidean nam Bian
            North Buttress of Sgurr
               Alisdair   .   .   . The Cuillin
            Parallel Buttress   .   . Lochnagar

WINTER Central Buttress of Stob
               Coire nam Beith .   . Bidean nam Bian
            D-gully Buttress   .   . Buachaille Etive Mor
            North Buttress   .   . Buachaille Etive Mor

GULLIES

SUMMER	Clachaig Gully . .	Sgor nam Fiannaidh
	Raven's Gully . . .	Buachaille Etive Mor
WINTER	Crowberry Gully . .	Buachaille Etive Mor
	Gardyloo Gully . .	Ben Nevis
	S C Gully . . .	Stob Coire nan Lochan

CHIMNEYS

SUMMER	Crack of Doom . .	The Cuillin
	Crypt Route . . .	The Church Door of Bidean nam Bian
WINTER	Deep-cut Chimney . .	Stob Coire nam Beith

SUMMIT RIDGES

SUMMER	A 'chir Ridge . . .	Arran
	Blaven	Skye
	Coire Lagain . . .	Skye
	Cuillin Main Ridge . .	Skye
WINTER	Aonach Eagach . .	Glencoe

PLATEAUX

WINTER	Braeriach and Cairn Toul .	The Cairngorms
	Ben Nevis . . .	Lochaber

1   *Twenty-four Hours on the Cuillin*

IT WAS TEN O'CLOCK at night, in Glen Brittle. The June sun had left our little cluster of tents, which nestled behind a screen of golden broom between the Atlantic and the Cuillin. Eastward, the peaks were written along the sky in a high, stiff hand. High above us, the brown precipice of Sron na Ciche, which reacts, chameleon-like, to every subtle change of atmosphere, was dyed a bright blood-red in the setting sun.

I watched the lights fade from the rocks and white evening mist begin to creep round the hills, then I thought of having supper and retiring with a pipe to my sleeping-bag. But in this hope I had reckoned without my friend, B. H. Humble; his head, adorned by a dilapidated panama, emerged of a sudden from the door of a nearby tent. The lighted eye, the mouth upturned at the corners, the warm colour—they all bore witness to a recent brain-storm. Humble had given birth to an idea. I regarded him with profound suspicion.

'It would be a fine night for a climb,' said Humble, tentatively.

'Well,' I hastily replied, 'there's going to be no moon, no stars—it will be dark, cold, cloudy, and every cliff in mist. Granted that, it's heresy to deny that all weather's climbing weather.'

But Humble was paying no attention to me.

'We'd start right now,' said he; 'go up Coire Banachdich, rest on the main ridge, then north along the tops.'

'And what then?'

'Leave it to me. . . .' And he looked away very mysteriously.

'On this very spot,' I protested, 'is to be had a hot meal, a quiet pipe, and an eiderdown sleeping-bag.' But I was merely according the flesh its privilege of free speech. The spirit was already aloft, I was pulling on my boots. . . .

I had faith in Humble. He is one of those men who brim with an incalculable alliance of ingenuity and energy. A rock-climb in his company has all the fascination of a mystery tour; one is likely to end, not on some nearby peak, but miles from anywhere in a rarely visited mountain stronghold. And if port be not made until all hours of the day or night, at least one returns buoyed by novelties and ballasted by exhaustion. Of one thing I felt certain: there was more in his taciturnity than met the eye. I knew him. What that 'more' might be I should have to wait for time to disclose. I packed a rucksack, picked up a rope, and we bade farewell to Maitland and Higgins, the two remaining members of our party.

A June gloaming in Skye is so long-drawn-out that one may usually climb on moderate rocks until eleven o'clock. But the mist had been brewing for an hour in the corries and now over-flowed round every peak, complicating the problem of route-selection through the wilderness of screes and boulders that carpet Coire Banachdich. Up the wall that backs the corrie a winding route gives easy access to the main ridge. To find that route in mist at late twilight was another matter. Indeed it proved to be impossible.

We climbed the face by guess and by God a considerable height toward the crest, until an unavoidable traverse brought us to a square rock platform, like a balcony. The situation had a dramatic aspect that appealed to us. Below, the rocks plunged into blackness; above, they rose sheer into the mysteries of the mist. We resolved to bivouac until there was sufficient light for safe climbing.

There was just enough room on the ledge to accommodate us in comfort. Like difficulty, comfort on mountains is a term relative to the individual climber. We could stretch out at full length, heads pillowed on rope or rucksack. The hard rock made an indifferent mattress and night cloud a somewhat chill

blanket, but luckily I have the capacity to sleep at will, any time
and anywhere, and

> Weariness
> Can snore upon the flint, when resty sloth
> Finds the down pillow hard.

Humble wakened me at two a.m. The darkness was appre-
ciably less but mist still enveloped us. We could now see to
move, and in ten minutes arrived on the rim of the main
ridge, at about three thousand feet. We turned northward and
scrambled over the three tops of Sgurr na Banachdich. Immediately beyond Banachdich the ridge takes a big swing north-
east, the first curve of the horse-shoe that encloses Coruisk.
The route at this juncture was by no means easy to find; four
ridges branch downward-bound, and it is only too easy to follow
the wrong line. The compass, moreover, is untrustworthy, for
magnetic rocks on Banachdich attract the needle.

After reconnaissance we saw close by the spike of Sgurr
Thormaid, projecting like a dragon's fang through streamers of
twisting cloud. We swarmed up one side and down the other,
secure in the knowledge that our route was now correct. A
traverse of the Cuillin ridge in mist is a stirring experience. The
jagged edge, picturesque enough when clear, then astounds the
eye with a succession of distorted towers. They impend suddenly through the clouds, grim, as wild in outline as any creation
of nightmare.

At three a.m. we reached Sgurr a' Greadaidh. The dawn was
well under way and sunrise might shortly be expected. Nothing
was visible save mist, so we halted to cheer ourselves with a bite
of food. I confess that I again fell asleep, curled up on a slab
that gently tilted over the southern cliff. In a short while
Humble roused me. He was justifiably in a state of high excitement. On every hand the mist was sinking, and slowly, one
by one, each peak of the Cuillin reared a black tip through
snow-white vapour.

Never again in summer have I seen a sight so magnificent.
The clouds had now fallen to a uniform level at two thousand

five hundred feet; just sufficient to hide the linking ridges and to isolate each pinnacle of the six-mile horse-shoe. From the mainland to far beyond the Outer Hebrides this cloud-mass formed an unbroken sea. Immediately beneath our feet the surface surged and spun as though impelled by inner vortices, rising and falling like the rollers of a mid-Atlantic swell. Over the submerged cols between each mountain the ocean poured and seethed in a never-ending flow.

The grey sky was steadily changing to cornflower blue and black rock to ashen. To obtain a still finer vantage point we moved east to Sgurr a' Mhadaidh. No sooner did we reach the top than the sun rose. Down in the basin of Coruisk, the cloud-surface at once flashed into flame, as though a stupendous crucible were filled with burning silver. The twenty turrets of the Cuillin, like islands lapped by fire-foam, flushed faintly pink. The shade crimsoned. Within a space of minutes, the rocks had run the gamut of autumn leafage, 'yellow, and black, and pale, and hectic red.'

Beyond such bare words one may say little. The mind fails one how miserably and painfully before great beauty. It cannot understand. Yet it would contain more. Mercifully, it is by this very process of not understanding that one is allowed to understand much: for each one has within him 'the divine reason that sits at the helm of the soul,' of which the head knows nothing. Find beauty; be still; and that faculty grows more surely than grain sown in season. However, I must be content to observe that here, for the first time, broke upon me the unmistakable intimation of a last reality underlying mountain beauty; and here, for the first time, it awakened within me a faculty of comprehension that had never before been exercised.

Humble indeed had not failed me. He had hoped for a noble panorama. But in the bleak hours around midnight not even he had dreamed that we should be led by cloud and fire to the land of promise. Since then I have always believed and repeatedly proved that the mountains reserve their fairest prize for the man who turns aside from common-sense routine. One might say that hills repay trust with generosity. In Glen Brittle, our companions when they awoke saw nothing but a steel-grey layer of low clouds, and not imagining that the peaks were in sunlight, commiserated us on such an unprofitable end to our waywardness.

Several of the best hours of our otherwise misspent lives thus passed away on Sgurr a' Mhadaidh. Towards nine o'clock the cloud-bank broke up and gradually dissolved. We scrambled down to the high col under Bidein Druim nan Ramh, and thence turned downward toward Coruisk by the Corrie of Solitude. Overhead, hardly a wisp of cloud remained; below, Loch Coruisk was a royal blue rippled with silver.

After winning clear of the screes in the corrie we walked the best part of two miles south, to the junction of the main burn and the loch. And here I add my voice to Humble's in exploding the myth of 'gloomy Coruisk.' The face of Scotland has so often been falsified by writers in search of melodrama that there is now difficulty in convincing people of the evidence of their own eyes. Far from being shadowed and overhung by beetling crags, Loch Coruisk has a fairly open situation, inasmuch as the Cuillin main ridge lies a couple of miles back. In spring and summer it is flooded by sunlight for the best part of the day. I have heard it further alleged that here grows no tuft of vegetation; yet when I stood beside the loch with Humble the very banks were alive with wild flowers, their hues offset by cool green shrubs and long grasses. We might have imagined ourselves transported to the land of Xanadu, where

> . . . . twice five miles of fertile ground
> With walls and towers were girdled round,
> And there were gardens, bright with sinuous rills.

A few of these flowers were rare, and Humble, who is an accomplished botanist, was highly gratified by some carnivorous specimens.

As I am ill content to rejoice in mountains yet not climb them, so I am compelled not only to admire lochs and rivers but to plunge in and swim. In either act knowledge of their charm is extended. Every condition for the ideal swim had here been satisfied, for the sun had more than warmed us on the four-mile tramp. There was no need to propose a bathe—of one accord we stripped and plunged. I have never known anything like it. The swim was unique in my own experience because all five senses were feasted to the full.

The sharp sting of that first dive cleared at one stroke the fogs of lethargy from the mind—at one stroke the world stood vivid. The corrie was full of sun and the song of the burn, gay with the flash of many colours and the dance of light on the loch, fresh with the scents of blossom and an aromatic tang of plants in morning air. I drank from the burn and the taste was sweet and lively to the palate. And these good reports, being gathered together in the mind, suddenly fused in image of the beauty we had seen during the supreme hour on Sgurr a' Mhadaidh: so that I knew, what until then I had not known, that the one Beauty pervades all things according to their nature, they having beauty by virtue of participation in it; and that in the degree of realizing its presence within us, so is life lived in fullness. The ecstasy of that morning is bright after eight years.

When at last we emerged dripping from the water we let our bodies dry in the hot sun while we ate our too little food. Our departure from camp had been just a thought casual. There is no appetite on earth to surpass a Skye appetite; one is permanently hungry. But now we were ravenous. However, shortage of food for a day is of no consequence; much more serious was Humble's plight. I was almost sorry for him. He is an ardent and expert photographer and he had brought a camera but no spools.

Our intention was to go down to the sea—one might almost say up to the sea, for parts of Coruisk are said to be below sea-level—and then go north up the far side of the loch to Sgurr Dubh, by the ascent of which we should return to the Glen Brittle side of the main ridge. Reviewing this project in my mind while we walked along the east bank of the loch, I began to regard the absence of spools as an unmixed blessing. On a fine day in the Cuillin there is no more insatiable devourer of the fleeting hours than a camera with Humble behind it. As it was, the surprising variety of plant life all along the two-mile bank of the loch caused many a halt and much botanical dawdling. I think we spent two hours over these two miles, for it was after noon when we arrived at Loch Scavaig.

All this while I had been promising myself another bathe. As befits a small sea-loch, Scavaig is green, deep and clear—a perfect swimming-pool in one of the most lonely and remote corners of Britain. What was our astonishment, then, when we arrived on the brink, to see a MacBrayne Line steamer sweep into the loch and drop anchor! Within fifteen minutes several boat-loads of tourists landed. They had arrived from Oban to see that world-famous view: Coruisk and the Black Cuillin.

At another time Humble and I might have selfishly resented this landing as a rude shattering of our solitude. Instead, we looked at each other with gleaming eyes. The same thought had simultaneously occurred to us both—food!

We negotiated swiftly with the officer in charge. In a few minutes we had been taken out to the ship in a motor-boat and were climbing on board. The first man I met on deck knew me, and to put the finishing touch to our luck he was officially in charge of the cruise. We explained our urgent need of a good meal. He introduced us to the captain and we found our-selves conducted as honoured guests to the first-class dining saloon. I must explain that my beard was a fortnight strong, that I was in shirt-sleeves and braces, bore a large coil of rope round my shoulders, and that my breeches were in tatters. Humble, I am glad to report, looked distinctly less disreputable, but any good effect was destroyed by his antique and sorely battered hat.

Having run the gauntlet of clean, cool, spruce, and inquisitive tourists on deck, we were mightily relieved to find the dining saloon empty. The stewards had never before entertained two starving climbers. They watched round-eyed while we polished off two helpings of every course throughout a lengthy menu.

Then followed a quart of cool beer. Ever since that day I have harboured tender feelings for the English tourist, and I raise my hat to the name of MacBrayne.

At three o'clock we went ashore and were introduced to a number of young ladies, who suspected that Humble and I were local colour engaged by Messrs. MacBrayne for their entertainment. The consensus of opinion regarding the view spread before us was this: that to set foot on the Cuillin either in mist or clear weather was certain death; and that Loch Coruisk was the deepest lake in Europe—otherwise, why had they been brought to see it?

The ladies were charming, and after a prolonged bout of photography we parted from them with regret. The time was now five o'clock and we should be hard pressed to reach Glen Brittle before dark. Our proposed route of ascent, by the east ridge of Sgurr Dubh, was over three thousand feet high, and one of the two longest rock-climbs in Britain. I would recommend that ridge as a paradise for a rock-climbing beginner. Apart from the initial trouble in climbing on to the ridge, one may thereafter proceed unroped up broad acres of boiler-plate slabs, whose rock is the roughest gabbro in all the Cuillin. In other words, it is so rough and reliable that only the grossest negligence could bring a man to harm. Here, too, one may learn balance and rhythm—the secrets of successful rock-work.

Humble and I kept our pace as slow as we could, consistent with continuous upward movement. The steamer slowly shrank to the size of a skiff and human figures became too small to be distinguished. White gulls wheeled and flashed across the green sparkle of Loch Scavaig. Meanwhile we sweltered under a grilling sun and were roasted by waves of heat reflected upward from the brown rock. The temperature must have been at least ninety degrees, and a raging thirst possessed our desiccated bodies. Beyond the summit, we threaded an involved descending route amongst huge crags, where we were obliged to rope down an overhang of twenty feet—our first use of a rope all day. At nine o'clock we stood on the rim of Coire a' Ghrunnda.

We were anxious to reach camp as soon as possible; our friends knew us too well to bother about a twenty-four hours' absence, but might feel less at ease thereafter. We decided, therefore, not to traverse Sgurr Alisdair and instead went straight down to Coire a' Ghrunnda. Here, if you like, lies a genuinely gloomy loch—a black and glassy sheet of water framed by a chaos of screes as desolate as one may find in all Scotland. In the stream that flows from it we at last quenched our agonizing thirst. Then we set off downhill, skirting those terrific slabs in the corrie-bed, convex slabs that pour seaward, scored and burnished by ancient glaciers.

At ten-thirty p.m. we strolled into camp, exactly twenty-four hours after departure. Maitland and Higgins had proved friends indeed and a hot meal was waiting for us. This time, no earthly power, not even another Humble mystery tour, could have wooed me from supper, a quiet pipe, and that eiderdown sleeping-bag.

2

The Cioch and Crack of Doom

PROLONGED DROUGHT and blazing sun have almost invariably blessed my climbing days in Skye. I go in June. But in June 1937, when camping with J. K. W. Dunn in Glen Brittle, my luck suffered the inevitable relapse. We were half-way up the south-west buttress of Sgurr na h-Uamha when a full gale sprang from the south and spread-eagled us on the central slabs. It was the last big unclimbed buttress in the Cuillin. Therefore we battled our way to the top, fled before the wind to Sligachan, and not an hour too soon retired west to Glen Brittle. Heralded by the gale, rain stormed over the mountains and found us much inclined to rest on our laurels and keep dry. There was at first an indisputable pleasure to be wrung from lying warm and dry in one's sleeping-bag, listening to the vain beat of rain upon the tent-canvas, and thinking 'God help the sailors on a night like this!' After several hours the sound became monotonous; after three days we realized that there were worse things than a wet skin.

I amused myself by reminding Dunn of the less creditable episodes of his climbing career. He is one of the most hopelessly casual and yet friendly of men. To cite but one incident, typical of his way of life, he once sent me a telegram from the wilds of Kintyre, commanding me to climb with him on Nevis next day—but omitting to state time or place of meeting. I set off by car from Glasgow, staking all upon a chance encounter somewhere in Lochaber. Half-way there I happened to stop at Inverarnan hotel in Glen Falloch—to find Dunn, large and fair-haired, sprawling before the fire and wolfing hot scones and tea. I advanced to unleash my thunder, when 'Good man!' cried Dunn, 'I knew it was two to one you'd stop at Inverarnan.'

You cannot damn and blast a man whose eye is sparkling with delight at meeting you. I tried; but it was no use.

Thus it was in our storm-bound tent that wrath at his care-free habit kept me lively and was yet stayed by his infectious smile and naïve geniality. Against these I have no defence. My own more irritating behaviour he regarded with the phlegmatic calm of a noble but lazy mastiff. Despite such accord in idleness, three days of stored-up energy brewed a restlessness that drove us to action. We resolved that regardless of weather we should go on the fourth day to the best rock-climb in the Cuillin. To my own mind this was the Cioch direct and the Crack of Doom, which lie one above the other to form a thousand-foot route up the precipice of Sron na Ciche. To climb the first half by the Cioch pinnacle was practicable; but whether in rain we could cope with the Crack of Doom—by repute the hardest climb in Skye—was a question that I was unqualified to decide. We had not been there before.

The following day dawned with a rain-squall. We wakened, listened—and hastily shut our eyes again. But after a midday breakfast our resolution triumphed. As we made our preparations the weather relented. The rain went off and we set out in weak sunshine for Coire na Ciche, where the wet flanks of the circling sgurrs gleamed as though sheathed in tinfoil.

We spent an hour climbing up Coire Lagain and following a stony track under the mile-long cliffs of Sron na Ciche. Rooted four hundred feet above our heads, in the centre of the cliff, the pinnacle projected squat and gigantic, yet hardly distinguishable from below against the background of the main face. Its very presence there went long unsuspected until Professor Norman Collie, observing its shadow cast upon the cliff behind, deduced the existence of what has become one of the most famous rock-spires in Scotland. We proposed to climb by the direct route made in 1907 by Harland and Abraham.

After a few minutes' rest we roped up on a hundred feet of line. The rocks were still very wet, but the weather was fast turning to the lively breeze and sun that housewives call 'a good drying day.' Moreover, the cliff was gabbro, the roughest of mountain rock, to which wetness spells added difficulty only where the rock is water-worn or interlarded with basalt, or by chilling the fingers. The latter has caused several accidents heareabouts, but is not a trouble to which I am readily susceptible.

I started up a slab at the base of a long shallow chimney. There was more water in this natural drain-pipe than I liked, so at the earliest opportunity I climbed over the left wall on to the open face of the cliff, perhaps fifty feet above the screes. I found myself in a splendidly free situation, with the gabbro unrolling before me like a red ceremonial carpet. Dunn joined me and for a hundred feet we continued parallel to the chimney until the slabs converged on a little corner beneath a vertical nose. To the right and left, bulging rocks prevented an avoiding traverse.

I had been previously counselled that combined tactics—a 'shoulder' from the second man—had best be employed to vanquish this severe pitch. But the holds are definite, if small, and for a tall man like myself no aid is required. The high angle threw me out of balance, so that determined arm-pulling and quick climbing to avoid numbed fingers were the key to success. There followed a hard corner and rib; we zigzagged from one to the other and slowly advanced up to a bulwark of overbending crags.

The immense bastion of the rock above was unscalable, and to turn it we had to ford a river of slabs that fairly poured from the bulge on our left, two hundred feet down to the corrie. I launched out on a horizontal line of stepping-stones close beneath the overhang, and half-way across happened to look straight down to the screes, where I saw a large cairn that marked the landing-place of an unfortunate climber who had once fallen from my present position. The abominable practice of erecting cairns at such spots can hardly be condemned in strong enough terms. At the same instant there came a loud rushing sound like the noise of a high approaching wind. For one hopeless second I believed that a line-squall was coming at me. I clung to the rock like a limpet, and breathed a thankful prayer that Dunn weighed fourteen stone and myself but ten, that the rope was new and Dunn one of the best second men in Scotland.

The rush of wind changed to a long-drawn-out roar, lasting a full minute, and punctuated by terrific crashes from close below me. I then had good reason to recognize that alarming noise. A week before, when traversing the main ridge with J. Banford, I had left Sgurr Dearg in dense mist. After descending steep rock, we had embarked on a hand-traverse on the upper ledge of an overhang, at which the mist cleared, revealing not the main ridge a few feet below, but a chasm eight hundred feet deep. Aided by the sketchiest foothold, we were gaily swinging by our hands over the north-eastern precipice. We hastily retired and were no sooner clear of the ledge than the overhang, ledge and all, silently heeled over into the void in blocks like cottages, then dropped with that rushing noise that I heard now; with just that same roar when thousands of tons of rock crashed on the corrie.

I stood fascinated on the slabs until the avalanche ended, waiting until the last hoarse rattle of the small shot had fallen still. A breathless hush pervaded the mountain. Then I called to Dunn to let out the rope and continued the traverse with exaggerated caution, finding problems in foot-placing where five minutes ago I should have romped freely. This delicacy of nerve was promptly restored to more robust condition by the sudden uprise of the crux.

The traverse ended at a wet and slabby wall of twenty feet lying at right angles to the bastion. The middle of the wall was worn smooth and white, both by water and my predecessor's boot-nails. There was no place here for sensitivity to noise or memorial stones; such rock had to be dealt with in a mood of businesslike determination. Dunn, unfortunately, was still on the far side of the traverse and I had already run out seventy feet of rope, the weight of which was growing noticeable, and would by now have been a serious drag but for his skill in keeping it dry. However, his stance was good, those close at hand bad, so I left with him orders to be ready for an instant move should my rope give out, and then turned to the wall.

The principal difficulty was the glossiness of the rock, which after the coarse gabbro below lent a feeling of insecurity to each movement, not only of the feet but also of the hands, which, chilled by running water, found the tiny holes inadequate. Upon reaching the white patch half-way up I was therefore delighted to find two vertical cracks, wide enough to admit my finger-tips. With these for assistance, the doubtful downscrape of boots on the polished stone was much less dreadful than it had looked from below. This vital move accomplished, I clambered to the top. Before my rope quite ran out I reached a good ledge, from which I brought up Dunn.

Thus far the climbing had been of the most physically satisfying kind, making big demands on muscle and energy. The golden rule of rock-work—use the feet as much as possible, the arms as little as possible—must on the Cioch be often honoured in the breach. One must fight out one's way. For an untrained man I can think of no route more heart-breaking; and for a fit man, none more exhilarating.

We had now outflanked the girdle of the overhang and climbed a further long stretch of slabs, on which we were soon able to move together and which led us to the terrace under the Cioch pinnacle. The terrace sloped unevenly from the eastern gully on our left to the base of the pinnacle on our right. Directly in front arched that hugest sweep of gabbro known throughout the climbing world as 'The Cioch Slab,' from whose western edge sprang the Cioch, leaning towards us like the head of a lizard.

The day was growing ever more sunny as blue rents in the cloud-woof grew more frequent. After that most glorious of Cuillin climbs this unanticipated sun came like a liqueur at the close of a banquet, a final touch that raised our spirits to un-precedented heights. The ordinary route up the Cioch by the Slab and nape seemed too tame a conclusion, so we traversed westward to the direct finish on the nose. After scrambling up

broken rocks to the right of the overhang, we climbed the left
wall of a corner, wriggled up a steep, rough slab with few holds,
and cautiously eased ourselves on to an awkward mantel-shelf.
Immediately above, on the very tip of the nose, were a series of
three knife-edges.   Looked down upon from the top, these
short blades, set one below the other like the teeth of a saw,
wear a spectacular aspect; their situation is an airy one.   But in
the climbing of them resides no difficulty.   Indeed, we found
ourselves deliberately lingering over them—and savouring to the
full that joyous sense of freedom they yield, that feel of hovering
over space as though the climber were a bird on spread wings.

We pulled ourselves on to the broad roof and relaxed.   Dunn
lit up his pipe,

> A trophy which survived a hundred fights,
> A beacon which has cheered ten thousand nights,

and lay on his back, happily gazing into vacuity, while I rolled
over on my stomach, head over the edge, and surveyed the
cliffs below.   Throughout the precipice of Sron na Ciche, in
particular the area around the Cioch, there is a peculiar atmosphere, clean and spacious, which I have never observed so
markedly on any other mountain.   It arises perhaps from the
free lift of the pale brown slabs and the unique bareness of them;
for no vestige of vegetation is nourished in their crystalline
rock.   One's heart goes out to them, for the cliff has the same
virginal purity as snow-peaks in a burst of sun, or green seas
breaking white on a skerry.

Half an hour passed in delicious ease.   And here indeed is the
fine art of idling anywhere: there should be a mountain of work
accomplished in the near past or instantly impending in the
future.   Where these twin conditions are both satisfied, as now,
one may experience a double dose of bliss.   At the close of our
half-hour I proposed that we try the Crack of Doom.   Dunn
was enthusiastic, for I had kept this part of the programme to
myself until I knew our day's form.   We could then contain
ourselves no longer and climbed down the nape of the pinnacle
to the cliff.

A sharp descent and right-hand traverse along a shattered ledge brought us to the start of our route. It began as a deep groove, gradually growing shallow as it curved for a hundred and fifty feet up rough and tumbled slabs. On this first section, advancing by easy stages and husbanding energy for whatever might lie ahead, we encountered no difficulty. On the last thirty feet the groove became harder; then the cliff shot abruptly up, the groove swung hard to the left, and came to a sudden end at a right-angled corner. We stood on a sloping slab, on either side of which the corner walls rose sheer for fifty feet. The right-hand wall was split from top to bottom by a hanging chimney, set slightly at a tilt from right to left. We had arrived at the Crack of Doom.

While Dunn secured himself in the corner I scrutinized the crack to discover the worst. The tilt was clearly awkward, but twenty feet up a jammed stone augured a brief resting-place. Below that stone the crack was wide enough to admit one's right leg and arm. Above the stone I could see no holds at all and the crack narrowed. Although the outside walls were dry, trickling water filmed the interior.

Whenever Dunn declared himself ready I set to work. Facing sideways toward the corner I wedged my right arm in the crack as a balance-preserver and climbed by foothold only to the chock-stone. Those twenty feet were hard but not severe. Nevertheless, I had no doubts of what must follow, and there being no need to hurry, I stopped on the chock-stone for some two minutes until I felt completely rested. On the slab below me Dunn looked up with that smile of unbounded optimism that has cheered me up many an ice-clad pitch in winter. No matter how grim the prospect or precarious his own situation, he has the remarkable capacity of appearing unshakably safe and solid. Indeed, he inspires a leader with the sense of mutual confidence, which means much to the success of a climbing team.

I began to climb again. With every foot now gained the crack narrowed and the difficulties increased. At intervals on the outside edge were microscopic incut holds, too wide apart to provide continuous footing. In between these havens I retained position and mounted higher by slipping a foot inside the crack and turning the ankle to jam the boot. I had also to fight against the tilt of the crack, which tended to thrust my body outward; and since an arm might no longer be wedged, I was obliged to force a hand into the crack and make pressure-holds by clenching the fist. I imagine that a shorter man might find less trouble with the tilt than myself. With jammed foot and fist I thus pulled up my body from one sparse hold to another.

Unfortunately I had done almost sixty thousand feet of climbing on the Cuillin in sixteen days and my boot-nails were in a sad state of decrepitude, being not only worn to shreds but loose into the bargain. There was one edge-nail, on the inner side of my left boot, which tinkled as merrily as a dinner bell whenever my foot was shaken. This nail had repeatedly to be used on the miniature holds on the outside of the crack. One placed it carefully and applied the strain gently, in constant preparedness for its breaking off. Like a true friend it did not fail me in emergency.

Meanwhile I had progressed to the top of the crack, where a tongue of stone jutted overhead as though to mock my weariness. I again jammed myself, and for a few seconds halted to gather in strength for the final tussle. I put out my hand and grasped the top of the stone. With a last strenuous heave I pulled myself out of the crack, dangled for a second, then swarmed up, drawing myself into a flat-bottomed corner.

I frankly confess that although by no means exhausted, I was muscularly very tired indeed. In comparison with this crack, the Cioch direct, everywhere recognized as a standard 'severe,' seemed child's play. Yet the crack is eminently practicable; it calls for no feat of esoteric gymnastic.

While my breath was returning I looked over the edge to give Dunn a signal of success. My eye flashed a thousand feet past his head, down a cascade of slabs to the corrie. So absorbing had been the climb that till now I had felt little or no sense of height. My eye wandered further, down to the green fields of Glen Brittle, where black cloud-shadows were driven in herds by following sun-shafts. Beyond was the Atlantic, its wrinkled expanse scored by a dozen golden furrows, as though the outer islands, like low Viking ships, had ploughed those gleaming wakes when they stood out to the west.

Intense power was given to this simple vista by the frame of crags to my left, and once again I was struck by the truth of those words of Mummery, when he declared that the best route up a mountain is a difficult one. Only there, rather than upon the screes of an easy route, may one find a foreground of bold rock whose noble outline does no less than justice to the distant view; and only there, rather than upon the plod up a uniform slope, which dulls the mind, is one's whole being glowingly alive and keyed to full receptiveness. After one is up, there can be no doubt that ridge-walking is the finest occupation.

Being fully recovered, I gave Dunn a shout to come on. Like me, he went well to the chock-stone. Thenceforward, and despite his exceptional strength, his much greater weight placed him at a disadvantage; for my own body, being relatively light, has a high power-to-weight ratio. But Dunn was too skilful a mountaineer to climb anyhow but gracefully, and the only signs of difficulty were some hard breathing, and when he glanced up, his fair hair tumbled over his eyes, an expression of acute anguish that almost choked me with laughter. His expression immediately changed to a broad grin, his more explosive mirth being held, perforce, behind glistening eyes—a triumph of mind over matter which those who know the Crack of Doom will appreciate. He came on slowly but surely, and in due course was prostrated by my side.

We sat together for a while, coiling up the rope and congratulating each other on the best climb we had had in Skye. Then we went up to a *glacis* or broad slabby ledge, which ran leftward like a corridor on to the crest of Sron na Ciche. Where we emerged on the *glacis* a short final crag rose above us. I understand that this gives a very hard finish to the climb; to me it looked more suitable to rubbers on dry rock than to loose

ON SRON NA CICHE

boot-nails on wet rock. We therefore turned to the corridor and walked on to the top of the mountain. We made there the brief halt that proper respect for such a hill demands, then pursued our way along the ridge to Sgurr Alisdair, descending thence to Coire Lagain, a thousand feet in five minutes by the rapids of the Stone Shoot—the longest scree-run in Scotland. On passing below the cliff of Sron na Ciche we threaded our way through hundreds of tons of new avalanche debris, and saw a fresh scar on the face a few hundred feet above the track. Gabbro holds may be the most reliable in the world, but in the mass, I fear, even gabbro is little more immune from decay than other rocks.

We returned to Glen Brittle, and that night I examined my boots. To an attentive ear the note they sounded had become unmistakably one of warning. Until I was new-shod there must be no more rock-climbing. Moreover, the very skin of my finger-tips was worn to a fragile tenuity. Next day we struck camp and departed for Glasgow.

3

Slav Route—Ben Nevis

FLANKED BY a cheerful fire, Dunn, W. M. Mackenzie, A. M. MacAlpine, and I sat round the breakfast table in the Scottish Mountaineering Club's hut on Ben Nevis. It was mid October 1937. I was entertaining myself with the hut's climbing register and speculating what was the full tale behind some of these cryptic entries: 'Observatory buttress—three hours rain and sleet,' or 'South Trident direct—half-gale.' They were succint enough in all conscience, but too tantalizing. They stimulated yet did not satisfy imagination. What tense moments, high on the mountain-wall, were hidden there? How many hard fights by a leader, silently witnessed by only a couple of friends on windswept ledges—and never again mentioned? I closed the book with a bang. 'What *are* we going to climb?' I asked.

'When the weather is foul,' said Mackenzie—and here he paused so that his audience could hear the wind soughing round the corners of the hut—'and the rain is coming down in sheets' —at which he looked pointedly out of the small window— 'there is only one thing to do——'

'Get back to bed,' I murmured.

Mackenzie's blue eyes flashed with indignation and the nostrils of his hawk-nose distended. He looked a perfect specimen of the intolerant man of action. 'The only thing to do,' he sternly continued, 'is to climb the hardest route on the mountain.'

'Why?' asked MacAlpine briskly.

'Why!' exploded Mackenzie. 'In rain you get miserable on an easy climb. But go to a hard climb and you forget the weather—all your interest goes to the rock.'

We could not deny there was an element of truth there.

20

A mild route would be dreary in the thick mist that choked this upper corrie of the Allt a' Mhuilinn: not a glimpse of the Spean valley two thousand feet below or of the cliffs rising two thousand feet above was vouchsafed us. We were housed like unwilling gods among the clouds. But there were limits to Mackenzie's theory; we were not like gods, immune from destruction.

'The hardest climb is Rubicon Wall,' I remarked, 'and that won't go in rain. You must have something else in mind.'

'Slav route,' said Mackenzie, sitting up very straight. But with these two words he had won me over. Like a magic charm they broke the spell of lethargy, for Slav route was then reputed to be the finest summer route on the mountain. The name Slav derives from two Czechoslovakian mountaineers with whom E. A. M. Wedderburn made the first ascent in 1934. So far as I knew, however, all ascents to date had been made either in rubbers or rope-soled shoes. And rubbers cannot be used on wet slabs.

'We'll try it in boots,' concluded Mackenzie. 'It's a full sixteen hundred feet—takes about four hours.' Then, brusquely, 'Nothing to it! Can't be more than very severe!' And his whole face lit up with infectious enthusiasm.

MacAlpine and I burst out laughing. Mackenzie is that happy companion, an unconscious humorist. There is a Confucian dictum that love of daring without understanding casts the shadow named rashness. If Mackenzie loved daring more than most virtues his understanding was commensurate, so that boldness of planning was balanced by prudence in execution, which in combine made him a first-class mountaineer. A party of four, however, was too large for so long a climb in wild weather. Dunn and MacAlpine therefore decided to go to Observatory ridge.

At eleven a.m. Mackenzie and I set out in a cold spit of rain toward the North-east buttress, the most tremendous cliff on the mountain. It marks the eastern limit of the two miles of precipice that ring the north face of Nevis. Its west flank and the east flank of Observatory ridge confront each other like opposing

B

pages of a half-open book, in the angle of which is the unclimbed
Zero gully.   Slav route runs closely parallel with the gully on
the rocks of the North-east buttress.   To-day this grandeur of
rock scenery was invisible to us, 'wrapt in dense cloud from
base to cope,' but we were not ill content.   We had the clean
damp smell of mist in our nostrils, and in our eyes the thrust
of a sudden tower through the veil, the looming and fading of
vague buttresses, the hurried flitting through thinning wisps of
unsuspected pinnacles, each gleaming with wet.

When we arrived in the great angle beneath Zero gully we
found a small snow-field left over from the previous winter.   As
we went across, boot-nails crunching on the rough surface, I
noticed that the snow was peppered here and there with stones
discharged down the conduit of the gully, and an instant later
the whirr and whine of a fragment was heard overhead.   It
went wide, like a warning shot across our bows.   In another
minute we were in neutral waters under the dripping protection
of the North-east buttress.

We roped up on a hundred feet of line, with Mackenzie as
leader.   The exact line of Slav route was unknown to us and
Mackenzie made a false start up pouring wet slabs, which grew
ever more smooth and precipitous until eighty feet up his hardy
optimism began to flag.   It became plain that he was tilting at
a watermill and he came down, chastened by the truth that Nevis
rocks and routes are not only as God made them, but generally
worse.   There could now be no doubt that the start of Slav
route was a prominent rib hard against Zero gully.   It projected through drizzling mist with a hostile aspect that sapped
much of our booted confidence, and I found myself counting
the hours of daylight to calculate the limits of attack.

Mackenzie's false start was in the end a psychological gain,
for after wandering half an hour on rocks that no mortal was
ever intended to climb, he found those that were so intended
unusually yielding.   Wiry and lean as a courtyard cat, he went
as though on midnight tiles, with a vigorous rhythm, up the
front of the rib.   I thought the rock bulged awkwardly at me

when I followed. Mackenzie was standing on a niche, which he vacated as my hand groped over its edge, and, since the rocks directly above overhung, disappeared round a corner to the left. I took his place, hitched myself to a rock-spike, and quickly paid out the rope over my shoulder, for he had clearly struck top form and was travelling with speed on rocks that were not easy. There came a long halt. Not a movement for several minutes.

I became aware why Mackenzie had been so very prompt in departing—a rivulet was pouring from the eave on to the back of my neck. And there was no room on the cramped ledge to avoid it. I could turn and twist, I could bend and stretch as I liked, but that stream found a joint in my clothing. Like Wordsworth's cataract, it haunted me like a passion. It passes my understanding how it is possible for October rain water on Nevis to be so cold and remain liquid.

After I was completely saturated I heard my call from above. I went round the corner and traversed narrow ledges on the gable of the rib. They brought me to a piton driven into a crack at the top edge of the wall. The piton was presumably a relic of the first ascent and Mackenzie was using it as a rope belay.

'He was no fool who nailed this place,' announced Mackenzie, eyeing the sloping roof which swept overhead parallel to our traverse. 'Take a look and tell me what you make of it.'

I peered over the top and saw a bare, yellowish slab spread with a film of water. Its lower half sharply dipped to the eave overlooking our last stance; the top half curled steeply upward to some unknown destination. At such a sight I could imagine a bishop turning apostate and cleaving to materialist philosophy. An air of stark reality clung to that slab.

'Slavs must climb very well,' I suggested. 'Still, it's not so bad but what it might be worse.' Although it is needless to encourage a leader like Mackenzie, it is a second man's duty not to discourage him.

We said no more, for Mackenzie climbed up to the slab and

waited while I tied myself to the piton. Then he crept out sideways, using one-nail footholds on a thin split in the rock. From the middle he began to move slowly up, carefully placing each foot, gently transferring his weight to it, and so balancing up by nail-friction aided by a minimum of hand-hold. As he arrived at the final upcurl I watched with breathless interest. He took one long look and climbed down a step or two. Then I saw what I had not seen before: a second piton in the rock immediately under the crux.

'A karabiner!' demanded Mackenzie, like Richard III calling for a horse at Bosworth, that he might 'enact more wonders.' I rummaged in my rucksack for the required article, a steel ring with a spring-clip, which I passed up to him. He clipped the ring on to both the piton and the rope, the latter freely running through the centre. Thus doubly protected against a fall, he advanced once more to the crux. The footholds were minute, but not too small to take the thin edge of a side-nail, or at least enough of it to support the body. The real difficulty, and the most trying, was the lack of adequate holds for numbed fingers. The wind, too, had chosen to swirl round Observatory ridge and drive the rain still more icily. It is usually thus; mountain nature is not chivalrous and wields the sword of cold most fiercely when the plight of the climber is sorest. At length he disappeared, and like a curtain drawn to close his performance a wreath of cloud floated over the top of the slab.

In a few minutes there came through the mist a muffled 'Phew!'—a short silence, then, 'I'm up!'—followed by a joyful laugh and later a few piercing whistles, which echoed weirdly against the neighbouring cliffs.

At last he shouted to me to come on. I obeyed with alacrity, and ten minutes later we had reunited on a spacious platform. I removed the karabiner *en route* but left the pitons behind. I generally hold that pitons should be taken out after use and the rocks left clean. But we had been thankful to find them there and thought that others might be thankful too. I have since twice led the pitch in boots in dry weather and thought pitons unnecessary; in rain and wind, when the slab is very severe, at least one is essential. There is no other belay.

The question before our meeting was whether the last pitch was merely a sample of the fourteen hundred feet above. It was a horrid possibility. If so, the best thing we could do would be to climb down it again. The last thought, and the fact that it was now my turn to lead, contributed to my illogical conviction that the worst was over. The route appeared to continue up an open corner to the left, where a grey column rose seventy feet between broken walls. I found the column technically hard. The holds were particularly small and ran with water, which poured up my sleeve to the chest whenever I was so misguided as to take a high handhold. With numbed fingers I felt the upper part of the column to be rather exposed. After we had relished its clean-cut intricacy and taken refuge behind a square block crowning its top, our thoughts became dominated by the threat of immense slabs ahead. They seemed to bend up and over in vast red sheets, streaming with water, and the only visible route ran by an eighty-foot shute to an overhung corner.

We reconnoitred along an easy traverse which led us to the very verge of Zero gully. On our left was the shute, on our right the gully, water-slides both, and repulsive enough to induce a shudder in examining climbers. They were impossible. Between them reared a high right-angled step which, were it climbable, must allow us to outflank either impasse. I made the attempt, floating up like a ballet-dancer, accompanied by the bubble and tinkle of water-music; my choir, a thousand treble voices. I was soon able to put the issue beyond doubt. After a hard climb I went up a low vertical wall to the crest of a rib overlooking Zero gully. Mackenzie then led through and vanished over a square-cut crest.

While these proceedings were in hand I was fascinated by the sanguinary appearance of the water that trickled over the red rocks to my left. It reminded me of that gruesome line of Tennyson's, 'The red-ribb'd ledges drip with a silent horror

of blood'—a line that rejoiced the bloodthirsty heart of my boy-
hood, disgusted my more tender adolescence, and which my
manhood now recognized with grim amusement as no extrava-
gance.   My poetic reflections, however, were disturbed by a tug
on the rope and some expletives from above, whose tenor was
more akin to the subject of my thoughts than Mackenzie knew.
I had, it seemed, been called more than once.   Perpendicular
rock with good hold is a rare pleasure to the climber, and the
party forgathered above the step in high spirits.

From now onward the difficulties abated.   Yet the route
selection remained all-engrossing and at one place we had to
use combined tactics.   For a thousand feet the climb continued
up a series of vertical walls, which progressively became shorter,
the average angle of the cliff being lessened by a myriad ledges,
broad and narrow.   Throughout this upper part of the route
we moved together, which provided me, as second man, with
much brisk work in managing a rope stiff and heavy with water.
From such rope management I always derive the greatest delight
—striving for a perfection that is, alas, never to be realized.

When the cloud locally thickened we appeared at times like
the most insubstantial of wraiths, drifting through the shifting
mists like the wolves in a Russian melodrama.   Climbing thus
through cloud we could not see what height we were gaining,
and the route gradually took to itself a sort of epic quality.   It
rolled on and on, magnificently and unendingly, until one thought
that since it had continued so long it must go on for ever.   On
subsequent visits I have observed the same quality.   It is the
sure sign of a great rock-climb, of mountaineering as distinct
from crag-climbing.

After four hours' ascent there became noticeable that strange
freedom of atmosphere, a lightening and movement of air, that
indicates nearness to a summit.   At four o'clock we arrived on
the boulder-fields of the plateau and went in search of the cairn.
Suddenly I noticed the rain.   Shafts of wind drew attention to
my clothes.   I was soaked to the skin as though I had newly
swum in the Allt a' Mhuilinn.

'You were right,' I said to Mackenzie, 'about forgetting bad weather on a good climb. But we knew it was raining at that slab!'

My honest tribute was suspect. Mackenzie was alert. He would make no damaging admissions that might be used in evidence against him.

'Raining!' he exclaimed. 'Not a drop—dry all day till now!'

And on that contention he took his stand, nor would he yield an inch. But later that evening, when we sat before a glowing fire in the hut, I observed him record the ascent in the official Climbs Book, and surreptitiously glancing over his shoulder, read this laconic narrative: 'Slav route—wet.'

4

On the Rannoch Wall in Winter

The Cliff and the Moor

OF ALL LOWLAND SCENES that which most compels my admiration is the stateliness of tall trees on a broad lawn. It is a harmony of the vertical and horizontal, simple, serene; its effect on the mind a perfect calm: ideas that in Greek architecture culminate in the Parthenon. Among Scottish mountains, and there alone, have I seen its most noble demonstration in the cliffs of the Buachaille Etive Mor, towering over the vast flatness of the moor of Rannoch. But the shape of the peak itself is happily not classic. From ten miles over the moor it reminds me of a neolithic arrow-head; from the road near Kingshouse Inn, of a Gothic cathedral, raised to a height of 3,345 feet, based in proportion, and spired.

Thus in the cliff and moor we see the classic calm; in the peak and sky the Gothic aspiration; opposed ideas, here reconciled in bewitching harmony. For the Gothic spire is an outward, visible expression of the inward, invisible soaring of man's spirit toward union with the beautiful. Therefore it is a form profoundly satisfying to the eye; for it fires the mind with thought of the eternal, and we call that fire the love of beauty, and the emotion it arouses the awe of God.

When there is created within our minds this state so difficult for mere intellect to understand—a blend in one of an inward movement of mind and a flawless calm—or when an artist is given grace to project it in outer forms, there emerges the highest beauty, peace. For in true peace there are ever present and reconciled two logically irreconcilable elements—stillness and motion, rest and love, silence and song. Wherever there is a union of the pairs of opposites so perfect that Reason confounded cries: 'Two distincts, division none!' there too is an exceeding and eternal weight of beauty.

From the porphyry of Buachaille the chisel of God has carved that for us in symbol.   And if it be courteous to say, until we are aware in the midst of our climbing that mountains are but the sign of things higher, we may be climbers but we have not begun to understand mountains, or mountaineers.

In consequence of this demonstration I admit (what is true of few hills) that the best of Buachaille may be experienced from the roadway.   It is a humbling thought for a keen rock-climber. On the other hand, the paradoxical harmony in contrast of the eastern cliffs with the moor is nowhere so well appreciated as from the Buachaille itself, either from the summit, or better still from the most perpendicular rocks—the Rannoch Wall of the Crowberry ridge.   In a lecture to the Scottish Mountaineering Club in 1939, I showed a slide of Agag's groove on Rannoch Wall, which depicted the mountaineer as a fly crawling on the face of a skyscraper, and with the words, 'This climb commands a magnificent prospect over the moor of Rannoch,' raised no little laughter.   The reader may have similar doubts.   Therefore I propose to show him the climb, not under too good conditions, so that he may know how photographs, by revealing only part of the truth, distort the whole.

AGAG'S GROOVE

From a tower close under the summit of Buachaille, the Crowberry ridge drops nine hundred feet north-east.   Its sheer eastern flank remained unclimbed until 1934, intimidating climbers so long as more obvious routes remained unexplored. In that year G. C. Williams opened up the cliff by a good but relatively short route, whose name, Rannoch Wall, has since been applied to the whole face.   In August 1936 the tallest part of Rannoch Wall fell to J. F. Hamilton, who used a groove, barely visible from below, to climb the three hundred and sixty feet from the lowest corner to the top centre.   From the delicate tread of Agag was derived the name of his new route.   I had the good luck to witness his first ascent.   No photograph can

* B

convey its sensational aspect as watched from below: on no short summer climb have I seen a bolder lead. But the 'fly-on-a-wall' appearance is misleading and constitutes a libel on a splendid route.

One morning in December 1937 I arrived at the Glencoe-Glen Etive cross-roads with Dunn, MacAlpine, and Mackenzie. We had made no definite plans, for new snow had come on the hills and a black frost held the earth spellbound. The air was still as death, so that sounds from a long distance came sharp to the ear, and our footfalls rang hollow on the roadway.

With nipped ears and much stamping of feet, we stood at the cross-roads in brief debate. It occurred to us then that a winter ascent of the Rannoch Wall would provide high interest, and we surveyed the Buachaille to see what opportunity offered. The colours of the rock showed unnaturally clear—dove-grey, brown, and palest red, projecting through a snow-sprinkle that sparkled like salt. Here and there a smaller crag, softly black as though smoke-stained, was girdled by the white ribbon of ledge and gully. Rannoch Wall stared down at us, more free of frost than any other part of the mountain. Its angle and a day or two of sun had kept it clean, but within the groove we feared that deadly combination, ice-glaze and loose powder-snow.

We resolved to inspect the conditions more closely from the foot of Curved ridge, so turned south to Coupal Bridge in Glen Etive and thence tramped the moor for an hour and scrambled among the lower rocks to the water-slide below the ridge. There was one little mountain ash close by, miraculously springing from a ledge of solid stone. Its twigs were exquisitely beaded with ice and it looked like a crystal chandelier. I have passed beside it well over a hundred times and regard it as an old friend of heroic fortitude—how *does* it contrive to wring life from its chosen block of porphyry, winter after bitter winter? One may only marvel in vain—and pass humbly on. The water-slide was frozen and step-cutting was required. Under the swing of my axe, an icicle on the left wall, twice the size of an elephant's tusk, cracked like a rifle shot; and left a sudden

THE SHADOW OF BUACHAILLE ON THE MOOR OF RANNOCH

silence, which for a moment seemed to brood over us like a hovering of wings, then as suddenly to vanish.

Ten minutes later our boot-nails were grating on Curved ridge and we drew up parallel to the Rannoch Wall. From all over the wall came a hard metallic glitter, emanating from invisible frost cressets. As a whole, the wall displayed a gratifying freedom from the snow that dusted the remainder of the mountain. Agag's groove looked most inviting.

'The sun has certainly been getting at it,' said Dunn with a delighted grin. 'But what about the groove? We'll probably find it lined with green ice.'

'There may be black ice at the crux,' said Mackenzie, in a tone that implied that such would be a point in its favour.

'But there's no snow,' I pointed out. 'Only the leader need carry an axe. We can always come down if it won't go.'

'At thirty-two feet per second per second!' added MacAlpine.

We honoured him with the half-laughing snort due to one's jesting friends; for in fact one may rope down the groove from any of its stances, which have first-class belays. Without more ado we crossed C gully to the cairn at the foot of the climb. We put on balaclava helmets and all available scarves and sweaters until we bulged like polar bears, then roped up with Mackenzie as leader, myself second, followed by Dunn. MacAlpine, who was suffering from a strained muscle, spent the day on Curved ridge. We all retained our rucksacks, but left two axes beside the cairn. Mackenzie carried the third slung at his waist.

The lowest end of the groove was eighty feet overhead, separated from us by a wall, which Mackenzie took in two pitches by bringing me up to a small half-way stance. That first eighty feet was not specially difficult; better than that, it was delightful. The rock lies indeed at a high angle, coarse, clean-cut, and well provided with little square holds—ideal both for boots and gloved fingers.

On joining Mackenzie in the start of the groove I at once looked around for ice, but save for straggling filaments, spreading vein-like on the main wall, there was none. No more than moderately difficult, the groove rose long, wide, and arching to the crux. At close quarters it is not so much a groove as a curving ledge, one hundred and eighty feet in length and about three feet broad, sometimes less and rarely more. As we climbed slowly upward we had a knowledge of complete safety that seemed at odd variance with our progress up the most vertical cliff in central Scotland. The feeling induced was pure elation —height and distance were a sparkling wine poured to the mind from a rock decanter. And to this blend of height and distance my attention was inevitably and repeatedly drawn as I waited on comfortable stances while the man above or below was climbing.

Near the top of the groove I came upon one especially well-upholstered couch—a hollow cushioned with crowberries, which in summer ripeness affords the climber both bed and board, but whose hoary counterpane gave me a chill welcome in frost. I sat there and first paid out Mackenzie's rope and then drew in Dunn's. I felt, perhaps, something of the pleasure of that raven, which as long as man can remember has nested on the neighbouring crags of Raven's gully—I looked straight out from the rock-wall, snugly conscious of the unseen drop below, as a man may nestle more happily in his bed when he hears the rainstorm beat upon his window. My gaze met nothing till it met the moor, lightly whitened as though veiled by frail lace, through which the brown heath glowed like an inner warmth. Along the farthest fringe, behind Schiehallion and beyond Loch Rannoch, ran between sky and earth a broad belt of brume, the colour of the Cuillin after rain on a still evening.

Meanwhile, Mackenzie had climbed twenty-five feet to find that our protecting groove had petered out in a nest of bulging rocks. He was still a hundred feet beneath the crest of Crow-berry ridge, and by a traverse to the left must now embark upon the open face. Immediately above him was the crux of the climb, twenty feet of almost vertical rock, the last fifteen of which, jutting like a squat nose, were split by a crack whence a climber may look between his legs to the screes. In this crack we anticipated ice.

'Look out for squalls,' Mackenzie said casually. 'If there's no ice then the frost has probably loosened some of the holds.' And with these parting words he stepped from the groove on to a ledge on the open wall. He climbed to the nose, where for a moment I saw him outlined against blue sky. He had stopped to strip off his gloves. Then he vanished like the boy in the Indian rope-trick.

I waited for the ominous sound of his axe, but five minutes passed without even the faintest noise from above. If there were loose holds I could trust Mackenzie not to use them; or to use them correctly. He was apt to leave loose holds rather than throw them down, arguing that loose holds are not of necessity bad holds. I was startled by a whirr, and a black shape dashed towards Curved ridge. It was my other old friend—the raven. He had watched many a climb of mine on Buachaille. He wheeled round the base of Crowberry ridge and led my eyes down to the moor. The Glencoe road ran like a grey thread to the Blackmount. It was absurd to say that this new road spoiled the scenery. As well might one say that a scratch could spoil the façade of Chartres Cathedral. The road was dominated by the scenery—lost in it. Perhaps, by comparison, it helped to lend some meaning to an immense scale of things otherwise beyond comprehension. A shout came from above. Mackenzie was up.

Dunn arrived and anchored himself in my former berth. I moved on to the face. The change from security to extreme exposure at once quickened up my pulse—a physiological advantage that assists one to climb well on the crux. I paused for a second to familiarize myself with the sweep of the rock, then climbed to a sloping ledge below the nose. So far as I could see there was not a vestige of ice in the crack, which errs on the shallow side: ''Tis not so deep as a well, nor so wide as a church door; but 'tis enough.' Like Mackenzie, I thought it well to remove my gloves. Foothold was available, not within the crack, but on either side. I thought the holds very small for boots, and the angle made it awkward to take them properly without leaning out on the finger-tips—which I wished to avoid as my fingers were numb. As I went up I tested each hand-hold before putting weight on it. It is good policy to regard a cracked bulge with suspicion, however secure it may seem; like Byron's column, this particular specimen has seen better days:

> By a lone wall a lonelier column rears
> A grey and grief-worn aspect of old days;
> 'Tis the last remnant of the wreck of years—

and as such one of the holds in the crack came away in my hand. I tossed it into space and looked down sideways to watch it crash into C gully. I could also see that my rope hung well clear of the rock and that our two axes seemed directly under-neath my heels. All sensation was now beginning to leave my hands and I lost no more time in reaching the top.

A noteworthy fact of that last twenty feet is that whenever one begins to climb, all sense of undue exposure vanishes before the great technical interest of the rock—unless one deliberately chooses to stop and look down. One forgets one's environment as one forgets it while reading a good book.

Mackenzie was sitting on a small platform on top of the nose. He looked cold, but refused to admit to any severe chill in the air, although his own breath was a visible witness against him. There still remained eighty feet of hard climbing, and since gloves could not be worn Mackenzie decided to take it in one run-out of rope, and by thus saving time, to temper the frost to the bare finger.

He went to the left on another ledge of traverse, carefully stepping over a large loose boulder *en route*, and once again I was alone. The sun was low down in the south and the shadow of Buachaille, which in summer is cast in a perfect cone over the flat face of Rannoch moor, fell now to the more hilly north. Kingshouse Inn, the merest white speck, was engulfed within the edge of the shadow. The Buachaille must rob that inn of a great deal of sunshine although the two lie two and a half miles apart. Great depth and immeasurable distance commingled in that subtle harmony of which I spoke, but which must be seen and felt before it can be understood in words.

AGAG'S GROOVE, RANNOCH WALL

Fully twenty minutes passed, and then with Dunn's arrival I was free to follow Mackenzie.   I felt the exposure here much more than at the crux, and the reason is not hard to discover: the climbing being less difficult one has more leisure to think of one's position.   The rock must lie at an angle of about eighty degrees; in other words, to the climber it seems practically perpendicular.   Although the face is basically sound, great caution was required in dealing with detached stones, and on the last six feet, the steepest of all, another hold broke in my hand. I was prepared for it and no damage was done.   It is none the less worth noting, for the benefit of others, that it looked absolutely secure.   Snow on the ridge and frost on the face are melted by the sun and trickle into the cracks, where the water in again freezing must inevitably prise loose some of the holds. Therefore in hard frost on Rannoch Wall every hold on the last hundred feet must be tested, even though its summer staunchness be known. I am anxious not to convey the impression that Agag's groove is unsound.   On the contrary it is excellent; as good porphyry as any on the mountain.   It ranks equal to most gabbro.

I emerged on the crest of Crowberry ridge on the gently sloping rocks above 'the slabs.'   Mackenzie, who was now fully gloved, took in Dunn's rope for me while I sat on the edge and tried to thaw my paralysed fingers.   Even to one much accustomed to rock-work, a man climbing those last eighty feet of Rannoch Wall made a startling sight.   The depth and sheerness seemed to suck both eye and breath into the gully, and Dunn's presence on the wall, as he climbed with studied ease above remote scree, appeared an incredible flouting of natural laws.   I know of no other rock-climb that strikes me in that way.

When the whole party had assembled we coiled up the ropes and advanced over the frost-hoared rocks of Crowberry tower to the summit.   The biting cold did not dispose us to linger and the sun was setting in a smother of frothy cloud.   There would be more snow on the morrow.   We retired down Curved ridge, and retrieving our axes, returned with all dispatch to a bright fire and hot dinner at Kingshouse Inn.

5

The Deep-cut Chimney of
Stob Coire nam Beith

ONCE EVERY WEEK, Dunn, Mackenzie, and I used to forgather for supper at MacAlpine's house in Glasgow. There we met on Thursdays to exchange yarns and hatch mountaineering plots. It may be deduced from a reading of Herodotus that the ancient Persians owed much success in war to the habit of planning their strategy at nightly carousals and revising it in the morning when they were sober. Imagination thus illumined method. On the same principle many a new route was first made in MacAlpine's sitting-room, where we never failed to find the cheering stimuli of a blazing fire, deep arm-chairs, and tankards of beer. If these schemes could afterwards pass the severe test of dawn-hour on the day of action, one could safely say they were practicable. These nights of merriment and discussion were something we looked forward to only less than the climb itself, and this was the only climbing-combination I knew that over a period of years consistently planned in advance. There was a peculiar appeal in such long-distance planning— a keen satisfaction in seeing deliberated efforts draw to fruition in face of many a setback.

One of our hardest campaigns was the struggle with the Deep-cut Chimney of Stob Coire nam Beith in Glencoe—the north-westerly peak of Bidean nam Bian. Underneath these two summits sprawls a northern corrie, whose west wall is the great east cliff of Stob Coire nam Beith, rising twelve hundred feet, broken by weather into a chaos of ridge and buttress. At the centre of the mass the biggest buttress is split to its base by a narrow gully named Deep-cut Chimney; to the left and right of which are No. 3 buttress and No. 4. The chimney ends four hundred feet above the screes in a small amphitheatre from which eight hundred feet of open rock rise to the summit. In 1936 there was still no record of any ascent of this chimney.

The first skirmish was undertaken in spring of that year by Mackenzie and Dunn, who were preceded on the climb by J. A. Brown and T. D. Mackinnon. They failed, being turned away by an ugly overhang at the second pitch, where Dunn was obliged to stand for half an hour under a waterfall, whose volume increases with the years. But with such men as these failure can generally be made to show profits. Not only did Dunn subsequently lead the ascent of a rib to the right of the chimney, but Mackenzie by careful study acquired an exact knowledge of the chimney's features. That same day Mackinnon and Brown made the first recorded ascent. But they by-passed the principal pitches by a shelf high on the left wall. A direct ascent remained to be done. In 1939 the seeds of discovery germinated in Mackenzie's fertile brain, and one January night, from behind a frothing mug in the depths of MacAlpine's arm-chair, he delivered himself of a revolutionary stratagem.

A direct summer ascent, said Mackenzie, was probably impossible. The overhang seemed hopeless. But in winter, when the gully walls and the four pitches below the amphitheatre were iced, one might carve holds to supply the natural lack. That was a plain enough proposition. Unclimbable summer rock may frequently be climbed by virtue of a snow or ice crust. He calculated, however, that on a short winter's day we could not expect to reach the amphitheatre before sunset. Therefore the remaining eight hundred feet must be climbed by torchlight.

That was a typical instance of Mackenzie's originality. With one bold stroke he cut through orthodox practice. At first the idea of climbing eight hundred feet of snow-bound rock by night seemed unusual; but the more we discussed the plan the more feasible it appeared. We knew by experience that climbing on whitened rock by torchlight is little harder than by day—provided that the proper line of ascent be known beforehand.

And as it happened, we had all made previous acquaintance with the upper face. Therefore the plan was adopted.

Three mornings later (January 1939), Dunn, Mackenzie, and I arrived in the north corrie of Bidean nam Bian. The hills were draped with new snow and a high ceiling of steel-grey cloud promised at least twelve hours of settled weather. We kicked a few hundred steps up a snow-slope to the foot of Deep-cut Chimney. It looked grim enough in all conscience. The first three hundred feet were of snow-ice packed between narrow walls, then the angle suddenly dropped and a hundred feet higher the snow spread out fanwise in the amphitheatre. Every pitch was thickly hoared and appeared to hold too little ice to assist us and just enough to augment its normal difficulty. We roped up and Mackenzie took the lead.

The bed of the chimney was choked with firm snow and the vertical walls floured with soft. In one and a half hours we climbed two ice-pitches and arrived at the overhang. Mackenzie cut up to the roof and belayed me round an enormous icicle. I then forced the remainder of the pitch up an ice-coating on the right wall of the gully. We had spent one hour on thirty feet of rock. Thereafter the rock was smothered more heavily than ever and the climbing became very hard and slow. Sweeping with gloved hands and scraping with ice-axes, we gradually forced a way, until at three o'clock, after five hours' climbing, our assault was broken on the fourth pitch. Mackenzie tried again and again to turn its overhang on the left wall. Straightforward methods and his repertoire of tricks and jugglery alike came to naught on brittle ice. He reached within a few feet of the top, but the rest was starkly unjustifiable.

When we turned to the descent we had only one and a half hours of daylight to get down what had taken us nearly five hours to get up. But the retreat ran as smoothly as clockwork, and by using combined tactics and hitching doubled ropes to minute rock-spikes, which were not at all easy to find, we roped down in one hour.

That we had been utterly beaten was of little consequence,

ICE PITCH

On Ben Nevis

but I was about to learn a valuable lesson, and can now expose a trap from which we narrowly escaped, and thus, perhaps, spare some future party a benightment:

At four o'clock we arrived back at the floor of the corrie, whereupon inner pangs recorded the elapse of twelve hours since our last meal. We sat down on the snow and I opened my rucksack in search of food. There, in the bottom, lay the electric torch on which our climbing plan had been founded, its three-hundred-foot beam reduced to a dying flicker. It must have been blazing full strength for the last six hours or more. When I looked round the corrie at the grey dusk, deepening by little shivering starts into darkness, and saw the cliff loom high and remote behind the murk, I reflected that had all gone well we should now be penetrating the amphitheatre—and upward bound for wide acres of rock and snow, be confidently fetching out our night-light. For once in my life I felt grateful to brittle ice and thankful for a last-minute failure.

The remedy, always to keep torch and battery separate until required, is too obvious to need labouring. It is such attention to detail that distinguishes efficiency from 'bad luck' on mountains.

THE FIRST WINTER ASCENT

Good Friday is always a fine day. In anticipation of this Mackenzie and I planned our final attempt on Deep-cut Chimney for Good Friday 1939. We were justified. The stars sparkled from a clear night sky when we left Glasgow at six a.m.; when we reached Glencoe hard frost and bright sun illumined the white face of the mountain world. Neither Dunn nor Mac-Alpine was free to climb, but otherwise the prospect was perfect. We reached the northern corrie at eleven o'clock with eight hours of daylight before us, and sat down on a warm slab to have second breakfast. I had brought a tin of sardines, and the high traditions of its species were upheld when the key broke. The time that can be wasted on an unopened tin of sardines is phenomenal. Realizing the danger of the situation we attacked with our ice-axes and triumphantly forced the lid while the sun was still high. The sardines by this time were sardines no more, as the rocks for yards around bore witness. But the tin had been opened.

At eleven-thirty a.m. we climbed the frozen slopes under the chimney, and looking up, saw with astonishment what was waiting for us. The character of the route had completely altered. Little rock and no snow save in patches were visible. From top to bottom the chimney was one long ribbon of gleaming ice, blue, grey, and white. We could form no idea whether any of the pitches would go. It looked most unlikely. One could only hope and try.

We agreed to lead alternately and then tied up on a hundred feet of rope. Under the influence of Dr. J. H. B. Bell I had come to suspect that many a stretch of rock or ice, blithely described as perpendicular, is in fact less so than it seems. The theory was probable enough to be worth investigating; therefore I had brought a clinometer with me to measure the *average* angle of the pitches. Thus the first of these was proved sixty-three degrees (I should have thought sixty-eight degrees) and on this Mackenzie opened his innings with half an hour of stylish axe-work. The ability to climb on steep ice with any appearance of grace, when holds must be cut one-handed and one's nose is not more than a few inches from the slope, is rarely seen and can be won only through long practice. Mackenzie at his best, and given good ice, can display a rhythmic motion most fascinating to watch; as Hazlitt says of such art: 'There is something in all this which he who does not admire may be quite sure that he never really admired anything in the whole course of his life. It is skill surmounting difficulty and beauty triumphing over skill.'

When Mackenzie's head came level with the top of the pitch, he stopped. He looked ahead for a few moments and then said that he did not think the second pitch would go. He was doubtful about the result of our climb, for the pitches would all be lengthened by the small depth of snow in the bed of the chimney. He therefore climbed down and asked me to go up and say what I thought. On putting my head over the top I was surprised to find that the second pitch, which had given us hard axe-work on our last visit, was in fact a 'pitch' no longer. It must have been formed before simply by an accumulation of snow and ice where the chimney steepened for several feet. Now it was merely a brief steepening of angle, and the true second pitch was the old third pitch. It looked grim. Height forty feet. The rock overhang was draped with icicles, while the right-hand wall of the gully, by which the overhang must be avoided, looked glazed and nasty. However, I could see no wisdom in retiring without an attempt on it. We had come prepared for severities—and here they were.

Being now above the first ice-wall I took over the lead, and was delighted to find upon the ice a tongue of shallow snow, hard as iron, on which I cut a staircase of three-inch notches, until a hundred feet higher we came to the next impending obstacle—that summer overhang of high renown. The shortage of snow left it much higher than upon our last visit, and the overhang was prominent thirty feet above; but the quantity of ice would have satisfied the most querulous. The angle of the lower half was seventy-seven degrees (without a clinometer I should have said 'vertical'), and we were glad to use specially short axes—slater's picks with the side-claws removed—which we find of great value in the cramped space of an ice-choked crack or chimney, where a swing with a full-size axe is hardly possible. Mackenzie attacked at first with two-handed vigour. His ashen shaft flashed as he opened his shoulders and the well-struck blows went home. A sharp crack as the pick drove in —a gout of white spray. The ice split and splintered. The tinkling fragments flew outward and whirred past my head, their hum rising in pitch as they shot into the void. Whenever he moved on to the first holds balance became delicate; his initial violence gave place to forearm and wrist strokes with the short axe, and as he gained height to a mere patient picking, which accounts for the length of time that such climbing demands. He climbed fifteen feet and retired. I again took over the lead and completed the route to the overhang, where I found a shallow recess of pure ice. I wedged myself between two pillars of ice at the back and brought up Mackenzie. He halted only to remove his rucksack and was then able, safely belayed by myself, to skirt the overhang on the right wall and cut up a curtain of grey ice to the top.

Mackenzie was now in high feather and constantly gave vent to a piercing whistle, whose tune, if any, was too shrill to be detected by merely mortal ears. Meanwhile, I paid out the rope and sat back on the icy scaffolding. There is an undeniable thrill in gazing out, like an eagle from its eyrie, through the slit of a lofty chimney. I felt it keenly as I glanced down to the sun-bright cup of the corrie. That plain view of the sweep of the snow-fields between torn crags is stamped in my mind with peculiar intensity. I can recall it clear and sharp at will, visualize a fragile snowflake on the wall and the sinuous curve of a drift in the corrie, when many a more noble panorama, which I thought unforgettable, has grown dim and misty.

The confined space of a gully may appear at a disadvantage, but within the smaller field of vision, whether the sun shine upon a filagree of frost, burnish a further crag, or flood some distant moor and river, one observes a quality in sunlight that cannot be properly seen in the open; one sees a peculiarly rich and mellow glow, which in open country is absorbed into the land-scape and lost to the eye. In fact, one more clearly observes sunlight's inherent beauty.

After brooding by myself for ten minutes I heard Mackenzie call me upward. We had already spent an hour on the pitch, so, relying on his rope-belay, I climbed swiftly on precarious holds to economize time. I discovered him, beaming all over and gaily whisking in my rope round an ice-axe, barely two inches of which were sunk into a strip of snow-ice. It appalled me into a quick heart-beat—until I found that snow tough enough to hold a ton weight. This absence of snow in the bed

SNOW

of the gully added to the tenseness of the climbing. One might never rest at ease between pitches, for the ice-layer was thin and foothold rarely more than a few inches deep. Every step of the climb had to be cut with the axe. We could not tell from one half-hour to the next, when we might be defeated. On the other hand, the brisk air seemed to brace us up throughout the day, and after our first hesitation we felt absurdly optimistic.

The snow in the chimney now became better and we went up speedily to the third pitch. This we regarded as the crux of the climb, since we had failed to get up before. A tape-like runnel of snow-ice, glossy and concave, rose gently from our feet and swept upward, quickly rising to verticality until forty feet above our heads it bent forward in a cornice. Above the cornice was a low rock overhang. There were thus two over-hangs, one of snow and the other of rock. Thus far we had passed over many a short bulge not included in clinometer readings, but this forty-foot overhang could be climbed direct only in the bar-parlour of a highland inn.

It was my turn to lead, and no other course being possible, I climbed to the centre of the concavity and then traversed on to the left wall of the gully. Straggling veins of black ice streaked the rocks, which stood out as a cheerful red between the white runnel and the blue sky. Higher up, a left-flanking buttress fell back and allowed the sunlight free play in the more open part of the gully ahead. I felt as though about to emerge from a region 'numbed by the slow snow-breath' into a rocky paradise of warmth and laughter.

The golden promise of the upper gully so filled me with *élan* that I made short work of an otherwise nasty wall, and drew level with the cornice that crowned the pitch. To continue up the wall was impossible. I tried and found that the ice was good enough where it bulged and bad to disappearing point where it did not bulge. The only route open to me was to traverse round a rib on the wall on to the overhang. It was from this particular move that I shrank. Quite apart from mountaineering principles, every instinct recoiled from such a step. To tread upon a cornice near the top of a steep gully is to shout aloud for disaster. Owing to the various shortcomings of the rock, the step was, moreover, a wide one: three and a half feet across the angle of a corner.

I asked Mackenzie what he thought of this predicament. A question purely rhetorical, asked for the satisfaction of making my own violent reply. Mackenzie tried to conceal an amused grin and studiously ignored me; very wisely he would encourage me neither way. I leaned round the rib and prodded the cornice with my axe. Its back, at least, was blue ice thickly hoared. There was a narrow joint between the ice and the rock behind. With all my strength I then hit the cornice a full blow with my axe-head. Not a move. It was like hitting granite.

Provided I could step on to the *back* of the cornice, then for once a rule might be justifiably broken. But the whole difficulty of the move lay precisely in stepping on the back rather than the front; for there were no pull-in holds on the rib to support me while I swung round out of balance. I worked out a method—speed and counter-press—but that cornice did look alarming. Reason said: 'Do it! It's safe.' Instinct said: 'Don't. The cornice and you will collapse outward.' I tried to rely on detached judgment rather than the instinct of self-preservation. On that I acted. I leant round the rib, drove my axe into the joint behind the cornice, and swung round the rib in a crouching position—balance retained by a press on the rib with one hand and a pull on the axe with the other. Then my foot came on the cornice, my main weight still on the rib. Looking between my legs, my eye went down to our morning snow tracks below the chimney. I let go the rib, flung my whole weight on to the foot on the cornice, at the same instant whipping the axe-pick into a crack in the rock above. There was never a safer cornice in all Scotland. A few more awkward movements and the pitch was climbed. Mackenzie joined me. The way was clear to the amphitheatre.

The most urgent question before us was whether we should find the amphitheatre a cul-de-sac. But our natural desire to

quicken the pace was frustrated, for though the gully rose uninterrupted for a hundred feet, the ice in its bed was so thin
that everywhere the glazed rock showed through.   This unpleasant state persisted until we penetrated to the snows of the
amphitheatre, which we found to be a beautiful little cirque
ringed by warm brown walls—a hanging corrie in the midst of
the cliff.   The time was three p.m., and thus far we had spent
three and a half hours on the climb, two-thirds of which still
lay ahead.

The amphitheatre was filled with downward-tilting snow and
backed by a high crag, from which the snowfield had shrunk
away to leave a twenty-foot chasm.   We stood beside the brink
and surveyed the scene.

To our front and left we were truly walled in; the only breach
was a forty-foot crack, lacquered in black ice and therefore
impossible; to our right, a snowy belt of more broken rock
offered a feasible escape over the north-west rim.   We were
then frankly jubilant and indulged in a joyous half-hour.   Sitting
like horsemen astride the lip of the chasm, we voraciously consumed our first meal for ten long hours and gave free rein to
merriment over past failures.   It is an odd thing in mountaineering that misfortune in retrospect provokes more mirth than
success; discomfort is but a sorry competitor against humour on
the time-track.   We wound up the feast with a panegyric on
the vanquished chimney and regret at the absence of Dunn and
MacAlpine.

When put to the test, our chosen route of escape yielded
readily and we emerged at last on the upper face.   Projecting
everywhere through the snow were bare ribs, broad walls, and
low ridges.   They were mingled in a general confusion and
gave us heavy work but not technical difficulty.   The choice
of route was wide, but to avoid dead ends it was very necessary
to select the way as far ahead as possible.   No such care is
required in summer.

In one hour we climbed six hundred feet above the amphitheatre.   Thus far we had found the appeal of this superb climb

to lie in its variety. First, three and a half hours of severe ice in the chimney, then as a pleasant change a long scramble unroped on an interestingly complex face: ice, rock, and snow in perfect proportion. We both thought that this twelve-hundred-foot route ranked next to Crowberry gully as the second-best winter climb in Glencoe.

Mackenzie and I were enjoying ourselves so much that a short way beneath the summit we turned and climbed back down the cliff. Choosing a discontinuous series of shelves, grooves, and gullies on a course further to the north, we made a tortuous descent to within two hundred feet from the corrie; when suddenly the mountain unmasked its batteries.

We were most luckily traversing a ledge under protection of an overhang when there came from above an ominous crash. Through the twilight there whizzed three feet above our heads an enormous boulder. It hummed and sang as it shot into the darkening corrie. A whiff of grape-shot followed; then all was still. One round only. I like to think of it as a shot fired in celebration: to commemorate a first ascent and to mark the close of a year's campaign.

6

Rubicon Wall

I HAVE NO WISH to embroil myself in that well-tried topic of the debating chamber: 'To travel hopefully is a better thing than to arrive'; but let me say, non-committally, that whether these words be true or not of the spires of El Dorado, they are not infrequently true of Ben Nevis in summer. A mist-cap and a rain-blanket, ample enough to dampen a Vesuvius, keep the mountain cool, too cool, in the heat of summer, the rocks too often slippery to the numbed hand, and Rubicon Wall unvisited.

By the summer of 1937, no second ascent, since the first by A. T. Hargreaves four years earlier, had been made of the Rubicon Wall on Observatory buttress. The route was classed as 'very severe,' and was thought to be the hardest on Nevis. Its neglect arose from the difficulty in getting the right party on to the mountain at the right time; for Rubicon Wall is throughout a slab-climb, impregnable in rain and amenable only to rubbers on dry rock.

In late July 1937 there came a west highland heat-wave. The right weather had at last arrived, and after an exchange of telegrams the right party assembled one evening in the Nevis hut. Mackenzie and MacAlpine came straight from the Cuillin. They were lean from much climbing and brown as niggers. In place of Dunn I was able to bring with me from Glasgow Douglas Scott, the most beautifully stylish rock-climber who has ever tied himself to my rope. It seemed too much to expect that the weather would hold. Yet the night came warm but not sultry, and the 1st of August dawned with a tropical brilliance.

At sunrise I climbed Carn Mor Dearg to get photographs of the cliffs while the sun was on them. I returned to the hut for breakfast, to find Scott scanning a guide-book.

47

'What do you think we should climb?' he asked innocently.

We all cleared our throats simultaneously, and save that I was a bar ahead, the answer came in four-syllable harmony.

We turned out at ten o'clock and went up the left bank of the Allt a' Mhuilinn, from which we diverged rightward into the wide bay between the Observatory and Tower ridges. From the back of this bay there arose a thousand feet to the summit the broad mass of Observatory buttress, whose left half constitutes Rubicon Wall. The wall looked very slightly less vertical than the Rannoch Wall of Buachaille; its pale face was coloured the same faint tint of red. There all comparison ended, for Rubicon Wall was twice as high, and here were no grooves or incut holds, but a rumpled sheet of smoothest porphyry.

After a short ascent upon screes we climbed on to a snow-field, which hung like a white apron from the cliffs. So far as home mountains are concerned, an August heat-wave is an odd time for snow-climbing and we had not thought an ice-axe necessary. But as the snow very considerably steepened as we neared the rocks, and as the surface was hard as a board, I found myself creeping sideways on my edge-nails and wishing that I had an axe for braking purposes.

We had aimed toward the left of the wall at a yellowish rib, which marked the start of our route. This lay close to the unclimbed gully that split Rubicon Wall from Observatory ridge. On approaching the foot of our rib we found our way unexpectedly barred by a *randkluft*, a chasm forty feet deep and six feet wide between the snow and the cliff. It circled the whole width of the buttress like a moat around a fortress. Its formation there was probably less due to melting by the radiation of warmth from the rock, for little sunshine ever strikes the base of the buttress, than to a downward sliding of the entire snow-field.

The obstacle it opposed was a serious one. For a while it seemed that we might have to withdraw. The thin lip of the *randkluft* overhung and could not be trusted as the springboard for a standing jump. Further to the right, where the lip was broken, a jumper would arrive on unclimbable rock. We made a close inspection to see whether one might lower a man into the blue depths with prospect of his climbing the rock from the bottom. We saw, then, that close to our rib the snow-lip was thicker. It seemed likely to bear the weight of a man with a margin of safety. As the lightest member of the party, Mackenzie was delegated to try the jump.

We roped up—myself second, MacAlpine third, and Scott last. I took up position six feet below the *randkluft* and Mackenzie balanced like a tight-rope walker on the upcurled rim. His landing platform was a two-inch foothold, with a handrail of smaller holds on the wall above. He eyed these with pardonable hesitation, braced up and measured his distance most carefully; then again wavered, like a reluctant bather on a cold day. Suddenly he leaped: a perfect landing. He clung for a second, as if surprised at his own success, then moved slightly leftward and more slowly climbed the rib to a stance fifty feet up.

There was room up there for no more than two men at a time, therefore we in turn made the jump and moved up only as accommodation in that transit area allowed. With one exception it was the most commodious stance of the climb and boasted the first of the day's two rock-belays.

We followed the rib, which is distinguished from the mass of the wall not by protuberance but rather by its creamy tinge, for but a short way further. Its trend brought us to a saucer-like stance at the edge of the unclimbed gully, into whose bleak recesses I looked closely for the first time. I saw a series of overhanging pitches, wet, water-worn and in high degree forbidding. As a summer route it seemed blankly impossible. In winter—who can tell? Its ascent will be the most brilliant feat in the history of Scottish mountaineering.

Further ascent on our present line seemed no longer feasible, and Mackenzie traversed along a ledge to our right. It grew more and more narrow, until at last it faded out in a faint score on the wall. When he could go no further I followed after, to give whatever moral support he might draw from my presence; for the place was exposed and there was no rock-belay. He turned straight up on a high-arching slab, with the utmost difficulty gaining five feet in height; but all his efforts were frustrated by the polish of the rock. I had, indeed, never before seen rock of such metallic hardness: when kicked with a boot it rang like the steel plate of a ship. Mackenzie came down and we retired along the ledge until we could again balance without handhold.

'It's rubbers or nothing from now on,' said Mackenzie, 'and you'll have to carry my boots as well as your own.'

I shouted 'Boots off!' down the rope. Then we fetched out our rubbers and I stowed our two pairs of boots in my rucksack, which now weighed a good twelve pounds.

The sun was beating full upon us, and one might say reverberated from the rock like sound from a gong. We removed our shirts, and only the already alarming bulge of my rucksack persuaded us to retain our breeches. When all was ready we traversed back to the edge of Zero gully and Mackenzie attacked the refractory slabs from a new angle, this time with complete success.

For the next two hundred feet we described a curving course over the slab-sea, cautiously balancing up from one rounded hold to another, rarely if ever finding a notch and never an edge or splinter for grasping fingers. The principal task of one's hands was simply that of maintaining, by sense of touch waist-high on the rock-surface, one's sense of equilibrium; and for the rest, by down-press of the palms, aiding the feet. As with all true buttresses the rock was indefinite, and the exact line of our route impossible to describe. On Rubicon Wall, however, the rock is everywhere severe, and our problem was not that of choosing the best route from many alternatives, but of finding any route at all. For that reason I believe that we could never have been very far from Hargreaves's original line.

All this while we were moving gradually away from the unclimbed gully until we took to an incipient gully or groove on our right. After climbing a short way up its right wall we were forced to make an awkward stride across the groove to the left wall, then to recross to the right wall and climb a vertical or even overhanging edge. The movements were all airy and nasty ones. One could not tell, from one movement to the next, whether the rock just ahead was climbable.

After two hours of such climbing, during which we met not one belay, I felt thankful that the tail of the party was not less strong than the head; little save purely moral assistance of the rope could have been given to any weaker member of the team. But the greater responsibility lay with Mackenzie; the higher we went the more clear it became that should he lay an incorrect course, and bring his party to an impasse, our plight would not bear thinking upon. Without rock-belays, to rope down was impossible; and to climb down——! Suspense mounted as the issue continued unresolved. I conceived a great respect for those who made the first ascent.

At one o'clock we arrived at the first genuine ledge of the climb. It could not have appeared more opportunely. A traverse had become essential. From furthest east to west Rubicon Wall upreared in a final rampart of a hundred and forty feet. Directly in front no weakness invited assault. One's inclination was to trend toward the unclimbed gully, where the rock, being overlooked by Observatory ridge, wore a less exposed air; but there the ledge appeared to lead only to the base of a rectangular face, high and grey as the hull of a man-of-war. We had no choice but to traverse to the right in search of Hargreaves's route.

In the meantime, MacAlpine and Scott were strung out for a hundred feet on the slabs below. We therefore indulged in the luxury of a seat upon a square-cut block, reflecting that after all we had done well to retain our nether garments, and waited there for the party to reassemble. I watched them critically as they gathered on the ledge. In their tanned skin and tatters, stripped to the waist, three civilized men never looked more like pirates from the Spanish Main. Mackenzie in particular, sitting cross-legged on his stone quarter-deck, had the alert carriage and predatory mien of an Elizabethan sea-captain.

Our situation remained too doubtful to lend itself to free conversation, and after the exchange of no more than a few pleasantries Mackenzie and I departed westward along the ledge. The ledge quickly thinned to a crease and petered out at the centre of the wall on rocks that were none the less still traversable. We stopped. The continuation of Hargreaves's route lay farther to the right, but more directly overhead, on a wall that rose close to the vertical for a hundred and forty feet, were indented two shallow grooves, about twenty feet apart. A third of the way up, each came to a clean-cut end at the base of a swollen slab.

'If we could get up there it would be a new variation,' observed Mackenzie. 'But God knows if it would go.'

'If you like the look of it,' I answered, 'have a try. If ever you were in form it's to-day.'

Mackenzie cast a brooding glance upward. Suddenly his eye caught fire. 'Come on,' he said, 'it's in the bag.'

We went up to a small corner at the base of the left-hand groove. It now seemed vertical and not a little exposed, but Mackenzie found a way up until brought to a halt at twenty feet. All further efforts failed. His descent of the groove presented an unpleasant problem; for there were no handholds on which he could lean out to see his footing, while the angle was so steep that to lean out was imperative. He therefore drove in a ring-spike and roped down.

We consulted. I urged him to try again farther to the right, not explicitly suggesting where. We moved twenty feet along to the second groove and Mackenzie climbed fifty feet to its terminus. He gave a loud 'Ha!' of delighted surprise, and shouted over his shoulder, 'There's a belay!'—the second belay of the day's climbing.

He drew in my rope and I went up to find him ensconced on a foot-plate, which was cut like the half-section of a crow's-nest. It was the only break in the upper face and would take only one of Mackenzie's feet. I placed my own foot on his and clung on while he tied me to a small spike. There followed some intricate contortions while he won clear of entanglement; then he climbed to the slab overhead.

The groove had been difficult enough, but the slabs were of an altogether different quality. Despite his sure movement Mackenzie's climbing of them was, to speak modestly, sensational. I stood on one foot, body and face hard against the wall, and paid out the rope as I watched him balancing above, stealing up the rock, occasionally pausing before gliding onward. Often my only view of him was a pair of heels stereoscoped against blue sky. I saw his body, incredibly foreshortened, only when he turned to one side or the other. As though sighted along a rifle-barrel, my eye lay close to the rope, which after sixty feet hung straight from his waist and clear of the rock, and tapered as does a white roadway into the distance of a plain—an effect that added greatly to his apparent height and loneliness.

He disappeared. Ten minutes of electric tension dragged to an end. Ninety feet of rope had run out. Then from far above came the faintest of shouts. The words were indistinct, but I knew every inflection of Mackenzie's voice, and the tone was jubilant. He was up!

I lost no time in fetching up MacAlpine and in his favour thankfully abdicated my uneasy station. Mackenzie was by then ready for me and I ventured up with high expectations. Nor was I disappointed. The slabs were built up in a series of very severe mantelshelves, widely spaced and usually shaped like inverted saucers, tilting outward. The rock was hard and sleek as marble, so that whatever the skill of a climber no bootnail could have stayed on the rock. Here was the purest of balance climbing: handholds at discount; complete reliance reposing in the friction of feet and the carriage of head and body.

In consequence I laboured under a disadvantage from the agonizing drag of my twelve-pound rucksack. Four hundred feet below was the gaping mouth of the *randkluft*, and I could see right into it. The typical move, which stays in mind with all the freshness of the day's encounter, was that of hoisting myself

c

up to a mantel by the down-press of my right palm, of lodging the left foot on that same mantel at hip-level, and then, without further handhold, straightening the left leg, my sense of balance preserved by hands fluttering up the wall above and the right toe lifting against the wall below. I discovered, too, why Mackenzie had paused from time to time—to draw a deep breath at the end of each movement.

Rubicon Wall suddenly ended on a broad stone-strewn ledge, from which the last six hundred feet of Observatory buttress fell back to the plateau. My first thought, as I stepped on to the ledge, was to congratulate Mackenzie on a great lead.

Now that our goal of pilgrimage was happily assured, and we might descry the celestial city of our mountain-top, my second thought was to cast off my load of worldly cares—of total weight twelve pounds. 'To bear the burden up the breathless mountain flank, unmurmuringly,' is not a virtue I share with Ruskin's Swiss peasant. My third thought went out in compassion for MacAlpine, perched like a stork on his roost below. I signalled him to take up Scott and come on when ready.

While MacAlpine was climbing I had to stand well back to give him a safe belay; but later I obtained a unique photograph of Scott, climbing, as it seemed, out of the very jaws of the *randkluft*. From above, Rubicon Wall reminds me in some ways of looking down from the great dam at Aswan; the rocks and concrete sweep away in the same clean fashion. Rubicon Wall is less even—but twice as high. Upon this down-rush of slabs Scott climbed with a feline flow of movement that enthralled me. I have seen no man so entirely at home on balance climbs.

I could not help noting the contrast of this route with my climb up the Cioch and Crack of Doom, which likewise abounded in slabs. There we ended weary in muscle from wrestling up on minutely inset holds. Here, after four hours' climbing on a more difficult route, we finished as fresh as paint; for we used not arms but feet—balance, not energy. These sheets of porphyry may be smooth, but they are sounder than gabbro, and any man who falls here falls by no defect of the rock.   This is the hardest rock-climb I know on Nevis.   The course is continuously difficult.   Experience in the leader is as vitally important as high skill.

Whenever Scott arrived we coiled the rope and devoted an hour to talk and tobacco.   At last we donned our boots and climbed the upper buttress, now broken like the rapids above a fall.   Upon the summit plateau we were gently cooled by the faintest stir of air.   We could see Ireland and a blue haze that I thought to be the Cheviots of England.   But most enchanting of all was the black bristle of the Cuillin, which leap to the eye of a mountaineer as lightning to steel, so that a hundred encircling hills passed unobserved.

Was this, our El Dorado, a better thing than our hopeful pilgrimage?   I experienced something of both that day—and still I cannot answer.   I think the question is such a vexed one because it is not, in the first place, legitimate.   The goal and the way are one; they co-inhere; they are not to be separated.

7
Defeat

IT IS THE CUSTOM of mountaineers to set on record their most successful climbs, but to say nothing of their reverses. The custom is an unfortunate one; there can be no doubt that one may sometimes gain more genuinely valuable experience from defeat than from the most brilliant series of first ascents. This consideration persuades me to set down in writing an unsuccessful attempt, on 13th December 1936, to make the first winter ascent of the Crowberry ridge by way of Garrick's shelf.

With this high task in view, Mackenzie, Dunn, MacAlpine, and myself assembled at Inverarnan on the night of 12th December. The following morning we drove north to Coupal Bridge in Glen Etive, where we discovered that once again Dunn had forgotten his boots. He drove that seventy miles to Inverarnan and back like a rocket, and we finally set out for the Buachaille at ten-thirty a.m. The hour was now late, yet we adhered to our original plans, although a defeat high up at dusk on a rock-snow-ice climb could hardly be contemplated with equanimity. However, the route was well known to us and we felt confident of success. We were all in excellent physical condition, exceptionally well equipped, and yearning for a first-class climb. These factors overcame our good judgment. The morning was cloudy, with the wind in the west-south-west. New snow had fallen overnight but was not lying in sufficient depth seriously to impede our progress to the foot of Crowberry gully, where we encountered a short difficult pitch that whetted our appetite for bigger and better things. Never was an appetite destined to be more harshly glutted.

We now left the gully and moved up the lower rocks of Crowberry ridge, where we traversed a ledge of steeply shelving snow on its northern wall. This movement brought us under the first big pitch of Garrick's shelf. Here we found a cave large enough to accommodate the whole party, and we gulped down our second breakfast hastily before roping up.

The construction of Garrick's shelf is peculiar. It is a narrow trough running up the northern wall of the Crowberry ridge, parallel to the Crowberry gully. The shelf itself, which is punctuated with steep pitches, terminates in precipitous rock some two hundred and fifty feet below the crest of the ridge. This last section, difficult in summer, ends in a steep scoop that debouches on the Crowberry ridge near the base of the Tower.

We found the rocks well plastered with snow, but ice was present only in small quantity—too small quantity, as we discovered later. The snow-covering on steep rock was not sufficiently frozen to hold, and had to be cleared away as we advanced. Our progress was much hindered by fierce blasts of wind from the south-west, which swept down the Crowberry gully and shelf, bearing great clouds of powder snow that completely filled all the holds after each of us had passed upwards. Woollen gloves froze to the holds, and were sometimes difficult to disengage.

Four hours of continuous climbing on the shelf found us at the top of the fourth pitch, at a height of some two thousand seven hundred feet. At this point I took over the lead from Mackenzie, who retired to the end of the rope for a rest. Henceforth the order on the rope was myself with Dunn as second man, then MacAlpine and Mackenzie. The shelf now began to narrow and steepen, while the snow was thinner and in worse condition than ever. The sun had already set, and the upper reaches of the shelf were pervaded by a grey and gloomy twilight. The need for haste had become urgent, yet the next fifty feet of plain, straightforward gully occupied no less than twenty minutes. The difficulty lay simply in persuading the snow to hold. There was no danger of its avalanching.

Garrick's shelf now ended and merged in the steep face of the final rocks. On our right, the shelf fell perpendicularly into the

depths of Crowberry gully; on our left rose the vertical wall of
the Crowberry ridge; before us the rocks swept up steeply for
sixty feet to a small, rectangular tower.   This tower was sheathed
in black ice and fog crystals.   It lent distinction to the place.

Our first problem was a narrow crack set in a corner and
packed with snow.   My first two attempts on it failed, but a
third and more determined effort proved successful, and I climbed
the crack by the lay-back method to a small ledge.   The time
was now four-thirty p.m.   The usual route into a square recess
at the base of the tower was unjustifiable, on account of its skin
of thin ice, and I therefore made an attempt to force the rocks
on the left.   After a great deal of manœuvring for position, an
outward-tilting mantel-shelf plastered with firm snow lying on
ice was laboriously overcome.   For a moment the position
looked promising; on the left only a short wall barred the way
to easier rock running past the tower to the crest of the ridge.
But my first movement to the left would of necessity be made
without handhold, a 'down-and-out' strain being placed upon
the feet, the foothold being a sloping slab coated with *verglas*.

I reported my position and the party consulted.   The time
was now a quarter to five; the weather was rapidly deteriorating;
to retire now would spell immediate benightment with the whole
of Garrick's shelf below us.   On the other hand, only six feet
of rock barred the leader from almost certain triumph.   The
decision we had to make was a grave one.   Should or should
not that next, very dangerous step be taken?   We decided that
it should not, and I retired.

Across the black chasm of Crowberry gully the wall of the
North buttress was now growing steadily dimmer in the gathering
darkness; already the rising storm was roaring across the upper
rocks of the Crowberry ridge.   Snow was falling steadily, and
this was reinforced from time to time by sheets of drift snow,
hurled upon us from the rocks above.   The situation appeared
to be sufficiently desperate, but the party had climbed too long
in combination to entertain any doubt of a satisfactory issue.
We carried with us three hundred and thirty feet of rope, a

torch, spare batteries, and sufficient food. We resolved therefore to continue to climb downwards rather than bivouac.

The descent of the steep section in the snow gully to pitch four was less hazardous than we had expected. The first three, secured by the rope, enjoyed a comfortable passage. They cheerfully urged me to slide, and trust them to field me if need be. I declined, and the party moved down in strictly text-book style to pitch four. A wide square-cut chimney, all three walls of which were vertical, now presented an interesting problem largely complicated by its invisibility. The solution taxed us for two hours, but we finally dug out a spike of iced rock, from which the others roped down, belayed from above. Having seen Dunn safely down and well established, I followed a thought too gaily. For the fixed rope somehow rolled off its hitch above. Down I went with a rush, conscious only of one fat blue spark where a boot-nail struck bare rock. A split second later I landed astride Dunn's shoulders. He was strongly placed, safe and solid as rock itself, and by grabbing my thighs stopped a farther fall. The party was working now at such a high pitch of concentration that we gave the incident not a thought until later.

We were by this time enveloped in darkness. The snow on the shelf and on the surrounding rock could be dimly discerned as a dull grey mantle, far too obscure to afford any indication of the route. We progressed slowly by torchlight. Creeping circumspectly down the shelf over snow and broken rock, we descended as much as a hundred and fifty feet in one and a half hours. Above the uproar of the wind and the flail of careering snow could be heard some unusual noises, which, had we not known each other better, must have sounded suspiciously like profane language. At nine a.m. we reached an open corner at the top of pitch three.

Here we were unable to rope down. There was no rock-belay, and the snow was too unsound to take an axe-belay, but we contrived a good anchor by jamming our axes in an angle of rock. Thus protected we climbed in turn down steep snow to a

point near the base of a rock-face.   A distinctly tricky traverse
to the right then led, after one and a half hours, to soft snow
below the pitch.   We could not afford to leave an axe behind us,
so I went down without a fixed rope.   I was coached over the
traverse in brilliant style by Dunn, who employed the effective
though inhuman device of ruthlessly skewering his victim with
the spike of an axe.

We were now back in the trough, hard against the wall of the
Crowberry ridge, and descended very slowly to a short chimney
that we failed to remember climbing on the way up.   A little
disconcerted, we climbed down from axe-belays and found ourselves in a narrow cave festooned with giant icicles.   This cave
was the most comfortable spot on the whole route, and we felt
loath to leave it.   I hailed the place with great joy, and after
ejecting the rest of the party urged disingenuously that any haste
in accomplishing the next section would be most unadvisable.
From the narrow recesses of the cave I could speculate as to
what was happening below, while I watched, with a certain
measure of perverted pleasure, the swirling snow pour in hissing
cascades over the roof and down the shelf, where my more
energetic companions would literally 'get it in the neck.'

Time sped on.   For over an hour there had been a great deal
of shouting below and singularly little movement.   But at long
last a faint call from Dunn summoned me downwards.   Sixty
feet below, we all congregated on what appeared to be a broad
horizontal ledge on the Crowberry wall.   An eighty-foot rope
had been fixed round a spike on the wall itself and Mackenzie,
after prospecting the route at the far end of the ledge, had just
announced that farther advance was impossible.   He was faced,
or seemed to be faced, with a bottomless abyss.   We had lost
the route.

A good twelve hours had now elapsed since our last meal, and
the thoughts of the party turned to hot soup and roast pork.
With freezing fingers we then extracted from our rucksacks the
handfuls of sodden crumbs that had formerly been jam sandwiches.   We reviewed our position as we ate, and came to the

conclusion that we were now above Garrick's shelf, on a ledge ending in a cul-de-sac. The torch-beam was therefore directed downwards toward the Crowberry gully. After some prospecting a lower route was pronounced practicable.

Our principal concern was whether the fixed rope would reach to the foot of the pitch. Mackenzie, belayed by the others, set off downwards; he went leftward down steep snow, and then swung into the mouth of a vertical shallow chimney. A long period of suspense followed. In half an hour there was still no movement of any kind from below. The party above gradually became aware that it was being kept waiting—a feeling never absent during the entire descent — and wrathfully inquiring howls were directed downwards. Several minutes later a muffled 'What?' drifted upwards, followed after a while by 'Yip!'—whatever that might mean. We gave it up.

Quite suddenly a shout of triumph assured us that our proper route had been regained below pitch two: the vertical chimney was, indeed, on pitch two itself. In half an hour we were all down. The fixed rope refused to run round the spike and was left behind. A further hour of vigilant toil took us all to a big outcrop of rock, which presented a rectangular face to the lower regions of Garrick's shelf. Immediately below us was the last great step in the shelf. We edged carefully round the right-hand corner of the outcrop, and near its base discovered an excellent spike-belay. The snow here was firm but excessively steep, so we stood face-in during the hours that followed.

Our plan was to attach a thirty-foot loop round the spike, to rope down on a hundred and twenty feet of rope, which we fervently hoped would reach the foot of the shelf, and to secure the first man down with a hundred feet of line. This two-hundred-and-fifty-foot maze of rope and line was thereupon possessed by an evil spirit and became tangled in the darkness. The whole shelf resounded with the most powerfully expressive oaths known to man. Incredible delays occurred. Violent bursts of wind-driven snow still came lashing down the shelf,

* c

Cuneiform Buttress
Raven's Gully
North Buttress

Crowberry Gully
Crowberry Ridge
Garrick's Shelf

D Gully Buttress

North
Buttress Route
Crowberry Gully
Garrick's Shelf

Crowberry Tower

THE BUACHAILLE ETIVE MOR

unendingly, and the last battery in the torch was fading.   By wriggling our toes continuously during these halts we contrived to avoid frost-bite.

At four o'clock in the morning everything was ready.   One by one we roped down a narrow chimney on the flank of an overhanging bulge.   This was appallingly difficult, for the rope declined to run, and our descent resolved itself into an exhausting struggle against friction.   The torch was now out of action, so a fitting climax was provided by an awkward left-hand traverse round the bulge from the chimney, a movement that we made unroped, and which led us into the cave below the shelf.   Upon reaching the foot of the chimney, I found myself unable to persuade the now obstinately vicious rope to run through the loop. I left it behind, with emotions closely akin to pleasure.   When at length I joined the party in the cave, I at once remarked in the bearing and attitude of my companions a striking complacency, the source of which was speedily betrayed by the crumbs adhering to their now incipient whiskers.   Thus gorged, these callous people had yet no scruple in demanding bites at my one remaining apple, on the pitiful plea that all their own food was finished.

We roped up on a hundred feet of line.   The absence of a torch was a serious handicap, and we experienced no little difficulty in the traverse along the Crowberry wall, where drift snow had piled up on the ledge at a high angle.   Shortly afterwards we gained the lower part of the Crowberry gully, where we found our difficult pitch of the previous day miraculously transformed into an easy scramble, but on leaving the gully we unfortunately lost all trace of the usual line of descent.

An hour of prospecting, both up and down, resulted in our finally defying orthodox tactics by committing ourselves to the mercy of an unknown gully, which led us with unexpected ease to the moor.   The latter imparted some wholehearted if concluding kicks, and we were all, at one time or another, immersed up to the thighs in bogs.   We reached Coupal Bridge at dawn, safe and sound, if not precisely hale and hearty.   We had been out for rather less than twenty-one hours, of which fourteen had been spent on the descent.

The moral of this is only too plain. It is one appreciated by none so well as by the party most closely concerned. But our defeat had in no way discouraged us in our determination to make a second attempt under more favourable conditions, when the shelf would be more heavily plastered with ice. By the end of March such conditions obtained and the route was climbed in its entirety.

GARRICK'S SHELF. THE FIRST WINTER ASCENT

An early start, a small party, good snow and ice, these were essential conditions for a winter ascent of Garrick's shelf. The last consideration delayed our second visit until March blizzards had been followed by a fortnight of sun and frost.

On 28th March 1937 Mackenzie and I arrived at Kingshouse on a perfect morning. A streamer of white mist ringed the Buachaille, whose upper snows were pink in the rising sun. We reached Crowberry ridge to find that from top to bottom, Garrick's shelf was masked in glinting ice—the longest ribbon of clear ice we have ever seen. The ropes we had left behind on defeat were still visible, the cores of transparent pillars two feet thick. We roped up and agreed to lead alternately. We went hard from the start.

In two hours of fast and furious cutting we climbed four hundred feet, passed over four very difficult ice-pitches, and arrived at twelve noon below the crux. This pitch had shrunk to fifty feet. Once again the moderate summer slabs to the left of the pinnacle were glazed and impossible. We attacked to the right on rocks overlooking Crowberry gully. Here, too, the ice was thin; axe-cut holds to the square recess under the pinnacle were painfully minute. Our escape from the recess, made on the pinnacle's right-hand edge, was unusually delicate. Splayed out on this bulging corner we had to change feet on a small sloping hold without handhold, and with a long drop below into Crowberry gully. The pitch was very severe and occupied two hours.

We then arrived in a broad groove which hung over the gully beyond the pinnacle. The groove was choked by an ice-fall of a hundred and fifty feet, twice bulging in fifty-foot pitches, which tried the leaders severely; for the ice was inclined to be brittle and belays poor. At three p.m. we debouched on the crest of Crowberry ridge—a sensational arête arrayed in shark's fins of translucent ice, which we shattered regretfully. Deterred from direct ascent of the Tower by ponderous snows, we traversed southward into D gully and won the summit at four p.m.

Our climb is not one I shall ever repeat in like conditions. It became too exacting. But our day's route led us through snow and ice scenery of deathless beauty. This lives strong in mind, while physical pains and trials, the so-called realities of defeat and victory, have long been forgotten.

8 *Coire Lagain*

I WAKENED AT MIDNIGHT. Although the tent flaps were tied back, I found June air in Skye too warm for a sleeping-bag. There was no moon, but the night was bright. I felt restless, absurdly energetic for such an hour, and had actually struggled out of my sleeping-bag and partially dressed, when I heard the low purr of a car approaching down Glen Brittle. I looked out, and very shortly after heard the swish of tyres and saw headlights glide to a stop two hundred yards away. From the roadway there came an inquiring shout, neither loud nor intelligible, as from one who had no hope of an answer.

I could have sworn that I knew that voice. There flashed upon my inward eye the vista of rock and a white climbing-rope. I pulled on my boots and hastened through the whin to the roadside. To my delight, there stood MacAlpine and his wife! Engaging the Mallaig ferry by telegram, and leaving Glasgow at four p.m., they had come to Skye for a short week-end.

We pitched their tent and brewed coffee. I wish that I could remember now what brand of coffee that was, for no sooner was it down than MacAlpine suggested a climb before breakfast. After his drive of two hundred and forty miles in eight hours, much of it over very bad road, this was more than I had dared to hope. Truly he is one of the elect. We set out at three a.m. for the precipice of Sron na Ciche, and one hour later, in the grey of first light, climbed the gaunt slabs of the Cioch pinnacle.

We returned to camp for breakfast. MacAlpine's visit was a notable occasion—his first visit to the Cuillin. He could afford one day's climbing, and this we had to dispose to best advantage. In other words, where could I introduce him to the Cuillin at their best? I surveyed the entire range, and without hesitation chose the traverse of Coire Lagain. It is the classic

66

RIVER
Strath Fillan

short day of the Cuillin, the Cuillin in essence—narrow ridge, distorted rock, 'jagged towers tossed aloft against the sky'—by judicious treatment one of the laziest long days. For our rock-climb to the main ridge we must choose one that combined length with shade from the sun. We had already climbed the gabbro of the Cioch; therefore I proposed the basalt of Sgurr Alisdair.

For a fortnight past the daily temperature had been consistently touching ninety degrees in the shade. We accordingly set off at seven a.m. to reach the shade of the cliffs before the sun grew too hot. We climbed some two thousand feet, passing through Coire na Ciche and crossing the upper lip into a little corrie that cups the green pool of Loch Lagain.

We were now within the most noble rock cirque of Skye. The cliffs of Sgurrs Alisdair, Thearlaich, MhicCoinnich, and Dearg formed a close ring around us, a thousand feet high. Yet there is no gloom in that corrie; rather an atmosphere of gaiety in which has perished many a too arduous plan, check-mated by the care-free waters of Loch Lagain. For though the loch be small, one may dive deep from a rock platform and swim fifty yards; on one side there is even a grass margin—a rare luxury in such a site, charming to the wanderer as the yellow sands of the lotus-eaters. Let a man but once recline there on a hot day, and he will no longer roam.

We skirted the loch and climbed up a long scree-slope to the north buttress. Our earlier notion, to climb by Abraham's route because it was harder, had been censored by the holiday spirit of the corrie. We now chose Collie's route because it was less difficult—and more openly situated. We roped-up and climbed easy slabs, which steepened as the buttress narrowed, until several hundred feet above we went up an abrupt face in whose middle we came upon a small recessed ledge. We sat there, sucked a thirst-abating lemon, and savoured the keen tang of freedom on a mountain wall, from which we looked high over empty space to the jumbled world beneath. Despite the heat the air was fresh and clean. On the glassy surface of Loch an

Fhir-bhallaich, one and a half miles away toward Glen Brittle, we could see the quick rings made by rising fish.

Half an hour later MacAlpine belayed me from the back of the recess, and I gingerly traversed on to the right-hand face. The rock was basaltic and smooth, somewhat exposed but of moderate difficulty. After a delightful little climb we continued steeply to the summit. Just underneath the cairn I was startled into a crouch as an eagle of six-foot wing-span skimmed over the crest. One could clearly see the golden breast-feathers. Eagles were common in Skye that June; one saw them daily, circling round Sgurr Dubh, where it is to be presumed they nested. I never saw more than four in the air at once, and this was the closest view I had yet been allowed.

The summit of Sgurr Alisdair is fairly pointed, but there was room for two of us at the cairn. Our firm intention was to traverse round the rim of the corrie to the Inaccessible Pinnacle of Sgurr Dearg. Meantime, we believed there was no need to hurry. Ten hours of daylight stretched before us. Thus we completely forgot the problem of thirst; for we were now in the full blaze of the sun, and the rocks were already hot to the hand.

We unpacked our rucksacks and disclosed our sandwiches. Within thirty seconds two hopeful gulls hovered overhead. In the Black Cuillin there are none of what an old writer calls 'God's jocund lyttel fowles.' These naked peaks are most frequented by ravens, gulls, hawks, and eagles—above all by the ubiquitous gull. I say ubiquitous advisedly, for a climber in the Cuillin need only stop and open his rucksack, and although not one gull be in sight, within two minutes there will gather a growing congregation to share the feast or pick the crumbs, according as their host keeps open board or niggard.

In such tropical heat our appetite was speedily satisfied, so we descended a few steps northward, and bit by bit threw our surplus bread over the precipice of the stone-shoot, between whose narrow walls a throng of acrobatic gulls performed vertical dives to retrieve the food in mid air. They never pounced as a hawk might, but dropped like stones down the shaft until beneath the falling scraps, when they suddenly stood on their tails, caught the bread, and swooped sideways and out between the gully walls. Not one mistake was made, nor a feather turned wrong.

We returned to the cairn, where I tried to persuade MacAlpine that I could see St. Kilda, the minutest speck on the line where sky and sea divided—a hundred miles north-west. But Mac-Alpine clung to his privilege as a relative and remained profoundly sceptical. The sea was quite as deep a blue as the Mediterranean in summer. It appeared gently to lean up to the horizon, polished as ice, so that one might well wonder the outer isles did not gravitate back to the mainland. There must have been, none the less, a gentle Atlantic swell, for there were snatches of foam around the shores of Loch Brittle.

A man who has not been to Skye in May or June has not, properly speaking, seen Skye at all; for there is an exquisite quality in the sunlight seen only during the three months after the spring equinox.

The gulls, meantime, observing that no more food was to be had, had taken themselves off and were engaged in harrying the eagle, which now soared over Coruisk. The scene was much like that of fighter aircraft attacking a heavy bomber. The eagle deviated neither right nor left, deranged not a plume nor flapped a wing, but in ponderous calm held to its slow course. The gulls flashed in and out, wove loops, swooped at all angles, at the very last moment changing direction with a flick of tail and wing. Their agility was astonishing. The eagle's impassivity wholly admirable. For it suffered not a few pecks before it passed out of sight behind the Dubh ridge toward Scavaig. Cuillin eagles appear to lead anything but a quiet life. I have rarely seen the wretched birds unharried either by gulls or by ravens.

About one p.m. we began an almost imperceptible drift round the cirque, a sort of northward dawdling rather than scrambling, enlivened by the ascent of Sgurr Mhic Coinnich by King's

Chimney, which ran fifty feet up an open corner to the summit overhang. This last we turned by a traverse on the bare right wall and climbed up to the cairn. Our thirst, which on Sgurr Alisdair had been kept at bay by a lemon, now possessed us like raging demons.

> O, for a draught of vintage! that hath been
> Cool'd a long age in the deep-delved earth.

It is inevitable that in the gabbro desert of the Cuillin green should most attract the human eye—it is even the green basalt that most strongly attracts the compass needle—and to a thirsty climber there is no more dazzling emerald than Loch Coire Lagain. Looking down upon it from the edge of the main ridge, we saw the cliffs stand round in tall-towered battlements, as though the loch far below were a drop of priceless green nectar that must at all costs be safeguarded. Thus we watched and moved by fits and starts—the long ascent to Dearg became unthinkable—and our last ambition, to scale the Inaccessible Pinnacle, lay in the bottom of the loch with a philosophic brick round its neck. Henceforward, our only possible destination was that green allure below.

Beyond Sgurr Mhic Coinnich the ridge narrowed to an edge, dropped sharply, then broader but riven fell away in a series of high steps to the bealach below An Stac. Some time in the afternoon—one takes no precise note of time in Skye—we launched ourselves down the rapids of the An Stac scree-run, the fastest in the Cuillin, and a few minutes later were projected in a welter of sweat on to the grassy bank of the loch.

We could hardly strip our clothes fast enough, and so parched were our bodies that on going in from the diving-boulder one could positively feel the water soak into the skin, to such effect that out agonizing thirst of a minute before was perceptibly lessened. For half an hour we dived and swam in a wild ecstasy. The delicious sting of chill water reinvigorated our limbs as could no course of massage. I felt that I had never awakened till now to that allegedly familiar quality of water—its wetness. That there was beauty in wetness had hitherto

SOUTHWARD FROM SGURR ALISDAIR

never penetrated my mind. From that moment I have learned the truth, that in fact there is beauty in everything; and that one is not always apt in seeing it. 'A thousand-mile journey begins with the first step,' and the discovery that beauty is in all, and that all beauty is the same beauty, is the first step to the highest peak of the universe.

At length the cold began to penetrate more deeply. We came out, and scrambling up the swelling flank of a slab, basked awhile on the sun-warmed rock. Through half-closed eyes I watched a fleecy cloud sail immeasurably high above the crags. Its snow-whiteness deepened the hue of the firmament, as the grey rock drew out the sheen of Loch Coire Lagain. There was refreshment of mind in the green water, and in the purity of blue sky, rest of heart.

9 *The North Buttress of Buachaille. Winter*

IN EARLY DECEMBER 1937 a great blizzard swept the central highlands. The roads were blocked, the mountains burdened, moor and river buried in deep snow. Then came the frost. On the 12th it broke all records for severity in Argyll. The conditions seemed not yet ripe for climbing in the confined space of rock-ridge or gully, but for MacAlpine and me, attentively hearkening, the hour had struck for a visit to the North buttress of Buachaille Etive Mor. Like Garrick's shelf it is not very difficult in summer, yet in winter conditions good climbing can be expected of it. Here we should not be confined to a narrow shelf but have available for route selection the whole breadth of a buttress. Snow in abundance was inevitable, but on open rocks so early in the season we little imagined that ice would be met in quantity or that any hard test lay in store.

On 12th December we left Glasgow by car two hours before dawn. Despite our wheel-chains and the good work of snow-ploughs in preparing the way, the sun had risen before we swung north-west from the Blackmount, and saw Buachaille. It burned like gold in the furnace. For the sun was still low and glittered across the snow-fields of Rannoch moor, rayed in streaming banners of light over the frozen wind-ripples, leaving blue shadows on the lee-side of drifts.

That was the coldest day I have ever known. The deer stood forlornly by the roadside, or collected in dazed herds around the Kingshouse Inn, pleading to be fed. They were given grain by a stalker. All noise was muffled by the snow, and all the Campbells in Scotland might have marched through the glen and no footfall given the alarm. The world had sunk

72

into a numbed stupor. Even the thermometer that hangs out-side the inn had given up the unequal struggle, and after recording its lowest possible, had withdrawn its thin red line within the bulb. Less ancient instruments elsewhere recorded eight degrees below zero (Fahrenheit), and the anti-freeze mixture in Mac-Alpine's car engine went solid before the day was out. To conclude these curious effects, unusual at least in my own short lifetime, the metal door-handle of the inn stuck to our bare fingers.

Although mercifully spared the usual delay of Dunn's hurtling southward for boots, we lost no little time in examining this strange new world, in photography, and in listening to our curiously muted voices. Ten o'clock was upon us before our preparations were complete and we set off toward Buachaille. The mountain was a uniform white. Not a black spot sullied the glare. We spent the first one and a half hours in wading through snow-fields and threading an icy maze among the lower crags. Not until we traversed towards Curved ridge and the ash-tree did we meet our first and surprising check. Confront-ing us was the waterslide, upon which one walks unthinkingly in summer, now bulging large in bosses of blue ice. The con-necting ledge, which overlooks a drop of twenty feet, was invisible under a mass of white ice inclining from the wall above. We had no choice but to rope up and spend half an hour's step-cutting, and I went at it like a buccaneer digging pieces of eight. Not a moment was wasted.

Beyond the waterslide we moved straightway into the foot of Crowberry gully, which severs Crowberry ridge from the North buttress. Good snow, surface-glazed, led us rapidly upward for a few hundred feet to a fifteen-foot rock-pitch, whose em-barrassing defence was frail snow superimposed on *verglas*. In consequence of such delays on the easier slopes of the mountain it was twelve-thirty p.m. before we drew level with the east wall of the North buttress. Not having fed for seven hours, and the cold having put a keen edge to our appetites, we each scooped an arm-chair in the gully and sat down to second breakfast.

Ten feet above our heads a ledge like an unrailed balcony girdled North buttress to Raven's gully, which demarcated the west side. For three hundred feet above that ledge the buttress rose abruptly, then gently curved back on its thousand-foot flight to the summit. Provided that I made no error in route selection we had ample time to pass well beyond the steepest section before sundown, and nearer to the summit we might rely on strong moonlight. Even MacAlpine was satisfied with our prospects, and he is renowned for his level-headed common sense. To climb in his company is a guarantee that a lively breeze will fill the sails of the party all day, but no high-flown ideas, no extravagant propositions cut any ice with him.

At one o'clock we roped up and climbed on to North buttress balcony. It was paved with a thick layer of sea-green ice, which dipped gently outward. The angle was just enough to make walking impossible. I plied my axe for a quarter of an hour, and in one run-out of rope (eighty feet) crossed the ice-band to a narrower continuation of the ledge. It was heavily snow-banked. We traversed to Raven's gully in search of the line of least resistance and finally returned to a corner crack near Bottleneck chimney. The crack was choked with snow. But for previous summer knowledge we should never have guessed that there was a route hereabouts. The buttress wall had every-where an even coat.

I confess that beguiled by previous visits I had underestimated the whole climb, and was not keyed up to a piece of mountaineering quite out of the ordinary. That first crack gave me a rude awakening. It was hard, very hard, requiring a full hour and a run-out of ninety feet. Those who know the route only in summer will be amused to hear that I found still greater difficulty in finding above the crack any stance to which I could bring MacAlpine. The old roomy platforms were there no longer. MacAlpine, disconsolate below, began to growl a little and I brought him up for company, if for nothing else; his fund of humour could cheer the most afflicted climber.

Having made the best of a bad job and dispensed with a belay,

WATER

Loch Duich and
the Five Sisters
of Kintail

we found that further progress straight up had become impossible, and that we must execute a delicate left traverse across a face.   The rope was here no protection and MacAlpine began to calculate the days of grace on his unpaid premiums, but we accomplished the move and the rock began to look easier.   This turned out to be an optical illusion.   The rock became in fact more difficult.   Ten precious minutes were wasted in a vain effort to get up a tempting corner, which would have straightened out our route; instead the trend of the crags pushed us more and more toward the left, until at last we overlooked Crowberry gully.

The mouth of the gully seemed like an icy courtyard, walled and turreted a thousand feet by ridge and buttress.   We have never seen the fantastic grandeur of its winter rock scenery matched by any other gully in Scotland.   Directly opposite to us Garrick's shelf stirred our recollections of a year ago, and we suddenly realized that this was the anniversary of our defeat. I hastily looked at my watch, but believing that there was still time to spare I described my subsequent ascent with Mackenzie, which was the hardest five hours I ever spent on a mountain. To-day the shelf was burdened with soft snow.

Our ten minutes' reminiscence was not without bearing on our climb: we became too anxious to waste not a further moment in following the route of least resistance, and that soon led to the error we had most need to avoid.   Meantime we climbed a short crack and flake and then had two long run-outs of rope, but still there was no sign of the buttress yielding; and the day was wearing on.   It became clear that the left flank of the buttress was going to be too much for us.   Therefore we traversed ledges back to the centre of the buttress.   The walls above rose in either rectangular steps or swelling slabs, covered even where vertical in snow with the sheen and pile of ermine.   It was beautiful to the eye, but hardly gladdening, for the labour of cleaning and climbing such rock seemed destined to be lengthy. It was then that we came upon a groove running straight as an arrow up the cliffs.   It looked moderately difficult.

I knew from experience that rock faults are often the worst routes. They are always the most inviting; they wear the very aspect of weakness. Into that trap I fell headlong, not stopping in my keenness to save time to reflect that if thin ice were to be found anywhere on the buttress it would most likely be here. Intelligence is as indispensable as an ice-axe in winter. However, one is wise after the event. The fact was that on looking up the groove I could see no ice in the lower part, whereas there appeared every promise of quick climbing. If there were ice further up, why, no doubt I could deal with it. Truly the 13th December is my bad day.

At two-thirty p.m. I started up the groove. From my own point of view all went well for twenty feet, but MacAlpine was not so happily placed. I swept the holds with my gloved hand, dislodging cataracts of snow on to his wrathful head. On the second twenty feet the difficulties mounted and progress sadly dwindled; the rock required study and no little imagination to combine its properties to advantage. On the third twenty feet I at last met black ice.

Melted by the sun, snow-water had trickled into the groove and frozen, spreading over the rock in a thick varnish. However, could I climb fifteen feet further, there seemed a possibility of my forcing an exit from the groove. I chipped out several notches and found them deep enough to support the edge-nail of a boot. I eased myself on to them, using for the hands press-holds against the sides of the groove. The cutting of further notches, while trusting only to a precariously placed boot-nail, which might be displaced by one quiver of the leg, proved an operation more delicate than I liked. To avoid the slightest body movement one had to tap the ice gently as though breaking toffee with a silver hammer. The carving of a hold occupied ten minutes. I cut three and climbed up.

'Ten feet of rope left and the sun has set!' yelled MacAlpine. 'What is it like?'

I estimated another hour to force the exit and get MacAlpine up. Were the ice to thin in the slightest degree it would become

impossible. I carried no piton and should therefore be unable
to descend in bad light. But *did* the ice thin out? It was
furred with snow and invisible. That decided me.

'It is magnificent,' I shouted back, 'but it is not mountaineering.
I'm coming down.'

But that was easier said than done. My lower body prevented my seeing the ice notches, nor could I lean out and look
down backward for them. They had to be felt for with insensitive boot-nails after a gentle lowering of the body from a
gradually, very gradually bended knee. Widely spaced holds,
or a muscle tremor from long standing in one-nail steps, would
have earned a summary verdict in the courts of mountain justice.
Resisting temptation, I had cut these holds close and happened
to be in perfect training. I therefore won acquittal from the
ice and faced the trial of the central section—when, like a last-
minute galloping of horses and the waving of a reprieve before
the aggrieved nose of a hanging judge, there appeared a small
spike on the outside wall of the groove. Before the vision
might dissolve my rope was round it. A few minutes later I
had roped down and joined MacAlpine on the ledge.

We looked eastward to estimate from the closing in of dusk
the daylight left to us. Many miles across the moor of Rannoch
the breath of frost had lain all day in a transparent haze; in the
morning, suffused with sun, like a pall of gold-dust; in the afternoon like faintest pearl; now, with the setting of the sun, it
spread from the furthest fringe toward the middle moor, blue as
peat smoke at dawn. We calculated that we had still half an
hour of good daylight to do something decisive.

MacAlpine must have been almost frozen to death during that
last and a half, and being a sociable animal, obliged to
freeze without company, might without blame have grown
despondent and pessimistic. Hope makes a good breakfast but
a bad supper. However, as always when I most need support,
MacAlpine became most cheerful and confident. Instead of
pronouncing for retreat he now backed me up in deciding to
make a quick attack elsewhere. It sounded as if long standing

on exposed and ice-bound ledges was the chief delight of his life. I was waiting for him to say that I was climbing like a chamois, but he disappointed me.

It was agreed that should I fail to find a route quickly we should begin roping down the buttress in the fading light as best we could. At four p.m. we traversed ninety feet westward with a bout of step-cutting on icy ledges. I chose the face of one high square block and swept off the snow with my arm. Small square holds began to emerge. The route was not too apparent, but neither was ice. I went up, clinging, scraping, excavating, mounting higher and higher until I passed that fifteen-foot wall and the one beyond and the slabs that followed them. It would be hard for me to say how difficult this part actually was; for I had taken the bit between my teeth and was keyed up to the fighting pitch that makes subsequent classification an impossibility. At the middle section I traversed high-angle rock on one-nail foothold without handhold, yet did not find the move awkward; although MacAlpine, who was properly not wasting time when he followed, took a vigorous pull or two on the rope. I was thankful for his workmanlike intelligence.

The light of day was still with us when the buttress became noticeably more broken. The exact art of precision climbing in the groove had no place here; honest hard toil and little more gained us seventy feet of height in thirty minutes. These slabs and walls, so deceptively smooth under fluffy blankets of snow, began to bristle on the slightest cleansing, so that we were soon able to move together, which we did with celerity whenever one-handed climbing had become a bare possibility. Intersecting ledges grew more numerous, one could easily evade obstacles to pick the easier line of advance, and the angle of the cliffs fell back.

Meanwhile the twilight had darkened into night, but before the last light drained from the snow the moon assumed the relinquished task of the sun. We made steady and tortuous progress for a few hundred feet, then stopped to take off and coil the rope. The cold had become extraordinary. I happened

to touch the head of an axe with my bare hand, and like
the door-handle of the inn, the steel stuck to the flesh as though
smeared with glue. Yet in that windless air we hardly felt the
cold so long as we kept moving.

From now onward we were able to choose the least troublesome course and move freely about the rock. The moonlight
cast our shadows long and thin upon the snows, and before us
the buttress swelled in a silver wave to the summit, bearing us
up firmly to the starred sky. We congratulated ourselves on
our lateness; for there was magic in the air. Towards the end
snow conditions changed markedly. Upon every crag and
boulder lay accumulations of fog crystals, shaped like fig-leaves
and overlapping in massed banks, which must have been a foot
deep on the last rock-ring under the summit.

We halted at the cairn to survey the softly shining world far
below, and the more brilliant sparkle above, then went south
along the glittering summit ridge to the crusted snow-slopes of
Coire Cloiche Finne, down which we launched ourselves in a
six-hundred-foot glissade on the first stage to Glen Etive.

10

The First Ascent of Clachaig Gully

A GREAT ROCK-CLIMB traditionally presents to its pioneers, before they ever set foot on the mountain, obstacles and delays as numerous as those they encounter on the rocks of first ascent; and these last are charged with an air of impregnability, which from the instant of victory miraculously and for ever vanishes. Such facts are rarely appreciated by those who follow after, and who, when the way is known, are often greatly puzzled why the route should have gone so long unclimbed. Clachaig gully was no exception to the general rule. Therefore it seems worth while briefly to preface an account of the first ascent with subjective matters.

From my first climbing days, when I explored the easiest hills with a thrill of adventure, the unclimbed gully at Clachaig, Glencoe, made a most powerful appeal to my imagination. Facing the front door of Clachaig hotel, it splits the south flank of Sgor nam Fiannaidh in a curving gash two thousand feet high—the longest gully in Britain. During the previous fifty years it had sustained at least a score of attacks, several by outstanding mountaineers, all of which met defeat at a great cave-pitch at six hundred feet.

Therefore my early relation to Clachaig gully was much like that of the invalid of whom Stevenson said, 'The mountainside beckons and allures his imagination day after day and is yet as inaccessible to his feet as the clefts and gorges of the clouds' —a fact which I knew all the more surely after my introduction to rock-work, for then I saw what expert climbers could accomplish on rock, and that seemed so much more than I could ever hope for myself that the wind was quite taken out of my sails. Moreover, when some of these mountaineers, whom at the age of twenty-one I regarded as men of heroic breed, cast in nobler mould than lesser humans like myself, declared in my presence that the great cave in Clachaig gully was impossible, I confess that I gave up hope. But from time to time the gully still lured my mind with the power of the unknown, and gave rise to many picturesque dreams, in which I cannot remember ever reaching the top—but passed always through rock scenery and over obstacles such as never met the eye of living man on mountain.

After a further three years of unbounded enthusiasm, during which I lost but two week-ends' climbing, my knowledge of men and mountains considerably increased, as a consequence of which I beheld them with no less respect but with a more cal-culating eye. I knew now from my own experience that the opinion of even the best mountaineer of what is possible and what is not possible in rock climbing is five times out of ten worthless, and that the truth of most physical problems has been expressed in one sentence by Nansen: 'The difficult is that which can be done at once, the impossible that which takes a little longer.' Therefore, in the spring of 1938, when I found the vision of Clachaig gully recurring with all its old force and frequency, I gave up dreams and cleared for action.

My first visit was made with MacAlpine and W. G. Marskell on 24th April. We reached the Great Cave, and there, after careful study and desperate effort, we failed. Yet, whatever impossibilities might be waiting in the fourteen hundred feet beyond, I felt sure that the Great Cave could be climbed. No trace of a route could I see, but I sensed that there *was* one. And a more disturbing feeling than that can hardly assail a mountaineer. Like all our predecessors, we retired discomfited. But henceforth my blood was up. As we climbed down to Clachaig in a rain-shower I was already praying for a spell of good weather and longing for the day of return.

Thereafter not a drop of rain fell in Argyll for seven days. By the end of that week I was in agonies of frustration, for as so often happens, the difficulty of getting the right party on to the mountain seemed insuperable.   Dunn, whose company is more pleasing than a first ascent, would join us only if we camped and climbed on Garbh Bheinn of Ardgour, a magnificent and little-known rock-peak to which he is passionately devoted. Usually so careless, he was now adamant.

Therefore, on the afternoon of 30th April, Dunn, MacAlpine, Marskell, and I sped by car across the moor of Rannoch—bound for Ardgour. Mrs. MacAlpine accompanied us to share our camp but not our climb. I could never hope to combine a stronger party and better weather for Clachaig gully, but I knew that nothing could halt the westward journey if once we passed Kingshouse Inn.   It came into sight, flanked by tall pines, white walls sparkling on the sun-drenched moor, like a quartzite pebble on a sea-drenched sand. We could not pass it by, and swung off the Glencoe road to be given our last chance and respite— and mugs of dark brown beer.

While we quenched our thirst in the lounge MacAlpine and I set about the conversion of Dunn, who was justly incensed in view of prior compacts. I fear that he scored most of the debating points, for MacAlpine's pitiful plea was our heat exhaustion after the long drive from Glasgow—we were too weak to go further—and as for my own, said Dunn, that boiled down to a pig-headed refusal to accept defeat! Climbers had been beaten in Clachaig gully for fifty years, but on Garbh Bheinn an abundance of new routes could be made on a thousand-foot cliffs of gneiss — on rock as good as gabbro. We cunningly stoked Dunn with a host of irrelevancies and fresh supplies of beer, then fanned the flame of debate with the breath of dialectic. Each quarter of an hour that passed carried a load from my mind, and at last the hour became too late for any hope of reaching Ardgour in daylight. When Dunn discovered how he had been tricked his face was a study, and a warning to all mountaineers to drink not a drop but water.

We drove down Glen Etive and camped by the river.

Not more than two or three times each year there comes a

day so fine that one will swear that never before have skies been truly blue, nor air keenly invigorating. Such was the first of May. At ten a.m. our car rolled up to Clachaig Inn in mellow morning sunshine. Far away in the woods lower down the glen we could hear the faint call of a cuckoo, wooing a man to idle sprawling and dreaming as does no other bird-song. But the huge bulk of Sgor nam Fiannaidh rose immediately to the north; and barely five minutes' walk away the Clachaig gully cleft the mountain in two. A more obvious challenge to the mountaineer could hardly be conceived. If this mountain be not the shapeliest in Scotland, it has yet, in the words of Elroy Flecker, 'a monstrous beauty like the hind quarters of an elephant.'

We moved up gentle grass slopes to the start. A cascade of water, flashing in the sunshine, foamed from the foot of the gully, and for eight hundred feet above a forest of small trees sprouted from the flanking walls amidst a profusion of luxuriant vegetation. The final twelve hundred feet were bare and stern. There was good climbing there, and on clean rock, but the lower part looks from a distance like a slice out of central Africa.

We skirted the torrent by scrambling up the rocky bank, then drew close to the entrance of the gully. The water in the bed was easily avoided and great walls rose gradually on either hand until we felt like insects at the bottom of a canyon. Long-cherished aspirations flooded my mind in a wave of enthusiasm for the climb. But could we possibly succeed where better than we had failed? Exaltation subsided to a subdued excitement. I felt as though treading those very clouds that Stevenson alleged to be inaccessible; mind and body were taut.

For five minutes we climbed easy rocks. The high retaining walls, splayed out and far apart in their upper reaches, steepened and came close together as they approached the bed of the gully, where the bare rock was exposed. The trees and vegetation were thus confined to the upper walls of the gully and rarely interfered with our climbing. The rock was now becoming difficult and we halted to rope up. To save time we arranged to climb as much as possible in two parties, myself with Marskell and MacAlpine with Dunn, each party using a hundred feet of rope.

Marskell and I set off first, and continued climbing up good rock through exotic jungle scenery. We had negotiated several mild difficulties, and had climbed some four hundred feet, when we suddenly overtook another party of three climbers. They were men of high repute and well known to us by name.

The leader of the party stood dripping moisture at the top of a narrow vertical chimney, where a waterfall foamed forty feet to a pool below. His second man, an accomplished Alpinist, was jammed half-way up the chimney. Icy jets of water poured down the open neck of his shirt. His breeches bulged and quivered round the accumulating volume, which at last spurted under pressure from the knees. We gaped in silence at the struggles of the victim, whose terrible contortions were at length crowned with success. He emerged weak and bedraggled from the top of the chimney, whereupon the dammed-up water, now released, surged down like a tidal wave. The surpassing fright-fulness of the scene put us all in excellent humour for the rest of the day.

The party above disappeared, and it gradually dawned upon me that we must not gaze all day at the waterfall. Marskell, in fact, was already looking at me with a far-away, speculative smile, as though enjoying something in anticipation. Dunn grinned gleefully from ear to ear. 'What about Garbh Bheinn now?' was written all over him. In none save me could be discerned any concern for his own immediate prospects in the chimney. Therefore I turned up my collar and paid the penalty of climbing with men made of sterner stuff than myself.

I edged cautiously round the pool through hissing spray, hesitated, retreated with a sensation of nervous shock in the solar plexus, then stricken with shame advanced more deter-minedly and found small holds at the outer edge of the chimney. The spray poured over my body, a constantly penetrating spur to hasten me upward. At the very point where total immersion had seemed inevitable, I discovered some rock wrinkles that

allowed me to push myself up, back and foot on opposing walls. My head, chest, and feet were thus clear of the main volume of water, which instead poured on to my stomach. In one more minute I was standing on top, damp but delighted, and looking forward to the discomfiture of the others. I was not disappointed. I have paid good money to see performing sea-lions give me a great deal less pleasure.

When all were up we reaped the benefit of the gully's southern aspect. The hot sun flooded in and began to dry our clothes even as we galloped across screes, swarmed up an overhang, and regained the first party below the Great Cave. This most perplexing of barriers, the limit of all previous exploration, was a wall fifty feet high; the left half being scooped out in a shallow cave, in outline like a thin-necked bottle; the right half, a sheet of discouraging sleek slabs. To either flank the gully walls rose two to three hundred feet. We could still see no possible line of ascent and bestowed ourselves on various rounded stones—I tested several by hand to select the warmest—while we discussed the problem over lunch.

Meantime we were still somewhat wet after the waterfall, but our partial ducking had had a pronounced psychological effect. The mettle of the party had been tempered by immersion. Each one of us had struck top form, such form as one finds but once or twice in a year's hard climbing. Therefore, despite the apparent hopelessness of the rock, we were incorrigibly optimistic. 'Where there's rock there's a route' is the arm-chair axiom of the climber incarcerated in the plains, itching for rough rock under his hands, doubting not that all things are possible, however smooth the slabs and high the angle; but when great sheets of stone rise uncompromisingly before his very eyes, they usually bring to the mountaineer a more fitting humility. To-day, we seemed to retain that abounding faith that supplies hand and foothold where none have previously existed; almost realizing in action the dream-world of the Kingshouse fireside.

We serenely munched our squashed and drooping sandwiches, dried our clothes in the hot sun, and watched the first party go

D

into action. The cave was forty feet high and topped by a ten-foot chimney. A little torrent burbled down this chimney and splashed the inside of the cave and surrounding rock. Still, this was the most direct line; as such it appealed to the leader, who declared his preference and stepped into the cave. The left wall overhung, but the right lay at a lesser angle, so he climbed the latter till the roof forced him out, when he tried to traverse on to the outer slabs, thus hoping to reach by detour the base of the final chimney.

From the position of his body relative to the rock I could see that even though he successfully traversed from the cave, access to the chimney could be gained only by a brilliant acrobatic convulsion, hardly reversible. Assuming, then, that he found himself jammed in the foot of the chimney, he would have to get up the remainder to preserve himself from extinction; and there was no indication that the chimney was climbable. On the contrary, it bore every visible mark of impossibility. His only line of retreat would thus be a clear drop of forty feet to the screes. When trying that very traverse a fortnight before I had suddenly realized that life was already sufficiently short without such measures being taken to curtail it further. The leader of the first party came to the same conclusion. After due reflection he climbed down again.

The competitive spirit is happily completely foreign to Scottish mountaineering, and although the leader of the first party was fully entitled to make several attempts before allowing passage to our party, he now most generously stood back and invited us to have a try.

The cave route being far beyond my own skill I turned to the right-hand part of the barrier, where merciless slabs converged on a grass corner near the top. That grass corner was the key to the problem—if one could reach it. That no human could climb from directly below I knew but too well from my last visit, when I stuck on rock smooth as ivory. Some other approach would have to be found. Since it could be gained neither from directly underneath, nor yet from the left, there remained but one alternative—an ascent of the right-hand wall of the gully, followed by a traverse round a sharp rib and then ten feet across an almost vertical wall, which looked holdless from below. This wall was our last hope. I had not tried it before.

I changed into rubbers and climbed the gully wall to an enormous boiler-plate slab, out of the middle of which a rowan-tree sprang from a crack. I followed the lower lip of the slab till it heaved up against the rib, which it licked with an up-curled tongue. Delicately balanced on the tip of this tongue, I swung a leg round the rib on to a sloping foothold on the face. To my great relief and delight, I then saw a sketchy line of dimples, which might connect my rib with the grass corner, now looming large as a green oasis in a desert of severe walls. I moved forward cautiously, clinging to in-cut notches with my fingers and more rounded knobbles with my feet, until the holds suddenly became too sparse and I had to stop.

In hope of encouragement I instinctively looked down at the rest of my party, but they now seemed remote and impersonal. Like some medieval theologians, who argued for years how many angels could balance on the point of a needle—their true goal forgotten—they were grouped together and wrangling on the moral justification for using pitons on new rock-climbs.

I turned again to the rock for more material aid, but could find none at first. The direct horizontal line could not be continued. Something had to be done quickly, for muscles were tiring with the strain of too long a halt on inadequate footing. A more anxious scrutiny at last revealed above me a square-cut indentation, just large enough to take two finger-tips. I pulled up at once in combination with a toe scrape, and the two sufficed for a quick lift that earned better holds. In another minute I reached the oasis, a downward-tilting patch to which I clung with hands, elbows, knees, and feet, all of which were used for upward squirms and wriggles, which by spreading the weight of the body over a wide area made such peculiar climbing safe and enjoyable. The grass corner was in truth the

key to the rocky heart of Clachaig gully.   Only one more bolt
remained to be drawn—a four-foot bar of rock, which yielded
to patient manipulation.   Then I drew myself beyond all verticalities on to the level top of the Great Cave.   The gate was
unlocked and the barrier down.   All the unexplored mysteries
of the gully lay open to us.

For several blissful minutes I knew the blaze of sheer delight
that follows the fall of a great obstacle on a new climb, firing one
with enthusiasm for life and mountains.   In small part it may
arise from reaction from nervous tension, but principally from
the wholesome sense of triumph after hard work—after effort
not only of muscle but of mind in application of climbing craft.

I brought up Marskell, then we threw his end of the rope
down to MacAlpine and Dunn.   They climbed with many
exclamations of astonishment.   The other party then decided
to abandon the climb and managed to force an escape up the
western wall of the gully.   Meanwhile, I had time to appreciate
the unique downward vista, the like of which may not be seen
on any other British climb.   The rocks we had climbed below
were invisible: only the level scree-floor of the gully could be
seen above each of the numerous pitches.   Therefore the gully
appeared to plunge headlong, as though its unsupported screes
were an avalanche petrified, for ever menacing the inn at
Clachaig.   The inn, now small and distant, like a grain of
chalk on a green baize cloth, stood neatly framed between the
gully walls.   These latter were most remarkable.   Two vast
parallel rock gardens, they rushed down on either side of a steep
and stony avenue—true hanging-gardens crowded with slender
rowan-trees and birches, cool and green in the burning sunlight, bright with wild flowers and all kinds of vivid moss and
fern.   Here, too, were many Alpine plants, amongst which I
could name only the yellow saxifrage.   All mingled in a riotous
confusion.   One must come in late spring to see this sight at
its best.

We hastily pulled on our boots again.   The party was now
fairly straining at the leash.   No one had ever been in this long

upper part of the gully, which curved like a scimitar in an eastward upsweep of fourteen hundred feet.   What should we find
—impossible obstacles or rock too unsafe for climbers with
pretensions to sanity?   Should we be able to get up without
further difficulty, or if we failed, could we hope to escape up
either of the retaining walls, themselves rising to three hundred
feet?   Pulled by curiosity and spurred by difficulty overcome,
we set to work on the next passage—a thirty-foot shelf.   It was
hard and awkward.   In a mossy corner near the top I was
pounded for five minutes to the joyful surprise of the party
below.   Elation must fly and sober respect for rock return before
one is permitted to pass on from this corner.

Lenient rocks flattered and soothed us for a further two
hundred feet.   Our minds relaxed in foolish unwariness for
several minutes, instead of stiffening in distrust of abating difficulties, which were no more than a lull, a gathering in of the
gully's might for another great resistance.   In consequence we
were unduly startled to find ourselves entering a high-walled
cauldron, where we were faced at last by a terrific chimney.   It
stood seventy feet high, streamed with water, and was circled
by rock bulwarks of unusual fierceness.

Our hopes sank to a low ebb.   The moment of defeat is
never pleasant.   We had now been climbing for nearly five
hours and were nearly half-way up the gully.   Therefore I
revolted at the idea of retreat without a determined effort to
force a route somehow or other.   I examined the encircling
walls quickly and critically, knowing that I must spot a line of
attack before it was clouded by the mists of prudence.

We stood in the centre of the cauldron, at the upper end of
which the stream fell sheer down the chimney from the invisible
continuation of the gully.   To the left of the waterfall the
cauldron overhung in black bulges; whilst to the right the east
wall rose perpendicular, the lower part perfectly smooth, the
upper deplorably loose—so loose that we thought a loud shout
might tumble the rock around our ears.   Unanimously, we
named it Jericho Wall.   Its face betrayed but one weakness.

Running up the lower smooth wall was a narrow corner, steep but not vertical, smooth but not holdless, petering out against the higher Walls of Jericho.   Here, then, was a route to try. I replaced my boots with rubbers.

By this time I was again keyed to the calm that inoculates a climber against high-angle rock and exposure, and progressed steadily up the corner on small holds, till I arrived at a platform the size of an ash-tray.   Before me was the unpleasant prospect of an upward traverse across Jericho Wall itself.   I proceeded step by step, testing every hold and avoiding where possible those that seemed insecure.   By good fortune few footholds were dangerously unsound, whereas an unstable handhold could be used by delicately pressing down on it rather than brutally pulling outward.   By virtue of this technique, loose holds could, after careful examination, be used with safety, provided due allowance was made for the fracture lines.   On getting over the top I found myself stranded on a rolling wilderness of grey slabs, barren of standing ground from which to take in Marskell's rope with security for us both.   I therefore went leftward to the waterfall, where there was an excellent stance near the lip.

I then discovered that my hundred feet of rope had been fully used up, and that while I was comfortably placed in the centre of the gully, Marskell, MacAlpine, and Dunn would have to climb well out on the right wall, so that if any one fell, the result would be a terrific pendulum swing against the wet slabs below me.   Therefore to follow would be no different from leading.   In the past I have climbed often enough with weak parties to realize how helpless must be every leader without strong support in such a position; he must avoid climbs like Clachaig gully.   That Marskell, MacAlpine, and Dunn negotiated the hair-trigger holds of Jericho Wall by careful and determined climbing contributed more to the day's success than the leader.   All of us cleared away much of the loose rock— Marskell especially threw down large quantities—so that the traverse is now safe and no longer severe.

When we had reached the top we again split into two parties.

It is most unusual for any route to present more than two points of supreme difficulty and we felt confident that the most formidable defences had now been pierced. The character of the gully had completely changed. We were well above the tree-line and there was little or no water in the bed of the gully; the walls were bare and narrower, the rock scenery stern and lofty, and the standard of climbing harder. But there was no passage of outstanding character until we reached a huge red slab, a wet, unbroken sheet of eighty strenuous feet. Immediately beyond, the gully narrowed to a level trough. The walls were nearly four hundred feet high, yet one could touch them both with outstretched arms. This singular formation could not continue far, and the trough in its last agonies gave a sharp double twist and reared in a short chimney. The right wall awkwardly overhung, requiring an expenditure of energy out of all proportion to the chimney's size and importance. We were beginning to feel our seven hours' climbing.

Thereafter everything went so well that once more we unwisely thought that all serious rock-work lay behind. We were transported with delight—at least I was—and imagined the gully as good as climbed. Actually we were little more than three-quarters of the way up.

Then came the next shock. A mass of dull red rock, higher than a city building, towered in front of us. We named it the Red Chimney pitch. A shallow cave, arching thin and high like a great cathedral window, rose thirty feet above the screes. From its apex sprang a narrow chimney, splitting open the walls for twenty feet above and thus overhanging the base of the cave. This wet, gaping crack was in turn crowned by twenty feet of red slabs. Total height, seventy feet.

We had come too far, however, to be easily shaken, and felt that the problem might be solved could we only force an entry into the bottom end of the chimney. Without difficulty I climbed the wall to the right of the cave, and one foot to the right of the chimney found a ledge that seemed specially designed for rest and reflection. The crux of the pitch was to get my body round the corner and jam it into the chimney. It was a most unusual situation; for the chimney being under-cut, nothing but good mountain air occupied the thirty feet of space between its lower end and the screes. Near the top that space would become fifty feet, and fifty feet of a clear drop is never to be sneezed at. At all events, as I craned my neck round the corner to look at the next twenty feet of smooth wet rock, and wondered whether it were climbable, I felt a pardonable anxiety to eschew any step too palpably irreversible.

On the opposite wall of the chimney, at the bottom, was one knobble. I placed my left foot on its hunched back as a provisional gesture, and allowed my back to rest on the near edge of the chimney. In the attitude of a public-house loafer, I was thus comfortably supported over space. Then I swung on to a small hold in the back of the chimney and the problem was solved. But the chimney was stubborn. I had to fight strenuously to reach the haven of two chock-stones near the top. The upper one was loose, was tested thoroughly, and was subsequently used for a strong arm-pull. But winter frosts may undermine its reliability for another year.

Above the chimney was a perfect stance ringed with low walls like a pulpit. One could imagine a lesser rock nesting there in prehistoric days. I had to rest for five minutes until my exhausted muscles returned to normal. On this first ascent I had undoubtedly used more strength than was necessary through an over-anxiety not to fall off. Then Marskell arrived and I tried the final slab. The various nicks and corrugations were not too well distributed and strained muscles, already tired from eight hours' climbing, gave us a higher opinion of the slab than it probably merits. It made a worthy finish to a superb pitch.

There seemed to be no end to Clachaig gully. We continued climbing up and up, and for several hundred feet the clean firm rock gladdened our hearts by its irreproachable conduct. We calculated that we had climbed nearly forty pitches, and as the rock yielded ever more easily we thought more than once that the last obstacle had arrived, only, on climbing it, to find another one ahead. Profiting by previous experience, I became more and more suspicious. The Clachaig gully has a character all of its own, and I felt in my very bones that it would not come to an end tamely. There would be a sting in the tail. I was even prepared for the tail to whip up and utterly rout us at the last moment.

Then we saw it. Beyond doubt the last pitch in the gully. An unspectacular wall of blank red rock. Its first fifteen feet were well broken, its upper fifteen feet so smooth that no holds could be seen from below. A glance at my wrist-watch showed that we had been climbing for nine hours; we were all weary and this last pitch was obviously very hard, assuming it to be possible—so I exchanged boots for rubbers, in hope of easing my labours. The lower half led easily to the smooth section, where bands of slab ran lengthwise across the wall, under-lapping, thereby exposing long, thin edges. On these I made an upward traverse to the centre of the gully, feeling most insecure until I could clap my hands on top of the wall and pull up with a last hard effort. I looked upward. The gully no longer rose purposefully before me, but meandered onward, scree-strewn, uninterrupted; the flanking walls, so high and formidable lower down, fell away in low easy slopes.

I could hardly believe it. We had made the first ascent of Clachaig gully. I shouted the good news down to the rest of the party, where it was received with great enthusiasm. But we were too tired to be demonstrative.

We made our descent down the true right bank of the gully, which is quite free from rock. But tired as we were, and urged to haste by hunger and fading daylight, we were first slowed, then brought to halt by the beauty of the westward hills and sea-lochs. The sun was down. There was no splashed colour and blaze in the afterglow, such as one usually sees in May. Between the light-starts on Loch Linnhe near at hand, and a sky of clear lemon in the west, the mountains of Ardgour rose in sharp out-line, yet without substantiality. One looked not *at* them, but

*D

into them, as through the mouths of caverns filled with purple
haze, and still one looked beyond. . . . They delighted not
by crude colour, breath-taking as that can be, but with atmo-
spheric subtlety and noble shape.   These were the mountains of
true vision, not of this world, causing one to mourn his lost
splendour during this life of exile, yet rejoicing him with promise
of a return.   But there is no way of explaining them. . . .

An hour later we briefly celebrated at Clachaig Inn.   Then
the pangs of hunger, as only the destitute and mountaineers of
this country know them, routed us out of Glencoe and back to
our camp in Glen Etive.   The evening we spent there stands
out clear in my memory as one of life's milestones of sheer
happiness, when we were absolutely content and had not a care
in the world.   An ambition of four years had been satisfied;
nerve and sinew had been hard tried on a long new rock-climb,
and now, in a clearing in the woods, we relaxed our tired bodies
on soft grass before a crackling fire—while our food was cooked
and served by my sister, Mrs. MacAlpine.   We were in high
spirits yet quiet, joyful yet wearied out.

Exploratory rock climbing is the best of all.

NOTE. On returning next year to Clachaig gully I repeated the
ascent in five hours.   Several other ascents have been made
in from four and a half to seven hours.   Jericho Wall is now
safe and sound.   I do not recommend the climb in wet
weather.   Rubbers are no longer required for any of the
pitches.

11 *Observatory Ridge in Winter*

DURING THE MONTH of January 1938 great quantities of powder-snow fell in the central highlands, accompanied by dry and bitter winds, which in Glencoe swept the rocks clear and packed the gullies deep with drift. In early February sheets of windslab formed on eastward-facing snows.

Mackenzie, MacAlpine, and I put our heads together to discover what especial benefit might be derived from this state of affairs. It seemed to us likely that if such conditions prevailed in Glencoe they might also hold good on Ben Nevis. Gullies might be either easy or dangerous, according as they were tight-packed or loose, but the great ridges ought to be in perfect order—swept clear of powder and encrusted with old frozen snow. Then Mackenzie had an inspiration. There was no record, he said, of any winter ascent of Observatory ridge since the first by Raeburn, eighteen years ago. We knew of one other ascent in April, but not in genuine winter conditions; the ridge seemed much neglected. Being two thousand feet long and reckoned difficult in summer, it was not a winter route on which one could wander with an old umbrella: we must strike at once while the snow was frozen.

Thereupon I sprained an ankle by slipping in a friend's drawing-room. After seven days' rest I was hobbling with a stick, feeling desperate and vowing like Bill Bones that 'Doctors is all swabs'—while my companions enjoyed a very severe climb, which they described to me in high, astounding terms. That was too much. Sprain or no sprain, my stick went out of the window and I to Nevis with MacAlpine and Mackenzie. We arrived at Fort William on the evening of 19th February. We stopped there to buy a bottle of rum (for my ankle), then climbed two thousand feet by the banks of the Allt a' Mhuillin to the Nevis hut, which we reached at midnight.

Intense cold wakened us at dawn.

We arose at seven o'clock, and our breath made columnar clouds of smoke in the icy atmosphere. Imagine our joy when we discovered a truly perfect morning! Not a cloud in the blue sky. Straight before the doorway stretched the two miles of precipice, crowned with flowing snow-cornices, which blazed in the slanting sun-rays. From our feet the snow-fields swept in a frozen sea to the cliffs, beating like surf against the base of ridge and buttress, leaping in spouts up the gullies. The rocks were laden with snow, but as we expected, there appeared to be less than usual on Observatory ridge. There were countless patches, of course, but everywhere the hoared rock showed through, except high up where the angle eased, and low down where the snow had been swept down by the wind.

One could feel a terrific power to attract in the perfect form of that ridge. It was broad and firmly planted below, but tapered through the first thousand feet to a delicate edge on the last thousand:

Icy in pure thin air, glittering with snows.

And all this was in accord with our belief that we should not find overmuch snow on the ridge until we were high up, where despite the narrowness of the ridge the rocks became easier. We calculated seven or eight hours for the whole climb. Our judgment of snow conditions, thus substantiated by every visible sign, was in fact wrong, and was destined to involve us in one of the hardest battles we have had the good fortune to wage.

We hurried back to the hut and made breakfast. Shortly before nine a.m. we set off.

The effect of weather upon thought and temper is most profound. And from the crackling air of a hard morning an electric energy seems to flow through one's body. There was no wind to shiver us or to shackle our minds to material things. Well clothed, and thanks to MacAlpine passably well fed, we revelled in the cold, and our spirits leapt to the gay colours of the mountain. Our eyes ranged in delight from ebony towers to pale brown ridges, from the cream of a cornice to the sheen of green ice bulging a buttress, from silver icicles to ice glinting grey in gullies; from the blue sky to the feathery powder squealing beneath our boots like harvest mice. Life is more than merely worth while on a fine morning with stirring work ahead.

We stopped to examine the great unclimbed gully on the right flank of Observatory ridge. Its awe-inspiring appearance compelled a halt. The first thousand feet were a continuous ribbon of unmitigated ice. From time to time a small powder-snow avalanche trundled down the gully and flashed on to the snow-field below. If ever a party tries to climb that gully it will have to be very sure of stable snow above.

We then gave our attention to Observatory ridge and decided that the speediest method of effecting lodgment thereupon was to contour its base into Zero gully, which bounded its left flank, and then make a right-hand traverse on to the crest. Zero gully had likewise never been climbed, and the cause of neglect was apparent when we moved into its lower reaches. High up, higher than we could see, the angle fell back, but the lower visible section bristled with pitches of green, overhanging ice. In point of severity there seemed little to choose between these flanking gullies, and once launched on our climb we should have no alternative to direct upward advance or downward retreat. We turned involuntarily and examined Observatory ridge still more respectfully, but we were no longer in position to see far ahead and our view was restricted to a race of snow-dusted slabs, freckled with dark walls and lined with ribs.

At nine-thirty a.m. we left Zero gully and traversed on to Observatory ridge by a convex terrace swamped with the foulest rice-like snow, which lay poised with devilish cunning above a series of crags. Breaking steps soon imparted the first unpleasant thrill to the day's proceedings. We stopped and roped up, with Mackenzie leading, myself second, and MacAlpine last. The rope gave us much needed confidence, for the snow was so unreliable in quality that one could not put down one's foot secure in the knowledge that one's step would hold—that one would not, if unchecked, accompany the breaking snow over the crags below.   This bad snow low down was only to be expected, and we remained confident that conditions would rapidly improve as we went higher.   Then we began to wonder if we should ever get higher.   Our ledge had thinned to a flake, and in order to escape from the dangerously poised snow, Mackenzie sought the first opportunity offered by the rocks near the crest of the ridge.   I tied myself to a spike and paid out the rope while he wrestled with a high wall of snow-speckled slab.

His artistry was delightful to watch, yet he never ran out more than fifteen feet of rope.   He tried straight up, to the left, to the right, tried every dodge of body adjustment known to an expert leader, but without avail.   Half an hour passed and we were still in the same position.

MacAlpine, impatiently balancing on doubtful steps thirty feet beneath on the terrace, began to question the wisdom of proceeding further if rapid progress were not possible early in the day.   For reasons of his own he was anxious to get back to the hut in good time.   In fact, we had the not unusual choice between daring and exceeding prudence.   On the one hand, I felt that if we were going to turn back at all we had better do it now—it would be our last chance.   On the other hand, we had looked for slow progress low down owing to the accumulation of powder-snow, and believed in finding rapid progress higher up to compensate.   Lastly, the party was in good form and Mackenzie displaying all his usual mastery; but his skill had to be transferred to climbable rock.   I therefore urged him to come down and traverse forty feet to the right.   He did this and met instant success.   The hunt was up.

Our immediate route lay fifty feet up a truly vertical rib, where splendid holds lay distressingly far apart and exercised our arm muscles more than we liked.   I remember that rib with affection as the last safe and solid thing that we met in a long day

THE HUT, BEN NEVIS

and night. Above, our troubles gathered thick and fast. Slab succeeded slab, and rib succeeded rib, but all were lightly covered with snow, which when dusted off revealed rocks glazed with frost; all were intersected by ledges piled high with powder-snow bearing a wind-slab crust, which peeled off and swished over the edge suggestively whenever a foot was placed on it. And this snow was invisible from below. It lay on what might be called the corbels of the ridge.

That such accomplished deception was true to the character of big ridges we knew, but on this occasion we had faith that recent winds had swept the rocks clean. Always we were led on and up in the reasonable certainty of mind that conditions would improve, and always we were disappointed. The snow did not improve—it got worse. For some reason the wind had not been getting at it, had not scavenged half as much of it as we had expected. Therefore, we had to go cautiously and take elaborate rock-belays, while we traversed back and forth on the treacherous footing in search of the line of least resistance. Our progress was correspondingly slow and the hours went swiftly by.

Mackenzie fared better than MacAlpine and I on these wretched traverses. Light and wiry, he went first and the snow would often bear his weight complainingly, whereas the further strain placed on it by a second or third man was more than it would endure. At one such ledge I was crossing above precipitous slabs on a ribbon of floury powder banked at a high angle against the rock-face, when my steps caved in without warning. My feet slithered to the edge, but just before the slip developed into a fall I caught two finger-holds on the wall above. Mackenzie was well placed to hold me had I gone further. The rope was an ever-present safeguard. Nevertheless, the possibility of repetitions of this incident was always in our minds and kept us in a state of constant anxiety; and such a strain, prolonged through many hours of hard work and technical difficulty, is at first not easy to bear with indifference. But one improves with practice.

MacAlpine's task at the end of the rope was not an enviable one. He climbed on the shaky remnants of holds left to him by Mackenzie and me—after we ourselves had experienced difficulty—with a superb confidence, most cheering to watch. There was one specially loathsome and slabby gutter, where Mackenzie, balancing with precarious grace on icy wrinkles, made upward progress by using delicate push-holds for the palms of his hands on thin snow frosted to the rock. The failing stability of this snow film just sufficed to see me to the base of a vertical crag: then the film flaked off, scuttered down the gutter, and fell sharply into space. How was MacAlpine to get up without that snow? My only rope-belay was a paltry knob, half the size of a thumb-nail, on the wall above me; my only stance a foothold; these had to constitute the justification for MacAlpine's further ventures.

Mackenzie entrenched himself somewhere above. I stood sideways and with all my strength pressed down MacAlpine's rope against its miserable belay. We both prepared for the inevitable moment when MacAlpine must 'come off.'

As for MacAlpine, he surveyed these preparations with polite interest. When assured that all was ready, and that my belay 'would hold the *Queen Mary*,' he calmly stubbed out his cigarette, carefully smoothed the corners of his moustache, tilted his balaclava, then with stylish glide came up that gutter like a Persian cat to a milk saucer.

But Observatory ridge had harder trials in store for us. Meanwhile conditions improved. For an hour we made sufficiently steady progress to notice our gain in height while we climbed. It was a most encouraging change to feel slab and ledge and face succeeding one another, slipping behind and out of sight as we moved up. We used every possible device to save time: as when Mackenzie, for safety's sake, climbed sixty feet up a thin rib of great technical difficulty, while MacAlpine and I, relying on a tight rope, followed more speedily by an easier parallel groove, which was in a highly dangerous condition. Then the ridge suddenly fell back at an easy angle, as though resting on its haunches before rejoining battle more fiercely. We felt that we had better do likewise. Of one accord we stopped, for by this time the rope was a telegraphic wire linking our three minds. We found an excellent stance, where we could all sit down at once and in such comfort as cold snow affords to the mortal hind quarters.

For ten minutes we ate sandwiches and enjoyed one of those bodily and mental contrasts that mountains grant liberally. The sky was incredibly blue, the air windless and still. Not the faintest noise could be heard. Straight before our eyes on the north skyline, the mountains of Wester Ross were ablaze in afternoon sunshine, a jagged wall of white cutting through lilac horizon haze. At our feet lay the hut, a speck of red roof.

Thoughts of what must be ahead at last hurried us into action again, although even yet we failed to realize just how great would be the volume of unstable snow on the upper part of the ridge, or that under such a covering the crest in its narrowness would prove impregnable. The rocks swiftly steepened and rose in a broad tower, seventy feet high, which we recognized as the last battlement on the middle part of the climb. It completely blocked the ridge and was cluttered with incoherent snow. No frontal attack was possible. Mackenzie worked up to the right across snow that broke away and then stopped breaking, keeping us in doubt from one moment and move to another. He disappeared round an awkward corner and I watched the rope creep out at an average rate of two feet per minute. We could just hear a soft scuffling as he wrestled up a snow-choked crack; an occasional expletive floated down to us through the quiet air; then all was silent save for the whisper of falling snow.

The sun was out of sight, but from the look of the sky it was obvious that the afternoon was wearing on. We waited in growing impatience for half an hour before receiving the call to follow. Altogether we spent an hour on these seventy feet of rock. Now we looked to make steadier progress. The ridge narrowed henceforth and was demarcated by terrific cliffs, but the average angle was less than hitherto. We climbed but a

NORTH EAST BUTTRESS

SLAV ROUTE

UNCLIMBED WALL

RUBICON WALL

UNCLIMBED GULLY

OBSERVATORY BUTTRESS

Observatory Ridge

ROUTES FOLLOWED
SLAV ROUTE ----------
OBSERVATORY RIDGE ×—×—×
RUBICON WALL o—o—o—o   R.W. Continuation o—o—o

THE OBSERVATORY RIDGE OF BEN NEVIS

Observatory ridge in centre. North-east buttress on left.
Observatory buttress on right

short way further, however, before we were brought to a standstill. The snow lay on that slender ridge in greater quantity than ever and in even less stability.

The situation was now truly serious. There was simply not enough time to clear this great volume of snow from the crest, and it became painfully clear to each one of us that no matter what we did we were going to have a long and hard fight to win through. The declining sun did little to cheer us on, but there was no gain in standing about, wondering in a flurry of anxiety what to do next. If ever bold and determined leadership was needed on a climb it was needed now, and Mackenzie rose nobly to the occasion. On the face of it the situation was hopeless. To cut away such oppressive thought, to wrest good result from bad circumstance, decisive action was called for and decisive action we got. Mackenzie resolved to abandon tradition and the crest of the ridge, and to make a three-hundred-foot traverse across the western precipice. An upward slanting shelf of snow and ice provided fair prospect of a route, although nothing could be seen of a way to regain the ridge when the shelf ended.

The shelf started unpromisingly with fifty feet of evil powder-snow. Wind-slab was again the danger. The crust broke off in chunks, which swished down the tilted shelf, leapt dramatically into space, hung there for a split second, then dropped out of sight with fascinating suddenness. The entire passage was well belayed, but any fall would have meant a pendulum swing into thin air and great difficulty in regaining the shelf. We trod our subsiding steps with the utmost delicacy. None broke away. Then we cut up an ice-fall and were committed to a traverse from which we could see no hope of regaining the crest of the ridge for a long time to come. We perforce worked doggedly along the face.

Two hours later the shelf spread out fanwise, steepened, and culminated in a knife-edged saddle on which we sat astride in cold discomfort. We took stock of our position. Our saddle was the crest of a subsidiary ridge, which came down at right angles to Observatory ridge, then fell with exceeding steepness to a snow-field under the unclimbed gully. Our route could not have been more clearly defined. We must somehow climb the knife-edge and get back to Observatory ridge. Mackenzie literally swam up these hundred feet, using the dog-stroke to to cleave a passage up the massed powder. Such tactics cleared away the great volume of snow that alone made them possible, and to save time MacAlpine and I used the rope freely. At sunset we gathered once more on Observatory ridge.

We had been climbing for seven hours and thought the worst lay below, therefore we sat back and rested for several minutes. It was well that the truth was concealed from us; for in point of time we were only half-way up that stupendous ridge. The very fact of sunset might be thought disconcerting, yet it over-came all apprehension. From zenith to horizon the colours hung across the sky in broad belts of blue, green, orange, and crimson. The nearby snow-peaks were afire.

After the hard climbing lower down we were peculiarly sensi-tive to the skyscape. For suspense is not distressing when one is free to act; therefore doubt of the issue stimulates enter-prise and perception. Great clearness of mind and an inner calm are part of the many rewards of adventurous mountaineering. The mind is purged of sea-level preoccupations and sentimen-talities, stripped of self-seeking, alert to beauty, open to truth, and quick to understand. It is not too much to say that the test of true mountaineering is the presence of adventure and beauty, the criterion of the one being often uncertainty of result, and of the other, always inner purification.

We prepared to start again. Mackenzie retired to the middle of the rope for a well-earned rest and I took over the lead. But the moment I set off there came an almost conclusive set-back. The narrow upper section of the ridge was unclimbable—the rocks were swamped with powder, which was held together by an egg-shell crust. One hundred navvies with shovels could not have cleared those rocks by daybreak. And according to the Scottish Mountaineering Club's guide-book to Ben Nevis it was not possible to escape from the ridge into either of the flanking gullies. Unless we could reconcile ourselves to remaining where we were permanently the guide-book had to be proved wrong.

In the fading daylight we saw that fifty feet above one might possibly cut a route into Zero gully. At all costs that must be done. Once there, we felt sure of getting up by torchlight, even although, as we could see, the gully was decorated with the outward heave of at least three ice pitches. The first essential was to force a route up the dangerous snow of the ridge for another fifty feet. Thus far we could surely go, if no further.

That short stretch of ridge was climbed rapidly, for it was highly precarious and not to be lingered over. We had been ascending or traversing unsafe snow all day, and the continual succession of false alarms that this occasioned amounted in their sum total to a considerable nervous demand on the party as a whole. I myself felt resigned to defeat at this stage of the climb. Unless one cultivates detachment in time of stress, reason responds to tiredness by losing hope in face of further trials ahead, all accentuated by the onfall of night and cold. I drew much encouragement from the example set by Mackenzie and MacAlpine, who appeared to remain supremely calm and optimistic. Whether such an attitude be well founded or assumed, its effect on a leader in emergency is incalculable and irresistible. To feel that the party behind you is strong and has confidence in you is half the battle on a big climb, when it is the strength of the team, not that of the individual, that carries the day.

At five p.m. precisely, as light was failing altogether, I cut my way into Zero gully. To learn our fate I prodded the snow in the gully-bed with my axe and was delighted to find a hard surface. The angle was fifty degrees. Several feet higher the snow gave way to opaque ice, then to clear ice, but I could open my shoulders to this stuff and hit out hard, with the comfortable feeling that I was on safe ground and was getting somewhere. Soon it became too dark to see how the axe was fashioning the steps.   I stopped, brought on the others, shortened the rope, and went on again by torchlight.

There was no moon, but the clear sky flashed with stars; nor was there any wind, though the cold was numbing.   Thus for a quarter of an hour our plight seemed not so bad as it might have been.   Then the gully hit back at us.   We ran into powder-snow at least one foot deep and thinly crusted with wind-slab.   This abominable mixture continued right to the top of Ben Nevis except where the ice-falls protruded in fat gleaming bulges.   When one is hard-pressed for time and energy there is a sore temptation to trust to soft loose snow lying on ice. But any one who yields in Zero gully enters a death-trap. (Especially is this true of Alpine climbs.)   The only tolerable way of proceeding was to excavate the powder and cut steps into the icy bed of the gully.

Needless to say we were already tired and cold, perhaps more tired than we knew, for the climbing demanded and received our unremitting care and attention.   We climbed in Zero gully without any protection, moral or otherwise, from the rope; for our axes could not be used as belays: the spikes would not pierce the ice stratum and were valueless in the powder stratum. Moreover, having seen the lower part of the gully from below, we were unable to push on with care-free hilarity.   We took no chances.   A single mistake by any one of us might mean the speedy end of both climb and party.   Therefore the step-cutting could not be skimped; the steps had to be well made, not too far apart.   This meant heavy labour; digging, excavating, cutting, and at last climbing, until one's arms and shoulders ached with the incessant work, whilst one's mind kept alert to the faultless control of body movement.   We grew more and more tired, and realizing it, more and more determined.   It was beyond the power of one man to lead throughout, so each of us took turns at going first, flogging out the upward passage, until his weariness resulted in too slow progress, when he would retire in favour of the next man.

In two hours we reached the first ice-wall.   Until my days

are ended I shall never forget that situation. Crouching below the pitch amidst showers of ice-chips, I fed out the frozen rope while Mackenzie hewed mightily at the ice above, his torch weirdly bobbing up and down in the dark and the ice brilliantly sparkling under its beam. Looking down, I could see just a short curve of grey snow plunging into the lower darkness, then nothing until the twinkling lights of the Spean valley, four thousand feet below.

The atmosphere was electric; the climbing spectacular. Mackenzie slowly cut his way to the top of the wall, where he dislodged an enormous plate of snow-crust, which flashing past me at high velocity, fell flat on top of MacAlpine's head. The plate smashed to a thousand fragments, which shot with a hiss down the gully. MacAlpine gave a hollow grunt, at which the hairs of our balaclava helmets rose up on end, for he carried the rum (for my ankle) and seemed about to depart with it hutwards by the shortest route.

A further two hours slid by in wearisome cutting and waiting. The waiting was worst of all, for one had time to savour the great cold, and to feel the strain on leg muscles of interminably standing on smallish steps. The slope was steep enough for one's knees to rest on the snow and be chilled and finally numbed by the constant contact. MacAlpine and I had to climb with our torches held between our teeth, for both hands were employed on axe, rope, or holds. Fortunately we both had light-weight torches, but our mouths being frequently open our throats became dry and parched. Mackenzie, no foolish virgin, had his bulb and reflector secured to his head by an elastic band, the bulb being wired to the battery in his pocket.

At nine p.m. we reached the second ice-pitch, the angle of which was about seventy degrees. After so much exhausting work I looked on this obstacle with extreme disfavour. Had the leader been fresh it would still have been very hard. Therefore both Mackenzie and I entered the fray, and thanks to the former we got up, but the effort cost us much reserve energy and MacAlpine took over the lead.

Far off, beyond the crest of Observatory ridge on our right, the dim outline of the Great Tower on Tower ridge loomed through the darkness. Its top lay three hundred feet below the summit of Nevis and we looked across to it every little while to gauge our progress. But the watched pot never boils. We climbed for a solid hour without detecting the slightest difference in our own height relative to the Tower. Each time we looked we felt the same keen pang of disappointment. I began to feel anxious about the life of our torch batteries; these showed us all we required to see and no more, which was sometimes just as well, but they were losing much of their original strength. And somewhere above was a third ice-fall. For all we knew there might be more to follow. These cheerless thoughts were abruptly ended by the appearance of the ice-fall itself, an immense convex boss, a tough morsel whose mastication took half an hour of axe-work.

Up and up we went, digging, hitting, carving, scraping, moving steadily and without interruption for an hour. Quite suddenly, the snow became firm and reliable. On our left hand, stark square-cut towers were silhouetted against the starry sky, and round them could be heard a mighty rushing of winds, the voice of the high and lonely places of the earth. Then Zero gully broadened out and debouched without cornice on the summit plateau. We went over the top one by one, our hearts filled with relief. The time was eleven-thirty p.m.

'Well,' said Mackenzie, 'we 're up.'

I answered 'Thank God!' And for once I meant it. Nothing more was said, then or later. But I had no doubt then, and have none now, that this was the longest and hardest climb in relation to sheer strain that we should ever do. We had learnt that when one stands on the summit after such a climb it is not the mountain that is conquered—we have conquered self and the mountain has helped us.

A bitter east wind snarled across the snow-fields and we hurried for shelter to the ruins of the Observatory. Only the roof and three feet of wall projected through the snow-cap, but we managed to squirm through the top of a window and to wriggle along a tunnel to a snow grotto inside.   Once again in high spirits, we sat cross-legged in a circle while MacAlpine, beaming like a lighthouse, broached my bottle of golden rum and decanted it into a thermos flask of steaming tea.   The festivities that followed lasted far beyond midnight, while outside the wind howled round the corners of the walls.

Then, bursting with all reserve clothing, we braved the blast and, in billiant moonlight, descended in two hours by Coire Leis to the hut, where we arrived seventeen hours after our departure on the previous morning.   We could hardly keep our eyes open, but were inordinately happy.   Much of my own delight I owed to Mackenzie, who had given us that day the greatest lead I have ever seen on mountains.   Indeed it was a magnificent and unforgettable spectacle; for he was confronted with well-nigh impossible difficulties, and by strength of will rose far above his everyday self, forcing an issue by bare courage and precision of mind and movement.   Each time I look back dispassionately on that performance, my respect for the human animal increases.   He has powers within him of which he knows too little.

NOTE. One year later we repeated the ascent in six hours. The rocks were encrusted with hard snow and there was no powder.   The difference in quality of snow alone caused the eight hours' difference in time.   The ridge then gave us the most splendid of winter climbs.

12

The Lost Valley and S C Gully

THE LOST VALLEY OF BIDEAN NAM BIAN

IN MARCH 1939 there came, as is customary in Scotland at that time, a great improvement in snow conditions with successive falls, thaws, and frosts. The course of that ideal cycle had kept me for some weeks to hill-walking and the shorter routes, but the frosty climax raised my hopes high and my spirit ached for a kingly climb; therefore I set my heart on the highest mountain of Argyll, Bidean nam Bian, 'The Peak of the Bens,' and resolved to climb if I could its north top, Stob Coire nan Lochan, by the renowned S C gully.

My hopes were shared by Scott, MacAlpine, and T. D. Mackinnon and approved by the weather clerk. We reached Glencoe at ten o'clock of a brilliant morning, the world such a dazzling white as to pain the eye; the air coldly dry, searing our nostrils until we learned to breathe slowly but deep. From where we stood on the Glencoe road, Bidean was out of sight two and a half miles to the south-west, its majesty screened from vulgar gaze by three guardian spurs, known to the world as the Three Sisters of Glencoe. But far behind the cordon, there was permitted an icy glimpse of Stob Coire nan Lochan, thrusting a princely triangle into cloudless blue.

We determined that our approach should lie between the first and second Sisters by way of the Lost Valley. That appropriate name is used only by a handful of mountaineers who are intimately acquainted with this almost unknown glen, the most genuinely remote and in autumn or spring the most beautiful hill recess in Argyll. First, however, we had to cross the river Coe, whose fifteen-mile length bars access to the mountain and helps to preserve the Lost Valley's sanctity.

We went downhill to the river's bank.   It was sullied by no
bridge hereabouts and we were faced with a knee-deep wade of
twenty yards.   Luckily the stream was hushed and muffled by
the heavy snows closer to the source, and ran here with unwonted
sluggishness.   Several protruding boulders wore snow-puffs,
those subject to splash bearing domes of blue ice.   Harrowing as the prospect was, we did not timorously linger on the
brink—not when we stood barefoot on the snow.   The slippery
shores of the river-bed forebade a swift crossing, despite the
support of our ice-axes, and we gained the south bank with
feet numbed to the bone.   Circulation was soon restored on
the uphill tramp.

Twenty minutes later we entered the lower reaches of the
Lost Valley, where a wooded ravine has been carved out by the
Allt Coire Gabhail.   At first we kept high on the west bank
and then followed a descending track through the trees, whose
silver-grey shadows stole across our path like spirits.   Where
we came to the stream the ravine widened, but the track along
the bottom was hidden in soft snow and we picked our way
among half-buried boulders.   The trees were loaded like the
most audacious of Christmas-card scenery; each gaunt branch
bent heavily to its burden and every twig hung fat as a rabbit's
tail.   The last time I had passed this way the glen was a haze
of red and gold leaf, and filled with the chatter of a now
frozen burn.

The glen steepened.   We climbed through a tangle of rock
and trees where the burn vanished underground, until we came
to an isolated crag under whose foundations burrow a warren
of caves.   We stopped there to investigate.   I had been through
the caves often enough before but had no knowledge of their
winter condition.   As I thought, the rock-corridor and chambers
were dry.   At any season of the year they afford a sheltered
bivouac.   A short way beyond the crag the ground levelled.
Around the dry bed of some ancient stream a little arbour was
formed, an outer porch from which we debouched at last on the
true sanctuary, the Lost Valley of Bidean nam Bian.

At a height of twelve hundred feet, it stretched flat before us, a narrow plain walled by the two northward-running spurs of Bidean. The head of the valley was dominated by an unclimbed buttress of the summit ridge, two thousand feet above. All along the western wall icy turrets and battlements caught the sun, gleamed and shone. On these cliffs no climbing has been done, and no doubt with good reason. In summer, the valley floor is a green mountain lawn, at whose farther end the stream draining the higher corries sinks underground—to reappear below the caves. The construction of the valley leads me to think that at one time a loch may have lain there. But now the meadow was covered a foot deep in snow, whose spotless surface, untrodden by man or animal, heightened the valley's loneliness and deepened its silence.

Spring or autumn—for these have greatest charm—a man might come here for a week and be alone. He might pitch a tent on that meadow and be as much out of sight and sound of civilization as if he dwelt at the North Pole. On his side, all the advantage of a noble mountain girdling him about. He might go up to those unclimbed cliffs, seamed with gullies and chimneys, precipitate stairways, and explore to his heart's content; down to the ravine, if he were a botanist; or climbing to the spurs, walk for a dozen miles on the high ridges of Bidean, with breeze, sun, and a hundred hills for company; perhaps he might wander along to one of the Sisters, and gazing over the edge, watch with compassionate eye the fast car of some busy human creep like an ant along the Glencoe road—and then, going down at evening to his tent on the meadow, trim his solitary candle and smoke a peaceful pipe. He would find himself, after all, less alone than in cities.

In short withdrawals from the world there is to be had unfailing refreshment. When his spirit is burdened or lightened the natural movement of a man's heart is to lift upward, and this is most readily done in the Lost Valley, for there it is easy to be still; and there one may approach the state of which Gerard Manley Hopkins wrote:

GLENCOE

SCALE IN MILES

I have desired to go
Where springs not fail,
To fields where flies no sharp and sided hail,
And a few lilies blow.

And I have asked to be
Where no storms come,
Where the green swell is in the havens dumb,
And out of the swing of the sea.

We passed on over the valley, leaving our track across the snow-field with an uncomfortable sense of desecration, a feeling that quickly passed, as such feelings do, once the deed was done. Upon leaving the valley we bore uphill to the left in search of easy ground: as the snow deepened with height gained so our desire to avoid drifts, into one of which I sank to my waist, deepened commensurately. Our route took us underneath a crag from whose wall hung an array of ten-foot icicles, precisely spaced, like a rack of shining javelins in some medieval armoury. Thenceforward, bearing west to the north-east corrie of Stob Coire nan Lochan, we went up broad snow-fields, whose every flake seemed to radiate a sparkle, a myriad crystal crumbs; the whole flecked by glare and shadow like a hammered platter. I was greatly enamoured of the delicate shade of blue within our deeper footprints.

On the last slope to the corrie we crossed sheets of thick crust, whereon we could walk as on pavement and tack about freely. Across the pit of Glencoe I saw the Aonach Eagach ridge as though for the first time. It ran for miles with the edge and sheen of a razor. Had I not walked and scrambled on its crest a week earlier, I should hardly have thought a man could have balanced on the edge. Not only did it barricade the boundary of Argyll and Inverness-shire, but like some cleaver of the gods fairly cut the air between. After a two hours' ascent to close on three thousand feet we climbed over a last hump, and were ushered by a light northerly breeze into the presence of our peak.

The S C Gully of Stob Coire nan Lochan

The time was twelve-thirty p.m., and we stood on the rim of a shallow corrie seven hundred feet under the summit of Stob Coire nan Lochan. We looked straight upon the side of its north ridge, which confronted us with three buttresses. The south buttress, which was then unclimbed, was divided from the central buttress by the five hundred feet of S C gully. We could see into its white interior, and as invariably happens when a steep winter gully is seen *en face*, it appeared perpendicular. The upper half hung like a silk ribbon from the out-curl of a cornice, the overhang of which seemed to form a complete barrier round the top; in the lower half two snow-pitches were visible. But what most fascinated us was the steel-like glint of a seventy-foot ice-wall in the middle.

One could understand the feelings of a Himalayan mountaineer who was once brought hither by Dr. J. H. B. Bell and who protested that to attempt S C gully was suicidal. And probably it might be were it in the Himalaya. Between three and four thousand feet, however, such a gully may be entered with good heart, although with prospects that cannot be foretold. Although we could see the main features we were quite unable to declare them surmountable. Nor is it possible in winter, unlike summer, closely to calculate the time for a severe ascent; time depends on details of snow and ice, which high on a long rock-climb may by unforeseen quality and quantity add to or remove from an estimate a half-dozen hours.

As our route was short, we guessed four to six hours for a party of two. Since it was already afternoon they might not reach the cornice, another unknown quantity, until dusk—if indeed they could pass the ice-wall. The implication was obvious; and with great generosity MacAlpine and Mackinnon volunteered to stand down.

We all crossed the snow-fields to the cliffs and kicked steps for a hundred and fifty feet up firm snow-slopes to the foot of the gully. The snow hardened there and an ice-axe came into play; after fifty feet of cutting we arrived below the first pitch. This was a great surprise to us. On our first visit in 1937 it had been only a short wall of small difficulty. Now it was twenty-five feet, at an angle of seventy-five degrees (measured by clinometer). Scott and I tied up on a hundred feet of rope and I offered the lead to him, as being a better climber than myself. He refused and I turned to examine the snow-wall. The snow was good—that tough and viscous kind called *névé*, which I refer to hereafter as snow-ice.

I exchanged windproof for woollen gloves; for the former are very apt to slip both on ice-holds and on the shaft of the axe. Then I cut hand- and footholds as far ahead as possible before beginning to move up on them—throughout to adhere to that rule is the prime secret of climbing a snow or ice pitch. Whenever I began climbing I found the wall sufficiently steep to force me into a sideways turn before raising each leg, otherwise the bent knee overbalanced my body. When I was well over the top I drove in my axe to the head and brought up Scott. Mac-Alpine and Mackinnon thereupon waved farewell, and with a shout of 'Good luck!' glissaded down to the corrie.

The bed of the gully steepened, and we continued, an axe-slash and two kicks to each step, up to the second snow pitch. Its height and angle were less than the first, and where the snow-ice bulged a hollow had formed between the shell and the rock. I could cut the shell, and thrusting in my hand to the forearm, thus counter the outward lean of each step-up. We had climbed one and a half hours from the corrie by the time Scott joined me. He looked quickly past my shoulder. 'This is where the fun starts,' he remarked. And he was right.

The gully at once became sterner. The snow rose sharply in front and hardened. I had to wield my axe in earnest and hew properly cut steps. Then we entered a narrowing lane in the left half of the gully, the right half being occupied by a raised and icy chute—the seventy-foot ice-wall that had filled us with doubt nearly two hours ago. Our lane terminated

ICE

under a tall overhang, where massed icicles hung like organ-pipes, and beneath which we hacked out a platform in steep snow. Scott entered into possession, tenant of a natural refrigerator. His lease was destined to be longer than we dreamt. He thrust in his axe until six inches down it struck rock. As a belay that was by no means good enough: further excavations revealed a spike in the gully-bed, and to this he tied himself.

Our situation was most exhilarating, for the gully walls rose high and sheer, the outer edges clean-cut. They were clad in breastplate and shield of gleaming ice, festooned with streamers of white powder. But my own attention was most engaged by the ice-chute above me. To climb on to it I had first to sur-mount its side wall, which was smothered in soft snow. Clearly, my best policy was not to climb up, but to traverse along it till the chute dipped to meet me. I swept off the loose snow and exposed brittle ice underneath; it was laid like wainscot and readily peeled off under the shock of axe-blows. Nevertheless, I spent ten minutes cleaning the wall, slowly traversing on an upslant, before I leaned over the upper lip and cut my first holds on the face of the chute. Then I climbed over the wall and looked up.

Fifty feet above, the ice-sheet thinned to what looked sus-piciously like *verglas* filmed with hoar-frost. One could see the faint rugosities of the rock underneath its veneer. It might take an hour to reach as far—and when then? It was useless to speculate. I decided to go on, but in greater doubt of the issue than before. At present I was lodged on good snow-ice, thick and easily cut, but after six feet this gave place to true ice —and to the sting of spiculae spraying into my face at each axe-blow. This cutting was of necessity one-handed, and to save our valuable time I exchanged the long ice-axe for my old friend the slater's pick. Between twenty and thirty feet up I began to experience the utmost difficulty in placing my holds. The ice bulged in conformity with rock underswell; at the very points where I required ice to circumvent such bulges, rock-slabs bared

E

rounded tips.   One had need to calculate peculiar body angles and stresses for avoidance moves, and engineer the route to suit.

Between thirty and forty feet up these troubles passed and new ones assailed me.   The chute was here rumpled by waves of white ice-plates.   If roughly treated, they immediately shivered vertically and left one, in reward for time and work expended, with ice too thin to use but most beautiful to look upon, shining with a dark gloss like calf's-foot jelly.   The most paying method was to trace the base of each hold with horizontal strokes, then deepen it with the gentlest of vertical chip-strokes.   But occasionally I met a particular brand of pale blue ice that insisted on the reverse process.   One quickly came to know the quality of a plate by its outward signs.

After one and a half hours, a period in which one might complete a football match or play half a round of golf, I had carved a line of notches up only fifty feet of iced rock.   But like Nelson at Copenhagen, I would not have been anywhere else for thousands.   Every moment was intense experience; for body and nerve life lived at the full.   I had arrived at the suspectedly glazed section, but the glaze was thicker than I had dared to hope—half an inch perhaps—and much of the rock protruded, dusted as the ice with hoar but quite unglazed.   My time was now less occupied with cutting than with a search for natural wrinkles that might be scraped clean.   These unluckily led me up to the left to a crux, a sudden bulge that threatened defeat.

I could not progress and remain in balance.   Therefore, standing on a rounded knob, I cut one finger-hold on the upmost curl, by its aid embraced the bulge, and stretched up to cut the first hold beyond.   I could not stay in position long enough to finish it, for the blood ran out of my axe-arm, and leg muscles ached dangerously.   The strain became unbearable. I returned to my knob and rested.   Then I tried again and finished the first hold.   I withdrew and rested.   Three more such efforts were required to cut the second hold.   Then I stood

THE NORTH RIDGE OF STOB COIRE NAN LOCHAN

back, placed a final two notches in the centre of the bulge and climbed up. This passage was, if anything, too exciting, and I was mightily relieved by the chance of a precarious balance step to the right, where the angle fell back.

I was now close under central buttress in a seam of gravelly rock, from which pricked out one or two embedded stones. They were well frozen in and withstood testing. On these I climbed to an iced slab at the top of the pitch, where the angle of forty-five degrees seemed mild indeed. A year had passed since I had relished so stirring a winter action, but I was full of sorrow that MacAlpine and Mackinnon had not shared the full tide of happiness.

I yelled down to Scott that all was well. But the snow was too shallow to afford an axe-belay. I climbed a further ten feet, laboriously kicking steps to the detriment of my toes, rather than using an axe and so smothering in debris my hard-won holds below. My hundred feet of rope had now run out. I drove my axe two feet deep, and taking a turn of the rope round the shaft, called on Scott to come on.

In the course of his half-hour climb the sun set. Between the vertical walls of the gully I looked out as though between blinkers. Yet that very restriction had merit. It gave to the hills, arrayed in keen edges against a pale green sky, and flaring a more fiery pink with each passing moment, a framed and focused power to strike for all time to the mind. The broader and more splendid panorama, prevailing daylong, confuses the eye with too great a mass of detail—suffers from a diffused interest that too readily fades with time and is forgotten. Moreover, that panorama is not lost through a gully-climb. It comes at the top, a sudden revelation; thus more memorable.

For a few minutes the mountains burned, white and red upon a field of green and gold. In low country one may see so rich and full a glow of colour in the cavernous nave of Chartres Cathedral, when the forenoon sun floods the stained glass and the vast brown flags are flecked by shafts of ruby and blue. But Chartres is not matched elsewhere. To seek such depth of colour, and to find it in yet more noble forms, one must go to mountains.   The light died from the ridges and was replaced by a ghastly pallor, as when the angel of death breathed upon the gleaming cohorts of Sennacherib.   The green of the eastern sky slowly faded and was invested by night.   Below me, I could hear the lonely ring of Scott's axe.

I drew in his rope, inch by inch.   Scott is normally a leader, and when second on the rope continues to climb with the care of a leader—a comforting thought for myself.   An unsteady partner is as unwelcome in S C gully as brittle ice.   His helmeted head at last appeared over the brink—the first I had seen of him for two hours.   He climbed to my own level, and then to warm him up after his age-long residence among icicles, I asked him to lead the last two hundred and fifty feet to the cornice.   A man long frozen and eager for swift exercise, he cut the slope with a vigour that showered me with chips.   By the time he had gained sixty feet the fragments came at me with no small velocity; those that did not register on my head and shoulders whizzed by like shrapnel.   I hastily called him to a halt and climbed up.   Thereafter we continued on a short rope, and dispensing with belays, moved together to the cornice.

The exit of the gully being fairly small, I had feared a complete cornice and much expenditure of time in cutting through the overhang.   And thus it had appeared from the corrie.   We arrived to find it sweeping overhead in a faultless volute, six feet high and complete save at one corner, where it joined the top of south buttress.   There the overhang had collapsed and left a vertical snow-wall.   Five minutes later, and four hours forty-five minutes from the corrie, we emerged on the back of the ridge, our boot-nails rasping on the frozen snow crust.

A bitter wind blew from the north.   Twilight was deepening, and sky and mountain were drained of all colour.   The peaks of Mamore and Lochaber no longer flaunted their crests with the royal bravado of noon; nor stared, menacing and livid as upon the ebb of the afterglow; but shrank toward the shadowed north, the most forlorn of ghosts.   In an hour's time, when the moon and stars shone, they would step forth in coruscating might, triumphant.

We untied and coiled the rope, walked south to Stob Coire nan Lochan, and below the final peak glissaded down an eastern gully to the corrie. We hastened to the further rim, sped toward the distant glimmer of snow-fields in the Lost Valley, and beyond, down to the velvet dark of Glencoe.

13 *Lochnagar*

THE FIRST ASCENT OF PARALLEL BUTTRESS

THE THEME OF OUR conversation was the illogical preference that most men betray for clean, sound rock. 'Any fool can climb good rock,' said Dr. J. H. B. Bell, as our car topped the Devil's Elbow and nosed down toward Braemar, 'but it takes craft and cunning to get up vegetatious schist and granite.'

I felt no inclination to contest the point: 'Before fording the river,' runs the proverb, 'do not curse the alligator's mother'; and the fact was that we were bound for Lochnagar—the greatest citadel of vegetatious granite. We hoped to climb at least one, if not two, new rock routes there. In the circumstances, a panegyric on lichened and mossy rocks savoured to me of judicious diplomacy.

We turned eastward and followed the track up Glen Callater until we came to an attractive camp site beside the river and within striking distance of Lochnagar's south-west flank. The May evening was well advanced, but all Scotland had been baking under a heat-wave and the air was still balmy. We decided to sleep out on the heather. Only the gentlest breeze stirred on the hill-side and there was no need to seek a sheltered hollow. We chose a springy couch near the track, and pulling a sheet of tent canvas over us to keep off the dew, lay back, with minds passive but alert, and watched

> the gold air and the silver fade
> And the last bird fly into the last light.

Then we set about the solution of those classic problems that have puzzled philosophers for ten thousand years.

Our talk gradually died away, becoming more and more intermittent as the sky darkened to navy-blue. The glow of our pipes grew dull while the first stars, faint and twinkling, grew slowly bright and steadfast. Silence fell. Just a whisper of wind over leagues of heather. And then I saw and heard no more.

We were awakened by the rising sun shining into our eyes. A fresh spring morning—the most joyous thing in life. Our primus stove was purring in no time, and then Bell and I repaired to the river. We found a briskly flowing pool and dived in. Once was enough. The water stung, but we came out glowing. After breakfast we packed up, and taking a couple of hundred feet of rope, set out for Lochnagar.

Our proposal was to go straight up to the summit, make a new route down the cliffs on the Tough-Brown ridge, and then, if all went well, make an ascent of the unclimbed Parallel buttress. The programme was ambitious enough, but nothing seemed impossible that morning. Our progress up the first slope was marked by the whirr and squawk of startled grouse. The cool of night still lingered in the air and the strengthening sun was only now drawing the dew off the heather. But the walk up to Lochnagar from Loch Callater is five miles, with two thousand two hundred feet of climbing, and even though we went slowly we were forced within the hour to strip to the waist. There was not a cloud in the sky. The heat had become intense but not enervating; it cooked the flesh round one's bones without sapping energy. In one and a half hours we topped Cairn Taggart. The stroll over its broad back to the White Mounth was sheer delight. The short grass and heather rustled dryly underfoot, the air shimmered; a sweet scent, enlivened by thyme and bog-myrtle, rose in waves from the warming ground. The scene typified the Cairngorms—an immense and rolling sky-line with snow-splashed peaks to the north-west. Any tendency to monotony in the foreground was sharply counteracted by the sparkle of the Dubh Loch on our right, framed between the crags of its corrie. Over a black cliff a raven glided lazily, yet with an alert poise that suggested a nestful of young among the rocks.

At midday we crossed the stony summit plateau and walked along the edge of the north-eastern precipice. At intervals, a cleft crag or a gully that bit into the brink disclosed dramatic vistas of the corrie twelve hundred feet below. The cliffs ended there in long scree-slopes, which converged on the waters of a glistening tarn. Glancing to the side, my eye swept a mile-long arc of plunging granite. It is alleged that one may see the Cheviots from Lochnagar—a distance of a hundred miles—but the farthest views had already been obscured by heat-haze.

At the top of the Tough-Brown ridge we halted, rested, and prepared for the climb. At twelve o'clock we began, unroped, the first phase of descent. The first hundred feet were well broken up. Then we diverged from the original route, which swung eastwards, and continued straight down. The angle quickly steepened, and tiers of vertical slabs, intersected by grassy ledges, obliged us to rope up. Our purpose was to find a more direct line of descent than that of the original route.

Throughout the central portion of the ridge we were entirely successful. The very nature of the rock lent itself to descent. It is less troublesome to drop down a series of short walls than to wrestle upward against granite and gravity. At first our new line involved a certain amount of traversing to and fro in search of the best route, then in search of any route at all, and latterly we were pushed off the crest until we overlooked Raeburn's gully at the western side of the ridge.

We had a simple choice before us: either to descend the west wall into the gully or to try to force a way down the true crest of the ridge. Our first desire was the crest, and we made a determined attempt. Only two hundred feet lay between us and the screes—two hundred feet of convex granite slabs, devoid of any excrescence that might serve as a rope-belay. Like the lower part of most ridges, this was the steepest part of the whole, where convexity achieved its maximum inclination. There were no intersecting ledges.

We made trial and reconnaissance, in the course of which I found myself stranded on one-nail rugosities, with insufficient

handhold to lean out and prospect for further footing; with the
disturbing awareness, moreover, of no good rope-belay and a
two-hundred-foot drop beneath. Even Bell, tough as granite and
long in the tooth, cast a ruminative eye over these proceedings.
He declared definitely for the gully.

The gully wall gave us a good climb of a hundred feet on
sound rock. It brought part one of our programme to fair
success and ourselves into Raeburn's gully, a hundred feet above
the base of the ridge. The gully was snow-filled.

We were now in the sun again, and hotter than ever. It
was then that our eyes caught the liquid glitter of Lochnagar.
Its colour was deep-sea green. I doubt if a loch can actually
beckon to parched climbers, but most assuredly it can merrily
laugh and seductively smile. In a few minutes we were pulling
off our clothes by the shore. A granite block made an excellent
diving platform. I curled my toes round the edge and plunged
deep for the bottom.

Then up I bobbed, to float in hydraulic comfort, while
watching small white clouds cruise across the blue sky, or
studying possible new climbs on the stupendous mass of rock
above. Thereafter we basked like a couple of idle seals on sun-
warmed boulders, until at length the trumpet-call of duty sounded
clear and insistent.

Before leaving the loch I looked more critically at Parallel
buttress. It lay midway between Eagle buttress and Tough-
Brown ridge, from which it was separated by Parallel gullies
A and B. Both of these gullies were unclimbed. Between
them the broad base of the buttress tapered as it soared, until
six hundred feet up it narrowed to a slender ridge, which curled
to the summit. The total height was seven hundred feet. There
seemed to be a particularly nasty section about five hundred feet
up—a short tower placed at one of the narrowest points of the
ridge. If one reached so far there seemed little hope of by-
passing that tower, and a problematical chance of climbing it
direct. The thought of failure so high was disturbing, but
doubts such as these are the spice of mountaineering, lending

*E

suspense to the climb and zest to success—and if one be philo-
sophical, consolation to defeat.

At three p.m. we started the climb up steep rock immediately
to the left of gully A.   After a short ascent we made an oblique
traverse across gully A on to Parallel buttress.   Bell went ahead,
working his way up grey sheets of granite while I selected my
own route twenty feet behind.   We had agreed to climb unroped until either of us felt the need of moral support.   This
lower part of the route was typical of the true buttress—broad
fields of rock with plenty of scope for variation.   For the first
two hundred and fifty feet our ascent continued obliquely toward
the centre line; then, as the rocks curved more and more precipi-
tously, we were once again forced from the crest, this time
toward B gully.   Needless to say, the rocks were lichened and
peppered with tufts of sparse grass.   I shudder to think what
the climb must be like in wet weather.   There is a notable
paucity of belays, and slime-coated granite, I should imagine,
would give pause to the stoutest heart.

Our way was now blocked by a ring of impending slabs, which
circled the whole breadth of the buttress.   Our only hope was
to turn them by a right-hand traverse along a thin and vegetatious
ledge to the extreme edge of the gully.   There, on the actual
brink, we found a breach in the defences and climbed for a
moment with our heels projecting over the gloomy depths.
A short upward scramble, a slanting traverse up a long scoop
in the gully wall, and the crest was ours once more.

From now onward the buttress tapered quickly, the crest
became definite, and our choice of route narrowed to a single
inescapable line.   In short, the buttress was all set for a 'show-
down'; the conditions were ripe for the uprise of one supreme
obstacle, which could be turned by no backstairs cunning, that
'dark sanctuary of incapacity,' but must be won by frontal
assault or not at all.   We knew in our hearts it must come,
and in due course come it did: in the shape of an ugly
tower, the same that from far below had looked but a
short wall.

The honour of leading the first attack was bestowed upon me. While we roped up I stood back and surveyed the situation. We stood on secure footing on the narrowest edge of the ridge, from which the rocks fell sharply on either hand into deep gullies. The tower rose thirty feet, its head shaped like a blunt diamond and bent gently forward, so that the last ten feet slightly overhung. This arrow-head was set upon a high bust of slabs.

I looked around both flanks in hope of detecting some weakness. They were perpendicular. Frontal attack was the one course open. But running up the left side of the bust was one exceedingly thin crack. It ended twenty feet up at the left edge of the arrow-head. There was just a chance that from there one might traverse below the final overhang to the right-hand side overlooking B gully, at which point it looked possible to climb on to the top angle of the diamond.

I failed on the crack. Eight feet up was the most I could make. After that there were no holds, not even a down-scrape on lichen or a pull-up on a tuft of grass. Bell tried next, but a brief examination convinced him of the worst. However, we still had one last card to play.

Bell dug into his rucksack and produced—I wish that one could write in a whisper—two pitons. Their use is frowned upon by many British mountaineers. Like the queen of Spain's legs, a piton not only ought never to be seen, but must not be supposed even to exist. Its use, in fact, should be sparing and reserved for exceptional circumstances. Bell and I solemnly declared that this was an exceptional circumstance. It qualified with honours.

Armed with his pitons and a small hammer, Bell climbed the wall as far as he could. Where the holds vanished he hammered a piton into the crack until only the ring protruded. Using the ring as a handhold, he pulled himself up, contrived to get one foot on it, and by a movement curious to watch, stood erect. He drove in the second piton and this he used as a handhold only. the rest of the crack was wider, still demanding a high output of energy, and then he reached a little niche at the left side of the arrow-head.

When he saw what remained to be done he wisely decided not to move further until I had joined him. On my way up I was able to remove both pitons and so leave the rocks in their pristine condition; which meant that I had to dangle like a marionette on the rope, ever a wounding experience for the ribs. There was little room on the niche and before I quite reached it Bell had to move out. While I settled in and coiled the rope, Bell removed his boots. There is nothing so comforting as stocking-soles for a traverse on smooth slabs, and this is Bell's frequent method of dealing with them.

He needed all the security he could get. When I watched him edge out on swift-dipping granite below the arrow-head, which tended to thrust his body out of balance, I realized that he trusted only to the friction of feet, for my belay would have been of doubtful value had any sudden strain come on the rope. However, the last trump had not yet sounded. He reached the right-hand side of the arrow-head, scrambled on to the sloping roof, and disappeared. I waited patiently, prepared to hear of some new horror beyond; then I heard a voice say, 'Well, I'm up,' in the detached tone one uses for 'Good morning' at Monday's breakfast table.

To save time I told Bell that I should keep on my boots and might therefore require a pull on the rope. He assured me his belay was a good one and I began my crab-like crawl. I was right—with boots I required a constantly tight rope. In a few minutes I was again by his side.

The very air seemed brighter, more full of good cheer above that thirty-foot passage—a reaction, I suppose, from difficulty overcome. Peering over the blunt tip of the arrow, my eye went straight to the gleam of the loch. Three hours ago I had wondered whether a bathe before a climb were too good a thing on a hot day; it often tends to make one lethargic. But to-day that was not the effect on me, nor on Bell, whose performance at the crux, alternately exhibiting furious vigour and delicate

LOCHNAGAR

Parallel buttress lies directly above the
highest point of the large snow patch

balance, bore striking testimony to the virtue of Lochnagar water. Were the full truth known, this matchless tarn might become a national Lourdes.

We crossed a narrow neck behind the tower and climbed a steep nose, which turned out to be a threat without substance. Then we stopped, and with an upward glance saw that no further tower barred the way to victory. The ridge meandered onward, narrow, shattered to blocks, but after another hundred feet no longer standing out in distinguished isolation, more a part of the general mass of the cliffs, into which it finally merged just below the plateau. We united and coiled the rope, then followed the riven crest, whose unresisting crags seemed to welcome us at each turn. At the very end was a knife-edge of frozen snow.

At five o'clock we stepped on to the summit and passed, as it were, into another realm. Far beneath our feet a mighty expanse of tawny hills and plains stretched to the utmost fringes of the earth, and faded there in unfathomable blue. Over all hung the breathless hush of evening. One heard it circle the world like a lapping tide, the wave-beat of the sea of beauty; and as we listened from our watch tower and looked out across the broad earth, our own little lives and our flush of triumph in climbing a new route became very trivial things. They were suddenly measured for us against eternity and the real, and in such perspective vanished away, of no moment. Yet in that same instant our climb on the granite crags, the bare summit and the lands below, were with ourselves idealized as though in a point out of time and exalted in oneness. We began to understand, a little less darkly, what it may mean to inherit the earth.

14 *Tower Ridge in Winter*

IT IS NOTEWORTHY how often the red-letter days of our mountaineering come as a complete surprise. One such December day I spent with Dr. J. H. B. Bell and Douglas Laidlaw on Ben Nevis.

We passed the night of 16th December in the S.M.C. hut below the cliffs. For once we had made no definite plans, feeling that at such a place and time they might be an undue tempting of providence. At eight-thirty next morning we therefore stepped from the hut in a mood of mild suspense, wondering how much of the world would be visible. Westward, across the Spean valley, golden moors glowed in the early morning sun; but the upper glen of the Allt a' Mhuilinn, where the hut lies, was deep in snow and the blue shadow of white cliffs. The sky was full of wind and sun.

The snow conditions appeared excellent and we discussed the possibilities over breakfast. There was a wide choice before us, but in truth our minds had already been made up for us by the stirring challenge of Tower ridge; two thousand three hundred feet high, triple-towered, encased in snow and ice, it stood forth from the mass of the cliffs, the most splendid feature of the mountain. We set off with rope and axe at nine-thirty a.m.

Within five minutes the first surprise of the day was sprung by Bell. He proposed a direct ascent of the Douglas boulder. This boulder is seven hundred feet high and forms the first tower of the ridge. It presented toward us a huge face of slabs, which never having been climbed in winter condition would therefore make an excellent appetizer for the main course ahead; or so we thought, such was our innocence.

The first phase of operations was staged on a broad expanse

of intermingled slab and rib draped in masses of powder-snow. At the end of two hours I doubt whether we had managed to climb as much as a couple of hundred feet. It was more than well, perhaps, that before we were too deeply committed we came to *verglas*, which forbade further progress. Eleven o'clock, therefore, found us once more at the foot of Tower ridge. Whatever the others thought of such an appetizer, I myself felt akin to that Scotsman described by Byron, who having heard that kittiwakes were excellent whets, 'ate six of them, and complained that he was no hungrier than when he began.' With all speed we repaired to the eastern flank, and climbing by snow-slopes and broken rock came at eleven-thirty to the crest, a little way above the Douglas boulder.

The ridge was here slender but level. In front of us it rose abruptly for several hundred feet to the 'Little Tower,' whose midway bastion guards the narrow ascent to the main keep— the Great Tower at four thousand feet. The rocks were everywhere inundated with snow, which clung even to vertical walls. The climbing to begin with was not difficult; a sweep with a gloved hand disclosed good holds. Our first and foremost enemy was time. In the previous winter a good mountaineer had spent sixteen hours on Tower ridge; we had now only five, and must hope for better conditions to reach the Great Tower before sunset. We thought we could do it, but even then there was no guarantee that we should find the Tower passable before dark. At that height accumulations of snow and ice would be much greater than on this lower part of the mountain, and the quality would be altogether different.

Meanwhile, Bell forged ahead by himself. Laidlaw and I roped up and followed behind. This procedure saved time and we made fair speed up the first section of the ridge. Each ledge held a steep pile of snow and each square-cut block wore a tall bonnet. But the snow was good and held an in-driven foot firmly. For the most part Laidlaw and I were able to climb together, thanks to excellent rope management by Laidlaw. Following twenty to thirty feet behind, he climbed with several coils in his left hand, his ice-axe in his right, ceaselessly letting out rope or drawing it in as distance between us altered, simultaneously taking his own holds, deftly whisking the rope clear of obstacles, and never allowing it to trail on the rock. A perfect demonstration of rhythmical rope-work, accompanied by delighted grins of pleasure in the climbing.

After an hour of such climbing we arrived below the Little Tower. Strictly speaking it is not a genuine tower, but an abrupt steepening of the rocks appearing as a tower from underneath: no cleft separates it from the continuation of the ridge. To-day it was muffled up in a thick fur coat, in the unbuttoning of which we spent much time. The holds then displayed were small and glazed, most difficult to detect and scrape clean. Ninety feet up Laidlaw joined me on a ledge; we traversed left-ward round a corner and discovered a much-perplexed Bell. He was held up by a vertical wall of unusual obstinacy. When at length the problem was solved I noted that a full hour had been spent on the last hundred feet.

After some more very hard climbing on the east face over glazed rock we regained the ridge above the Little Tower. The rocks then assumed a more benign angle. Nothing could stop our reaching the crux of the ridge. For one more hour we kicked, swept and cut our way up encrusted blocks until at three o'clock we were brought to a halt under the ponderous mass of the Great Tower. Two more hours would decide our fate. Meantime, we had still no conception of what difficulties lay in wait. A few years before, Bell and F. S. Smythe had been turned back at the *further* side of the Tower at sunset, and Bell was not looking forward to a second defeat. However, no winter climb is ever the same climb twice: and therein lies the superiority of winter over summer mountaineering in Scotland.

The Tower rose almost sheer for a hundred feet above our heads. Its armour of snow and ice plate was complete. Not a chink showed anywhere. But circling round the eastern wall and overlooking the chasm of Observatory gully, there is, in summer, an easy ledge by which one may walk and then scramble up a slab until one comes to a face of sixty feet, which may be climbed to the top of the Tower. This eastern traverse was now banked with hard snow at an exceedingly high angle. It looked a mere frieze on the wide wall that dropped far out of sight into the gully.

Still unroped, Bell began step-cutting on the eastern traverse, until twenty or thirty feet along he was stopped by the first down-twist in the ledge. The snow thinned out there and it looked sensational. Bell looked at the twist, looked down at the gully, and waited for Laidlaw and me. He then tied himself to the middle of the rope; therefore I took over the lead and continued cutting until we came below the summer route.

The whole face was congested with heavy bulges of pale blue ice. Bell was against my trying the route at all, on the ground that I should take an hour to get up. However, no other route was likely to take less than an hour, and being obstinate in the face of such challenges I made an attempt. The ice was laid down in stout boiler-plates, awkwardly angled and linked by high steps of more thinly iced rock. Five minutes' cutting sufficed to show me that one hour was an underestimate; nor was I getting any encouragement from below. 'It's a waste of time,' said Bell repeatedly. 'This should be our last resort, not our first.' It was absolutely essential that we should be across Tower Gap before dark. Some other way must be found.

At three-thirty p.m. I withdrew from the ice and we decided to prolong the eastern traverse, if we could, on an upward-slanting line for a couple of hundred feet. We might then be able to climb back to the crest just before Tower Gap, whose U-shaped gash cleaves the slender ridge between the Great Tower and the main cliffs.

We moved a few yards further along the Tower wall and found our way obstructed by a twelve-foot flake of rock, split from the main mass by a crack just wide enough to admit one leg. The flake gaped like a partially opened clam and tilted outward toward the gully. With aid from Bell, who gave me a push from behind and then held me in balance, I managed to wriggle up the slippery film of the edge and find a secure stance on top. Indeed, I could not have found myself a safer position on the whole mountain, for I stood chest high within the crack as though wedged in a rock pulpit. The others came up on a tight rope and I vacated my pulpit to Bell, who was thus well placed to protect my more dubious operations beyond.

From the rim of the flake I climbed to the wall above, where a jutting corner made the first step or two troublesome, then I passed out of Bell's sight and emerged upon the white face of a long cliff, seamed by thin and icy ledges. Much step-cutting was required, mostly one-handed cutting with the left arm: to retain balance I had to use handhold on the wall above. Being not insensitive to exposure, I remained constantly aware of Observatory gully yawning hungrily at my heels.

I made slow but steady progress. To Bell and Laidlaw, the long delay, approximately an hour, was thoroughly exasperating. They could not see what I was doing, nor what the difficulties were, but could hear the metallic ring of the axe and occasionally glimpse the scurry of ice-chips into the void. The inch-by-inch movement of the rope stood in horrid contrast to the swift flight of time. The eastern sky was growing coldly pale in prelude to night.

From time to time I heard low growls, urging me not to dawdle, or muffled barks of alarm, drawing my attention to the revolution of the earth and the corresponding need for speed by climbers. But I felt greatly cheered when I thought what my taskmasters would say upon treading these ledges themselves. Eventually the hitherto impossible wall above me lay at a climbable angle and I started straight up for the crest. The rock was thickly fluffed with snow, which I laboriously scraped off with my axe, disclosing slabs wrinkled like the hide of an elephant. I found woollen gloves of great advantage over bare hands, which would simply have slipped off the rock; whereas the wool lightly froze to the wrinkles and gave a fairly secure hold. I crawled twenty feet up the slabs and drew level with the crest ot the ridge. The coping of snow was wind-moulded to a delicate knife-edge. I popped my head over the top and looked down the other side.

A strong westerly wind smote my face. The corrie was roofed by an even fleece of cloud, which lapped against the wall of the ridge several hundred feet below and ran down the full length of the Allt a' Mhuilinn glen, where the surface was sunset-fired. The red-gold of the sky, coming so suddenly after hard climbing along an ice-clad wall, literally stopped my breath. Knowing how fleeting such a wonder may be, I was filled with anxiety lest the others should miss the full splendour. I scrambled to the crest, called to Bell to come up quickly, and driving my axe into the snow, took in his rope round the shaft. Carn Mor Dearg and the Aonachs were rose-pink against a bright green sky.

After his long wait Bell required no exhortation to hurry, but by the time he joined me the most brilliant hues had quietened. None the less the effects were still hectic enough and Bell's astonishment gratifying. As Laidlaw arrived, a more rare phenomenon occurred. The sun on the far side of Nevis was right down on the Atlantic, and the shadow of the mountain was now projected like a gigantic gnomon across the face of Scotland, devouring at one stroke the breadth of Inverness-shire, until the apex not only reached the utmost rim of the world but climbed into the fringe of brume above. The effect was then not of a shadow thrown by the mountain toward the horizon, but of a broadening beam of dark directed by the apex in the sky toward *us*. For a few moments it hung there in the guise of an anti-sun, radiating not light but darkness. None of us had witnessed this phenonenon before, and only once had we known it reported —by Leslie Stephen—of a sunset on Mont Blanc. Then the anti-sun vanished. At one stroke the earth was in twilight.

Immediately after sundown the wind grew in strength each minute and we hastened to attempt the crossing of Tower Gap before the last light died. Between the Great Tower and the upper cliffs the ridge hung like a tight-stretched curtain, but the snow-blade was comparatively soft and for twenty feet we stamped it underfoot. Then we came to the brink of the Gap. It made the most savage cleft I had seen on Scottish mountains. The icy flanks dropped sheer into deep gullies, and on the far side, rising twenty feet, was a frost-hoared wall shaped like a canine tooth. The wind tore through the open jaws with a pulsing roar and thunder-beat, like a charge of cavalry, intermittently relenting only to rush again with increased force.

'This is where Smythe and I were beaten last time,' Bell shouted in my ear. 'I don't want a repetition now!'

'It looks tough,' I replied. 'Give me a tight rope till I'm down.'

I climbed into the Gap. The floor was curved and edged like a sickle. I kicked out a platform. But when I attacked the wall beyond I could make nothing of it. The tooth was enamelled in thinnest ice, which bore a top-dressing of fog crystals. In perfect calm I question whether it might have been climbable: with a half-gale tearing at my body and the rope billowing over Tower gully, I could not even effect lodgment on the lowest rock, nor could I see any method of dealing with it. Despite the limited standing-room both Bell and Laidlaw joined me; for the situation was serious. We tried each flank of the tooth without success. Every movement was made highly precarious by the wrenching wind and the thinness of the ridge. After half an hour of vain effort we were no closer to any solution and dusk had fallen.

I faced the unpleasant facts and began to think out ways and means of retreat, swiftly speculating whether we could climb down the eastern wall on to the tilting snow-fields below Tower gully—a long, steep, and uneasy procedure—or had better follow Bell's old line of retirement by the secondary Tower ridge. I asked Bell what he thought. He looked down the east wall and shook his head. 'Not that!' said he. 'Better go back as I went with Smythe.' But the idea of returning along the eastern traverse dismayed me. Quite apart from darkness, the cold had become piercing.

It was then that Laidlaw suggested lassoing the tip of the

BEN NEVIS

Tower ridge is seen on
the right-hand side of
the photograph with
the Great Tower in
bright sunshine. The
ridge is 2,300 feet high
and the lower part is
not visible

tooth. I was doubtful. It seemed a waste of precious minutes. We were not cowboys. However, the alternatives were bad enough to make it worth one trial. I untied my rope, doubled it into a loop, and climbing half-way up the short side of the Gap, cast the rope high and hard into the teeth of the wind. At this very first attempt the loop whipped neatly round the top of the wall. Life is like that. At another time in such weather one might spend an hour in fruitless effort.

Bell was now tied to one end of the doubled rope, the other being in my own hands. 'He was scant o' news that telt his faither was hanged,' say the lowland Scots; but in the highlands a man can string up a friend and be unashamed. Feeling very much like Mr. Ellis, the public executioner, I hauled at my own end of the rope, while Bell went skyward. In ten minutes he was up and the day was saved.

Laidlaw followed next. While he was climbing, my attention was drawn to a sudden, visible ebb of the twilight, several times repeated. The snow-swamped mass of the upper cliffs retired into thickening night; the rocks took on a gaunt and ghastly aspect, until one might say most aptly that 'Echo, here, whatever is asked her, answers Death.' The scene returns with faultless definition to the mind in after-days, although at the time, in a freezing wind, but a quick impression seemed to be registered.

In all, I had spent one hour in the Gap before my turn came to follow. Almost paralysed by cold, I partly climbed and was mostly dragged up the hoary skin of the tooth. The remaining three hundred feet of the ridge gave a straightforward climb in knee-deep snow, but care was required to avoid being caught on the wrong foot by the greater gusts. We skirted the last riven crags by a steep snow-slope to the right, then with a final tussle scrambled on to the summit plateau at six p.m. Our climb had lasted seven hours.

To our surprise we found ourselves in calm. For the wind, baffled, struck upright from the cliffs. Before us stretched vast snow-fields, shining frostily under the stars; beyond, rank upon rank of sparkling peaks. A great stillness had come upon the world.   We seemed to tread air rather than crusted snow; we were light of foot; we walked like demigods in joyous serenity. The intensity of our exaltation seems peculiar to the following of a great rock-climb to a climax of supreme beauty.   After the hard fight on Tower ridge we were elated, by the miracle of sunset, steadied; for in profound beauty there is more solemnity than gayness; so that our faculties were in balance yet highly keyed, therefore abnormally alive to the deep peace of the summit.   Its grace flowed in upon the mind with a touch soothing and most delicate.   We need feel but once the spell of that enchantment to understand Schumann's declaration that the true music is a silence.   In the quiet I felt something of the limitation of personality fall away as desires were stilled; and as I died to self and became more absorbed in the hills and sky, the more their beauty entered into me, until they seemed one with me and I with them.

Later, while we walked slowly across the plateau, it became very clear to me that only the true self, which transcends the personal, lays claim to immortality.   On mountains it is that spiritual part that we unconsciously develop.   When we fail in that all other success is empty; for we take our pleasure without joy, and the ache of boredom warns of a rusting faculty.

At last we turned toward Achintee and went down like fallen angels, with an ever-mounting reluctance, from a spiritual paradise to the black pit of Glen Nevis.

15 *Cir Mhor*

THE EVENING OF THE FIFTH OF AUGUST 1939
found R. G. Donaldson, M. Mackinnon, and me toiling with
swollen rucksacks up Glen Rosa to the high pass that looks
down to Glen Sannox. We had come to the Isle of Arran for
two days' rock-climbing and ridge-wandering. In tribute to
the notorious properties of Arran granite, whose 'cyclopean
walls' make high demand of time and energy, we proposed to
camp fifteen hundred feet up in the north corrie of Cir Mhor.

It is not my policy to 'rough it' on the mountains unneces-
sarily, for hard times need no seeking; therefore, in addition to
much climbing equipment we were heavy-laden with tent,
sleeping-bags, eggs, bacon—the luxuries of a comfort-loving
world, when hard tack and a couch on the heather might have
served our turn as well. I kept remembering a certain climber
who had lived for ten days in the Cairngorms on peasebrose
alone; at which I warmed with indignation, telling myself that
pseudo-toughness had roots in laziness. But I thought wist-
fully of iron rations and the light load they entail as the sky
darkened and dusk closed upon us on the long windless slopes
below the Saddle.

These symptoms of weariness may bear on a phenomenon
that arose later. Donaldson, brimming over with vitality,
inspired no doubt by this being the start of his summer holi-
days, had reached the pass ten minutes ahead of me. I could
see his tall figure on the rim of the ridge against the night sky.
He was staring eastward and I automatically followed his gaze
when I stepped up beside him. Before me, the waning moon
was just clear of the far rim of Cioch-na-h-Oighe, and thus
perceptibly rising. A few stars peered and twinkled round the
fringe of a travelling cloud. Even the sea, visible only as an

inky blackness, had a motion felt rather than seen.   Everywhere
that sense of movement.

After two hours of uphill tramping in sultry air I felt released
in a world lively and free, which awakened in me the illusion of
watching the spin of the earth and its flight through interstellar space.   This sensation sprang from both sight and touch:
the brush of the wind on my cheek, the lift of the moon, the
glide of some wisps of cirrus, and more especially of the stars,
which seemed to race behind them.   From the lofty pass I
watched this sweep of the earth through a chartless universe
with the added sense of a majestic rhythm of movement, which
may best be likened to the greatness of rhythm in a Beethoven
symphony.   The illusion lasted half a minute and disappeared
with the arrival of Mackinnon.   On reflection, I remember no
other mountaineers reporting that experience, which on subsequent nights I have tried in vain to recapture.   Yet so naturally
did it come and go that I thought nothing of its rarity at the
time.   And my attention was at once claimed by the hard work
in front.

Half a mile away on our left crouched Cir Mhor, beneath
whose ebony wedge the north corrie lay like a dark pool,
screened by Cioch-na-h-Oighe from the low moon.   We went
down to it by a long traverse of the mountain-side, groping our
way in pitch blackness through a confusion of heather and rock
outcrops.   A man's opinion of this world sadly deteriorates if
he gets much of such work.   My thoughts, so exalted a short
while ago, sank very low indeed.

Many a time Mackinnon and I stopped on the lip of some
drop, which for all we knew might be five feet deep or fifty, or
sat on some obstructing boulder, and comprehensively cursed.
We cursed the mountain, the moon, and in particular Donaldson,
whose most heinous crime was that of being alive and visible—
and in front.   At the end of a tiring day I have at other times
known weary men unwisely keep silent, allowing vague and
baseless resentments to gather over the party like a thunder-
cloud.   A discharge of invective is to be heartily recommended

at such times. It clears the air. Most salutary of all is a friendly word; but most difficult.

We arrived in the corrie at midnight and pitched the tent on a patch of turf midway between the cliffs and a small stream, whose plentiful supply of water made the corrie a first-class base. Inside the tent our cramped quarters were soon reduced to the cheerful chaos that attends supper. At one o'clock I disentangled myself and went out for a last look round. The moon stood well toward the zenith, and infinitely far below drove a golden furrow across the jet expanse of the sea. The sky was swarming with stars; and Cir Mhor, which an hour before was no more than a painted shadow lurking in the background, had taken a great stride forward; its cliffs now rose directly over us like the palm of an uplifted hand, raised not in threat but in benediction. Everything seemed propitious for the morrow and I pulled on my sleeping-bag with that delicious sense of work past and pleasure before, which yields a present of pure content.

I know few mountaineers who are good risers. It was broad daylight before we bestirred ourselves and not till nine a.m. did we set out and take stock of the day's battleground. It was a glorious summer morning and every detail of the cliffs stood sharp in clear air. The huge granite slabs lapped upon each other like the plates of a suit of mail; even in photographs Cir Mhor may be distinguished from all other rock-peaks by this unique armoured façade. Our plan was to attack the slender buttress named B C rib (thus styled from the B and C gullies that flank it) and thereafter follow a direct route on the upper face to link with Bell's groove near the summit. This course would give us the longest rock-climb on the mountain.

I was anxious to investigate B C rib. Many years ago, in a paper read before the Alpine Club, this rib had been described as the most dangerous of Scottish rock-climbs, mainly, I think, on account of a paucity of belays. However, the times change and I felt certain that the stigma could no longer be held true: we hoped to find the climb of great interest yet not severe. So far as we could judge from below, the main difficulty lay in the smoothness of slabs in the central section and an unavoidable overhang at the finish.

A short uphill walk brought us to the base of the rib. We roped up with a hundred feet between each man, myself as leader and Donaldson second. By cutting out a long preliminary ascent of the lower mountain, our high camp should, in theory, have brought us to the rocks fresher and better able to deal with them. As now, I have generally found this belief a partial fallacy, inasmuch as one is neither warmed up nor worked into that smooth upward rhythm of movement as essential to good rock-work as to hill-walking. I began to climb the easier rocks like an old cab-horse, and on the more difficult bestowed too great an output of energy. After sixty feet I was stopped by an awkward corner at the right-hand edge of the rib. Its tall grey wall bristled with unsuitable projections, whereon I struggled like one in an evil dream; until of a sudden I struck form. Eye, mind, and muscle co-ordinated, and I felt myself drift up the cliffs like smoke. It is a delightful sensation and one of the incidental joys of rock-climbing.

When I reached the stance above and watched Donaldson climb, and again from a still higher ledge when I looked down like a roosting gull while he brought up Mackinnon, I saw from the smooth progress of their tousled heads that each was in good climbing mood. The knowledge reassured me. For the principal obstacles were drawing close. Should belays be few and far between, not the form of the leader alone, but that of the whole party, must determine safety or danger. Shortly afterwards we came to a tilting grass platform, and there, hard before us, sprang the great slab which had drawn my suspicious eye from the corrie.

The pitch was an unbroken sweep of granite, shield-shaped, bare of feature save for one long groove, too thin for hold, which ran diagonally from the low left to the top right corner. In this shallow score were lodged at intervals a few tufts of coarse grass, whose cushion might accommodate the edge-nail of a boot. On these, it would seem, must depend a climber's further progress and 'the continuity of his cervical vertebrae.' With a quickened interest I instinctively cast round for belays. Not a spike, not a knob however diminutive, gladdened the prospecting eye. Donaldson, who as second man was most affected by this deficiency, was trustfully unconcerned. He was clearly sustained by those twin pillars of mountaineering faith; belief in the axiom that the leader does not fall; and more practically, that if he does, then the most secure of all belays by a second man is his sitting down on a ledge, whence he may feed out the rope round his waist—*not* round the rock.

Conscious of being safely belayed, I stepped very gently on to the first tuft, and before it might think of subsiding passed with stealthy tread to the second tuft. And so swiftly on till at length I glided over the top. There is no real difficulty in the pitch, but the grass must be tenderly treated and the foot set down as though on egg-shells. Nothing would persuade me to venture on it in wet weather.

A Lakeland climber to whom I described this simple slab was horrified. To place trust in grass-holds seemed to him a dangerous flouting of first principles. But this is not so. Grass and loose rock are natural inhabitants of the mountain precipice, and mountaineers must be able to use them; like snow and ice, their condition may be judged in advance—with practice.

When Donaldson and Mackinnon had rejoined me we climbed without further incident to the final overhang. There was a little recess to the left of it, like the niche for a saint under the eaves of some cathedral spire. I am uncertain of the height of cathedral spires, but our own niche was about two hundred and fifty feet above the screes, say four times the height of a city tenement. The ascent of the overhang, therefore, promised aerial thrills. But of this I was confident: there must surely be some very fine handholds as yet invisible to us; for it is manifest that no overhang may be climbed without them. Donaldson tied himself to a stout rock-spike at the back of his niche, and although lamentably unsaint-like, gave me a seraphic smile and the word to go forth.

I edged out to the right on small notches, taking my hand-holds low down to preserve arm strength, then went straight up until the overhand stopped me. At this vital point I found an undercut hold at waist-level, on which I was able to lean out of balance and stretch the left hand over the top. My hurriedly groping fingers at once closed round the ideal handhold, the same that has ever charmed my dreams, but which never till now materialized in the living rock—a jug handle. One vigorous pull up and my chest was over the brink, legs dangling in thin air; then with a few press-holds I pushed myself up to the easy rocks beyond. Like many an impending obstacle in life, it fell at once when boldly tackled; and the joy of swarming over this brow of space was out of all proportion to the technical difficulty. One's blood spins and the spirit sings. No melancholy in a man can survive such rock.

It is to be noted that at no time throughout the route had I climbed without a good belay. The standard of climbing was very difficult.

The whole upper rock-face was now at our disposal, like a splendid book stored with secrets of varied lore, of sudden beauty and essays in brisk adventure, of which, most sadly, we had time to read but a chapter and that quickly. We were, in fact, free to select one route from numerous alternatives, for the rocks were much riven and abounded in hidden nooks and crannies, and tantalizing corners with who knows what beyond. The face demands several days' exploration.

The line we ultimately followed led us tortuously to an inclined passage, which bored into a sudden upheaval of slabs. It appeared that we had reached a cul-de-sac and must turn back, but a disappearing tunnel called aloud for examination. We discovered that it ended in a rock chamber roughly shaped like a beehive. Fifteen feet above the down-hilt of the floor the arched roof was pierced by a hole—a hole wide enough to admit the body of a man. I caught a glimpse of blue sky and the white flash of a gull breasting the sun. They drew one's spirit upward, but to raise the flesh even to the foot of the chimney seemed beyond the ingenuity of man. No abundance of good holds could serve our purpose. None the less, and despite the plain evidence of our eyes, some intuition of a practicable solution held us there.

The problem was an intellectual one, and as such had its fascinations. We examined the construction of the chamber in a spirit of detached speculation, with something of that purely objective curiosity by which Galileo, observing the pendulum swing of a chandelier above his cathedral pew, surprised and formulated one of the fundamental laws of physics. The analogy would appear unduly flattering to Mackinnon and me, for this objective thinking bore fruit only in Donaldson.

There was a crack at one point of the wall, and where the roof began to overhang the crack held a chock-stone. Donaldson climbed up and threaded a rope through it and we viewed the situation anew. My own attention wandered again to Donaldson, who is at all times an absorbing study. He is much given to reverie and had fallen into a long abstracted stare, his lips slightly apart, as though breathing had momentarily ceased. Then his face suddenly warmed as the glimmer of a secret thought, rising like a bubble from the depths, broke through his eyes in a smile. At once he was alert. The rope hung clear to the floor; he seized one end and tied a loop there, adjusting the rope till the loop hung midway between floor and ceiling. The top end he tied securely to the chock-stone: after climbing the crack to the chock-stone he pulled the loop toward him, inserted one foot, and then with a powerful lunge catapulted himself from the wall. The forward and upward swing of the pendulum carried him close below the hole in the roof, whereupon he let go the rope and, swift as thought, grasped handhold in the opening. In a trice he had jammed his chest and shoulders in the chimney. After a noble struggle of some minutes he squirmed up and was free in the open air.

Had this feat of acrobatics been performed twenty feet above sawdust in a circus, it might have brought down the house in applause. High up on the face of a mountain cliff, it passed off with no more than a cheerful 'Good work!' Belatedly, I pay tribute to the quality of Donaldson's mind, for imagination and realistic thought rarely correlate. The actual acrobatics looked spectacular, but in fact were of little merit, for I had no difficulty in repeating them. An end of the rope was then thrown up to us by Mackinnon, who tied himself to the other end but had no way of joining us by his own volition. We therefore pulled him up like a sack of coals to the chimney, and thence like a cork from a bottle.

There seemed to be no serious barrier between ourselves and Bell's groove, so we sat a little in the sun and coiled up the rope; then continued, each to his own line, up the pale grey lanes of granite, whose flanking crags were sweeping in more closely to the final cone. I imagine we must have been following one of the joints in the armour, but we were too close to the vast scale of things to know this certainly, as an ant in a jungle, perhaps, may doubt whether it crawls in a track or a clearing.

A short way beneath the summit we made a descending traverse to the right and were confronted with our last pitch, Bell's groove: a great slab cleft by a diagonal crack. I recall no definite holds. The friction of cloth and skin and the jamming of the right boot in the crack were the means of adhesion and propulsion. Thinking in our folly that we could climb Arran rock without using our knees, we had this day discarded breeches for the greater freedom of shorts, and in much the same way as we had disgorged pier dues to land at Brodick, so here a toll of cuticle was exacted at the gate to the summit. Thus, each in turn spread his body over the edge of the groove, and wriggling like a caterpillar, forced his way up by inward pressure of foot, knee, and forearm. Feeling slightly the worse for wear, we left the groove behind and mounted the last few feet to the cairn.

Cir Mhor has one of the sharpest tops in Scotland. There was no room for three of us, so we went a little way down on the far side and enjoyed a spell of sun-bathing. An hour later we felt compelled to traverse the A' chir ridge to Beinn Tarsuinn.

CIR MHOR AND THE N.E. CORRIE

The A' chir ridge is the finest in Arran, and has attained much fame by virtue of the sensational photographs which may be taken at the *mauvais pas*. I myself, never having traversed the ridge, looked forward to it with high expectations.

At one o'clock we set off. The air was still and a hot sun beat upon the crags. We therefore went shirtless and enjoyed one of the most invigorating ridge-walks that have fallen to us in summer. The 'bad step' resolved itself into an easy stride across a cleft in the thinnest part of the ridge. Throughout we walked in the authentic mountain atmosphere, where a climber feels poised in the middle air between heaven and earth, and knows himself most close to the former. The crest was narrow and bold, like some of the less riven parts of the Cuillin; the rock clean; deep glens fell away on either hand and carried brawling streams to the sea, which in return sent wheeling round the hills a sparkling halo of gulls—those birds of in-human beauty, whose wild eye and stainless plume seem to me to have been evolved from the world expressly to embody the true spirit of seaward mountains, and by their cry, forlornly echoing among the rocks, to sound the inner music.

At three p.m. we came to the summit of Beinn Tarsuinn. Half-drugged by sun, I curled up on a rock beside the cairn and, closing my eyes, let my mind take me where it would. I soon balanced gloriously at ease on a spar of granite, and like a wizard on a broomstick, drifted far over the western isles with white gulls for escort.

16

The Cuillin Ridge and Blaven

I ARRIVED IN SKYE for the first time in June 1936. I hardly knew what to expect. I had heard much of the Cuillin and read more, and my imagination had run riot. It speaks volumes for the character of the range that my wild dreams fell short of the wilder reality. Climbing from Glen Brittle to the summit of Sgurr na Banachdich on a clear day of great heat, I saw them at last, by myself. Twenty peaks of naked rock shimmered in the heat-haze; a horse-shoe of light grey spikes linked by a six-mile ridge of gabbro and shattered basalt, narrow, rarely sinking under three thousand feet. Eastward, beyond the main array and across the deep, long-running valley of Glen Sligachan, the bulk of Blaven rose high above wisps of whitely curling mist, which glided up the west buttress and vanished. From its summit a sharp and pinnacled ridge fell and swept up again to the curving crest of Clach Glas. After an hour of silent admiration I took a wider sweep with the eye, disclosing a feast of sunlit seas and distant islands, and still later, a still wider sweep to embrace skyscapes that rocked the mind with wonder. Time spent in failing to fathom a blue sky is never spent in vain. Let the mind soar like the highest-mounting bird, self-surrendered to the infinite, and an infinite spirit seems to flow into one. This is the law of grace. Thus seeds are sown from which a rich harvest of philosophy may be reaped in its season. But I was too inexperienced to reap then.

Nor was I elderly enough to find in beauty an excuse for inaction. In fact that day inspired me to plan more tumultuous outpourings of energy than ever. How doubly excellent, I thought to myself that night, would be a combined traverse of

both eastern and western Cuillin!   Like many great rock-climbs
of the past, the one-day traverse of the Cuillin Main Ridge was
long held to be impossible (it involved ten thousand five hundred
feet of ascent) until in 1911 it was accomplished in twelve hours
by Messrs. Shadbolt and Maclaren.   Since then it has been many
times repeated.   But twenty-five years had elapsed without any
attempt on the traverse of the whole Cuillin.   For although the
Main Ridge traverse of the western Cuillin is now acknowledged
to be the best day's mountaineering in Britain, and the traverse
of the eastern group, comprising Blaven and Clach Glas, gives
four thousand feet of the best mountaineering in Skye, yet
the two had not been combined.   East was east and west was
west, and Glen Sligachan lay between.   Such was the position
in 1936.

The varied attractions of the double traverse fairly jostled for
attention inside my mind.   Firstly, the course lay through the
grandest mountain scene in Britain, and granted the prerequisite
to success—skill to maintain the steady rhythm of climbing
movement that slowly annihilates height and distance—then, no
matter how long and hard the day, we should lose nothing of
enjoyment, then or in retrospect.

Secondly, I was fascinated by the problem in mountain-
craft.   One must inevitably start or finish in darkness; therefore to turn ground to best advantage, where should one start
and where finish?   Should one bivouac on the ridge beforehand?   And where descend after—to Sligachan, Broadford, or
a previously pitched tent at Coruisk or Glen Sligachan?   Should
food and water be cached on the ridge, and what kind of food
had best be used?   What bodily training would be needed in
preparation?

Thirdly, since success must depend on untested qualities of
mind and body, the issue would remain in doubt till the day was
nearly done.   The great physical strain would afford valuable
data concerning one's ability to master an exhausted body, to
discipline temper and judge calmly under stress.   I thought
then, and now I know, that every man should have such know-

F

ledge of himself. And in 1936 I had no idea what my own limits were. Thus there was a double problem to solve, strategic and personal.

But above all, it was a good climb.

The first practical difficulty was to convince my own mountaineering friends that the proposition was not an impossibility. And for three years I was unsuccessful. 'It can't be done,' is a phrase one hears too often. One cannot stop its impinging on the ear-drums, but one should refuse it admittance to the mind. For it is demonstrably untrue. I had no inclination to attempt the ridge by myself, and had to find a companion who was not only an excellent rock-climber but an enthusiastic mountaineer into the bargain. The problem continued unsolved until December 1938, when on one of the luckiest days of my life I met R. G. Donaldson. He was very quiet and reserved. My first impression was that I had met a man in whose company no unwholesome thought could exist. It was not an experience I had had before. He had the reflective, unusually clear and steady eye of a man who can dream and plan boldly, and act with energy. Moreover, he actually entertained the idea of trying the two Cuillin ridges! I was astounded. Within six months I knew him for what he was—my plans for an Alpine holiday were discarded in favour of Skye, and mid August 1939 found Donaldson, M. Mackinnon, and me encamped in Glen Brittle. Mackinnon decided not to accompany us on the ridge, but most generously helped us in other ways.

We imposed on ourselves no special training, and our first ten days were spent in climbing ourselves into good form. Most of our excursions involved long traverses on the Main Ridge, preceded by a severe rock-climb and followed by a gargantuan feast at the base camp. Huge as our meals undoubtedly were, the abounding hordes of midges dined still more sumptuously. Skye in August is no fit place for man or beast. The entire island falls into a state of midge-ridden anarchy. Life in camp was often wellnigh unbearable, and almost every night witnessed scenes of disorder and sounds

THE CUILLIN

½   ¼ 0

SCALE IN MILES

of torment, dire enough to pour balm on the soul of a Torquemada.

During these days of mingled bliss and hell we evolved our plan of campaign. We should start at Garsbheinn in the south, traverse the ridge northward to Sgurr nan Gillean, descend to Glen Sligachan for two hours' rest, then traverse Clach Glas and Blaven. There were sixteen hours of daylight available and the traverse might take twenty hours—perhaps more. Thus we might have to spend four hours' rock-climbing in darkness. We decided to allot the first three hours of that period to reaching the first real obstacle on the ridge—the Thearlaich-Dubh Gap —where we should arrive at dawn; the final hour of the four we transferred to the end of the day, to the traverse from Clach Glas to Blaven, in the hope that by making good time earlier we might, after all, reach Blaven in daylight. The ascent to Garsbheinn at the beginning, and the descent from Blaven at the end, might take a further six hours, making a total of ten hours' climbing by night. The total was formidable, but we felt confident of overcoming all difficulties by torchlight. Bad weather would mean failure. We trusted to the happy combination of luck with judgment.

Were we fortunate enough to reach Blaven, we should certainly not care to stagger up five miles of boulder-strewn path to Sligachan, so we decided to pitch and provision a small tent in Glen Sligachan, as near to the foot of Blaven as we could. This we did on 22nd August, a day of roasting sun, when we found a perfect camp site at the north end of Loch an Athain, below Coire Dubh. We stocked the tent with two days' food and devoted the afternoon to the traverse of Blaven. This reconnaissance was essential, because the route-finding on the north ridge, notoriously difficult in mist, would be hopeless for two exhausted climbers did they strike mist and night combined, unless they knew the route in advance.

Furthermore, it was important to find an easy and fast descent to Glen Sligachan. Therefore, on our way down from the summit we reconnoitred two routes. Donaldson went straight down the west buttress and I down a gully to Coire Dubh. We consulted afterwards at Loch an Athain. Either route was direct, but the ground too awkward for easy negotiation by night, and we knew that our descent from Blaven after fourteen thousand feet of climbing would be a somewhat harrowing experience. It seemed best to find an easier route, even though it were longer. Therefore, Donaldson suggested the long, easy ridge running southward to Camasunary, a route that led not toward our tent but two miles in the opposite direction. Then we should return up the path in Glen Sligachan, thus defeating exhaustion by rhythm. I baulked for a while at choosing any route that took us so far out of our way, but the alternatives seemed even less attractive. We decided, reluctantly, that our descent should lie down the south ridge. The decision was a bad one, and would not have been made had we known the mountain better. Having omitted to bring any food, we then retired speedily on Sligachan.

Our next two days were spent in skirmishing with the weather. The first day was cloudy and we made no move. That was a great misfortune. For the aurora borealis roused us from our sleeping-bags before midnight. Directly over the Cuillin one of the gateways to heaven had swung loose, and beams of celestial light swept back and forth across the earth. This wonderful display lasted for hours. How we wished we had been up on the ridge that night! But the next morning was again cloudy, and we spent the whole day resting. We were anxious to avail ourselves of a clear night. For the moon was waxing in the second quarter and we should have good illumination. There is added delight in the climbing when black peaks point to a starry sky.

Then, at eight o'clock, the cloud-cap lifted. Could we now rely on the weather for a day or two? For some days the wind had been south-easterly. In Glen Brittle a movement of the wind from south-east to south brings rain, but there was no sign of change. I therefore proposed an immediate start. Our decision was sudden. We ate dinner and packed our rucksacks.

We had decided not to cache food or water on the main ridge, therefore in addition to the usual sandwiches we carried a one-and-a-half-pint water-bottle and vita-glucose.

We left our tents at ten p.m.   We had each looked forward to this night from our first climbing days, and as we moved slowly uphill in the gathering darkness we felt that tenseness of mind and body that enlivens the opening hour of a long-delayed venture.   For the wind and weather conditioning our efforts were as unpredictable as our ability to stay the marathon course.

Our first misfortune was not long delayed.   Mist had been gathering round the mountains, and as night fell the clouds sank into the corries and obliterated the peaks.   The moon, which had given promise of lighting our four-mile walk round the base of the Cuillin to Garsbheinn, was now obscured.   The wind had moved to the south and the weather had won the first round.   We moved slowly, not only to conserve strength, but because boulders, heather, and deep-cut streams were so inextricably mixed that we could not with safety move fast.

After an hour and a half of disagreeable walking we crossed the lower slopes of Sgurr nan Eag into the western corrie of Garsbheinn.   The prospect was bleak and gloomy. Far below, a flashing lighthouse on Soay exposed the island's flat outline against the darkly crawling sea.   It was hard to believe that men lived on ground so bare and desolate.   In front of us, scree-shoots rose into thick mist.   Fifteen hundred feet of perpendicular scree (I had no clinometer) in mist at midnight is a realistic foretaste of what awaits climbers in another world.

We climbed in silence, in stony silence, for my part inwardly cursing mountains and this the foulest of them all. The ascent seemed interminable, and the fact that we reached the top merely put us in worse humour, for we arrived there at one-thirty a.m. in a keen moist wind.   Somewhere in front lay twelve thousand feet of climbing, and already we felt too spent to put one foot in front of the other.   A crag below the cairn gave us shelter while we pulled on gloves, balaclavas, and sweaters before settling down to rest. Shivering with cold and crouching on damp rocks below the cairn, we were surrounded by a thick wet mist, which precipitated a fine, just perceptible drizzle; and far away in lonely Coruisk the staccato bark of foxes roused mournful, lingering echoes.

At two o'clock in the morning we dragged ourselves to our feet and stumbled sleepily down through the mist to find the ridge to Sgurr nan Eag. Donaldson had been unable to get a fresh battery for his torch before leaving Glen Brittle, and wa soon forced to rely entirely on mine. I therefore went first. We slowly scrambled along the narrow crest while grey tentacles of mist writhed and twisted round our bodies, diffusing and blanketing the powerful beam from the torch, so that little advance choice of route was possible. Donaldson followed as best he could in the feeble back-wash of light, but as always he made no complaint, although the effort to follow for three hours in semi-darkness without stumbling must have been an irritating strain. I have yet to hear him utter a disparaging word of any man or mountain.

We reached Sgurr nan Eag at three a.m., which was later than we had hoped. The level walking on top was a great relief after the long ascent, but if we were already tired enough to find relief in a little level walking, when we had barely started our day's work, then our prospect of success was surely not very bright. The fact of the matter was that we both felt despondent; that I was not outspokenly bad-tempered as well was probably due only to hard exercise. Human vitality drops to its lowest ebb in the hours before dawn, and no mountaineer is ever cheerful at three o'clock in the morning in mizzling cloud. If he were, his maddened companion would push him over the edge.

We struggled down to the col above Coire a' Ghrunnda, climbing automatically, but failing in darkness to strike that rhythmical movement so vital to long-distance mountaineering. Befogged in mind as well as body, we were almost trapped into the ascent of a rectangular tower, which overhung on its far side. We side-stepped just in time by traversing ledges on its

west wall and began the gruelling ascent to Sgurr Dubh.   We
reached the top thirty-five minutes behind schedule.   A halt
was essential, and we stopped for some food and water. Throughout, we were determined to go no faster than we found natural.

On the descent from Sgurr Dubh to the col below Sgurr
Thearlaich the inconvenience of having but one torch between
two became most apparent.   At every crag or boulder I had to
stop and shine the torch backward for Donaldson. This reduced
our speed to a crawl and we went as slowly as though tied
together on a ten-foot rope, each impatiently waiting for the
other to climb up or down the crags before he himself could
move.   I became more and more convinced that our expedition
would end in failure, unless by a miracle the weather cleared
and we received impetus from awakened vigour.

Meantime we floundered up the ridge to Sgurr Thearlaich,
until the broken slabs and scree steepened into solid rock.   We
swarmed up a gabbro tower, traversed a level ridge, and were
faced with a vertical wall of basalt, wet and grey in the gloom.
We tied on the rope.   I adjusted my head-lamp and placed the
battery in my trouser pocket.   The ridge was narrow here and
fell away with great steepness on either hand.   Directly in front
the wall was unclimbable.   I traversed a few feet to the left,
and had gone half-way up when, unluckily, just as I reached for
a handhold, the rucking-up of my breeches switched off the
electric current.   The hold promptly vanished, leaving me to
grope in blackness for a substitute, while my body contorted in
the effort to retain a sense of balance.   This happened twice in
quick succession before I reached a stance where the angle eased
off.   Donaldson, with no torch at all, climbed here with less
fuss than I, for his eyes had become used to the bad light.

The mist was lifting slightly from the hills by now, and the
darkness was lessening.   But we were still climbing in heavy
twilight when we reached the Thearlaich-Dubh gap.   On its
lower short side a basaltic wall fell thirty feet to a horizontal
edge, the flanks of which plunged several hundred feet to deep-
set corries.   On the upper side was an eighty-foot face of

THE CLIFF
Route I, Rannoch Wall

gabbro, split for half its height by a crack, the sole breach in its defence. This great gap, the first of four principal obstacles, causes no hesitation to competent rock-climbers, but no one may deny that in twilight hours the gap is spectacular. To save time, we adopted time-honoured tactics by roping down the cleft. There we tied on the rope, squirmed up the crack on the long side, crawled up the slabs above, and reached the top at daybreak.

The rocks became easy and we made good time to the top of the Alisdair stone shoot, where we broke off from the main ridge to climb Sgurr Alisdair. At ten minutes to six we reached the cairn. We were very far behind schedule, but the miracle for which we had prayed was now enacted before our very eyes : the last shreds of white mist were stripping off the peaks, and the sun was up and out. The sky steadily grew more blue and cloudless, a cool breeze blew—*from the south-east.* And as the sun, low, but shining clear, lifted the last rays of morning mist for the light wind to scatter into nothingness, so it lifted our mental fogs for the mind to whip away all lethargy of body. We were stung to action by the freshness of the morning. The joy of life returned to us.

Donaldson led off with a speed that interpreted our change of mood, and within six minutes Sgurr Thearlaich was behind and Sgurr MhicCoinnich in front. Moving rhythmically at last, we sped along the clean slabs of the ridge and swung down the steep drop to the MhicCoinnich col. Like an enormous cobra with its head extended, the summit tower reared two hundred feet overhead. Up we went, eighty feet to the base of the tower, where a right-angled corner, sixty feet high, was topped by a great overhang. We roped up and climbed the corner by King's chimney, a narrow crack adorned by small jammed stones. Upon nearing the overhang we traversed out on the right wall, where a sweep of slab avoided the projecting head and brought us speedily to the top.

Donaldson was revelling in the climbing. He led the way along that ridge and up the south rib of An Stac at such a steady

*F

pace that I was forced to concentrate on the rotten rocks to avoid getting left behind.

At last we strode over the crest of the Stac and arrived at our third point of difficulty, the Inaccessible Pinnacle of Sgurr Dearg. We climbed the pinnacle by the eastern arête, which by an old tradition, from which no man may depart, is ever to be described as 'a knife-edged ridge, with an overhanging and infinite drop on one side, and a drop on the other side even steeper and longer.' We roped down the perpendicular west side.

The time was seven a.m. and we had gone so well from Sgurr Alisdair that we felt free to halt and feed. We were tired, but were cheered by our good luck. We had time in hand and were graced by perfect weather. Half an hour later we started on a long easy ridge, curving like the sharp rim of a bowl to Sgurr na Banachdich. As we left Sgurr Dearg behind us I could not help looking back with some emotion to the plunge of the north buttress, where the overhang collapsed beneath my feet two years before. I seem to have had a most efficient guardian angel, and I never withhold a word of congratulation at the scenes of his master-strokes.

We arrived at Sgurr na Banachdich at eight-fifteen a.m. Our camp in Glen Brittle, a tiny cluster of tents in a green field, still lay in shadow; for the sun had not yet rounded the southern spur of the Cuillin, and no sign of life could be seen anywhere in the grey glen. Up on the ridge we climbed in golden sunshine, feeling a genial superiority to our bed-bound brothers and sublimely forgetful that our own earliness afoot was hardly habitual. The peaks and pinnacles of the Cuillin, no longer black but steely grey in sunlight, surged eagerly into a light blue sky. Across the Minch the Outer Hebrides were strangely near and clear-cut. But they lost none of the aloofness that has ever entranced men of sympathetic mind. Where they rose from the sea, earth there was transfigured and its form eternal, and the searching light of morning failed to disturb this sacred mystery; which is not, though seen here most readily, of them

THE
PLATEAU

alone; nor, as is said so often, is it peculiar to the cloak of their atmosphere, infinitely variable to hour and season, responsive to wind and cloud, rain and sun; but a thing steadfast through change, in everything that is.

The Cuillin, and all that one may see from them, are at their best in the early hours of a fine morning.   The stillness and silence have a profundity unknown to any time of night.   For at no time does the earth sleep less than at night; then more than ever it is contemplative and expectant.   But at sunrise the mountains are enrapt, like Wordsworth's nun, breathless with adoration.

We were now half-way along the ridge and had reached the first great bend in the horse-shoe, which here changes direction from north-west to north-east.   An hour of steady climbing took us over the slender needle of Sgurr Thormaid and the long thin edge of Sgurr a' Ghreadaidh on to the thrice-cleft comb of Sgurr a' Mhadaidh.   By this time we were most definitely tired —as yet a pleasant muscular tiredness: we had maintained rhythm and were buoyed up by the keen air and wind.   Where the ridge was cleft our minds found interest in the choice of route over wall and rib; or where the ridge was easy, on the ever-changing face of Coruisk, where drifting cloud shadows mottled the blue water of the loch.   Nevertheless, our tiredness grew as we approached Bidein Druim nan Ramh, and was only held at bay by the delight of grasping the rough gabbro of the triple pinnacles, so that when at last we hoisted ourselves on to the summit-tip we felt that a short rest had been well earned.

The time was ten o'clock.   Looking south to Garsbheinn, we seemed to have covered an enormous chunk of the ridge, but Blaven, our ultimate goal, looked distressingly high and distant as ever.   The secret of an easy mind on the big days of one's mountaineering, as elsewhere, is to concentrate on the work immediately in front, not to let imagination run riot on hazards far ahead, for that way lies discouragement.

I dragged my thoughts back to the present, and an excellent present it was.   The three pinnacles of Bidein lurched out of the ridge in close company.   We were squatted on the apex of the trident's centre tooth.   To the north, and contrasted with the throng of peaks to each side, was that most exalting of panoramas—a vast and uninterrupted sky, towered with lofty clouds and melting into a gossamer horizon-haze in faultless graduation of blue to silver.   Half an hour passed.   During that time I doubt if Donaldson and I exchanged more than a word or two, nor had we done so since leaving MhicCoinnich. Save in special circumstance, conversation and mountaineering go ill together; the more one breaks the precept the less contact is there, other than physical, between the mountains and one-self; and thus the best part of mountaineering is not experienced. The worst companion one may have on a hill is a talker.

We left Bidein at ten thirty-five and launched ourselves at the long expanse of ridge toward Bruach na Frithe.   Good scrambling on the descent to the col was followed by an inter-minable ascent, more than an hour of hard drudgery in sweltering heat.   The wind had died, and for the first time we suffered from 'a thirst like that of the Thirsty Sword.'   Our growing exhaustion was marked by slow progress on short obstacles and weariness of muscle at the top of them.   On the long scree-ridge below the summit our legs had to be driven to their task by conscious effort.   Bruach na Frithe is one of the easiest mountains in the Cuillin; its summit one of the finest view-points.   At a glance we absorbed the wild sprawl of gabbro architecture, from the boulder-spattered desolation of low corries to the soaring beauty of sun-washed ridges—a moment's glance that has endured through years.   The sun was standing still at high noon and we pressed onward to Sgurr Fionn Choire, our minds centred on a little oasis of bright green moss in Fionn Choire: 'Go but a little way over the ridge . . . thou wilt find bubbling through the fountained rock a spring colder than northern snow.'   These words of Leonidas describe the spring we found shortly after midday.

Sitting together on each side of the pool, which was no bigger than a chalice, we filled ourselves up with the purest and highest-sited water in Skye.   It never fails to give me a severe pain across the forehead, yet I am never truly thirsty without thought of longing for it. We stopped no more than ten minutes. Before climbing back to the ridge we each ate two tablets of vita-glucose, which we had carried for refreshment before attempting Naismith's route on the Bhasteir tooth. Their effect, normally unnoticeable, was on exhausted bodies immediate. Within ten minutes there was distinct improvement of muscular efficiency due to the refuelling of the blood with sugar.   Later in the day, when our exhaustion was much greater, the effect of glucose became still more prompt and powerful, acting as quickly as brandy but lasting no more than half an hour.   Glucose was the only food we carried during the remainder of the expedition. We consumed between us twenty-four tablets, taking two each at a time before long ascents or short difficult obstacles. They improved our time by cutting down the length and frequency of halts.

We regained the ridge under the Bhasteir tooth—

> The peak that stormward bares an edge
> Ground sharp in days when Titans warred;

it threatened us like a battle-axe, the uneven edge opposing advance with an overhang of a hundred and fifty feet.   Its savage appearance will rarely fail to intimidate tired climbers. We were glad of our glucose, still more so of the rope.   After roping up we traversed several feet from the overhang across the south face of the tooth.   The almost vertical cliff above could then be climbed by Naismith's route.   We enjoyed that climb.   It was more sensational than strenuous, and the last few airy feet, where one trusts to edge-nails on a shelving ledge, freshened us not a little.

Abutting against the tooth were the higher crags of Am Basteir.   We worked up them to a ten-foot overhang, normally of small account, which made us pant for the first time that day. At one p.m. we passed the summit and rattled down to the col below the famous west ridge of Sgurr nan Gillean.   The ascent of this ridge is the craziest section of the traverse, reminding one of the Bridge of Sirat, which according to Attar spans hell with a hair-line. The crest grows steadily more acute until it thins to a hanging tapestry, leaps in fantastic pinnacles, then swirls up and onward to a finely sculptured peak. At one-thirty p.m.—eleven and a half hours after leaving Garsbheinn —we stood together at the cairn. Our traverse of the main ridge was ended. The speculative part of the day had begun.

We rested a short while, then followed the ridge southward toward Sgurr na h-Uamha. We soon found that we had to contend with reaction, and by the time we struck down An Glas-Choire to Glen Sligachan our pace had been reduced to a painful crawl. The sun was blazing, hotter than ever before, and there was no wind. However, we struggled down by slow degrees, the boulder-strewn floor of the corrie stimulating exasperation until the wearisome descent seemed far worse than it really was. And then, down in Glen Sligachan, where the moorland quivered through the warm air-currents, there was the long rough walk across heather to our camp at Loch an Athain. I reached the tent at four p.m., and Donaldson, who preferred a slower pace, arrived an hour later.

I had waited for him rather anxiously. Until now I had been sure of him, but we had reached a stage beyond which he had never been tried, for this was the testing time, when bodies fatigued with ten thousand feet of rock-work come whining to the inner self to be left in peace, and strength of will was tried by the luxury of camp on one hand as against a further four thousand feet of scree and rock on the other. The first thing that Donaldson announced when he joined me was his determination to continue with me on the traverse of Clach Glas and Blaven. He looked as cool and unconcerned as though talking of a short stroll before lunch. How he does it I can't imagine.

Mackinnon welcomed us with hot chicken soup, followed by chocolate. It was delicious to lie flat out in the sun, one's mind a pleasant blank, recording nothing but the body's gratitude for rest and food. After Donaldson's arrival we enlivened our diet by consuming between us one pint of 'Mummery's blood.' This

THE CUILLIN RIDGES

mountain elixir consists of equal parts of navy rum and Bovril, served boiling hot. Its effect on both mind and body is nourishing, warming, strengthening; it lowers angles, shortens distances, and improves weather.

At five-forty-five p.m. we set off for Clach Glas. Our route lay up Coire Dubh, notable even among the corries of Skye for its evil mixture of stone and heather. But the black ridge far above, ruffling round the head of the corrie in a great arc between Clach Glas and Blaven, gave us heart to face the preliminary toil. A man would have to be dead before pleasure failed him there.

The evening had grown close and sultry. With so much climbing behind us we had expected this further ascent of three thousand feet to be the hardest part of the whole day. Our surprise was therefore all the greater when we felt ourselves climbing comfortably and with more dispatch than during the ascent of Garsbheinn at the very beginning of the expedition. The truth is that fatigue is rarely caused by tiredness of body; almost always by tiredness of mind, which is not to be refreshed by a mere flogging of the will. The will is indeed no great asset until it be fired by feeling—whereupon all things become possible.

Meanwhile, evening clouds were gathering in a dark pall over the Western Cuillin. We felt some anxiety lest mist should fall round Blaven and complicate the route selection before we could get to grips with the last uprush of its ridge. The food and rest we had had at Loch an Athain stood us in good stead as far as the north col of Clach Glas, then with weakening effect along a tormented ridge that broke in a spray of pinnacles against the slabs of the summit spire, which rose like a lighthouse from a stormy sea. The climb up its wrinkled slabs reduced us to our pre-camp state of physical exhaustion; but nevertheless there was a difference. As we stood on the rocky top and looked across to the Promised Land of Blaven, we had the knowledge, denied to Moses on Mount Nebo, that the goal could be won in our own lifetime.

We left Clach Glas at eight p.m. and enjoyed an effortless rhythm of climbing movement down the saw-toothed ridge to the col below Blaven. We stopped there to refuel on glucose, for seven hundred feet of rock lay between ourselves and the summit. Our anxiety on the score of mist was now removed and we had no trouble in zigzagging up the lower crags to the vital chimney cutting the central cliffs. Above and beyond all was plain plodding. We had drawn the last tooth of the Cuillin hills. At nine p.m., exactly nineteen hours after leaving Garsbheinn, we walked up the screes on the open brow of the summit and sat down thankfully beside the cairn.

The clouds which has been gathering two hours earlier had now vanished. The sun had set behind the bristling back of the main ridge, and all surface detail was lost in the dusk. But each bold peak of that far-flung chain, every great cleft and tooth, was painted clear and black against the faded blue of the evening sky. As the eye followed the incredible silhouette, from the far and lonely outpost of Garsbheinn, mile upon curving mile of splintered edge and spurting crest to the noble climax of Sgurr nan Gillean, it won a reward exceeding anything for which we had paid that day in physical energy. Later, when we came back to earth, and looked again, it seemed beyond belief that two infinitesimal animals, standing a minute six feet high, could pace out the length of that vast and jagged outline. We gaped at the ridge and wondered if our day had been a dream after all. The cold fact of the matter was swiftly supplied when we rose to go down. Only once before on a mountain had I been so physically tired; Donaldson never. Our feet felt flayed and raw, although they showed not a blister when examined later.

We had chosen for descent the long easy ridge running south to Camasunary, but the boulder slopes prevented us in our exhausted condition from striking anything resembling rhythm. We crept jerkily downhill, every step costing an effort of will. Dusk gave way to night before we were half-way down that endless ridge. Our mistake in not choosing the more difficult but short descent into Coire Dubh became more and more evident.   We despaired of ever getting anywhere on our present route, and at last had recourse to our map for some way of shortening our purgatory.

Direct descent to Glen Sligachan was barred by the western precipice, but some way further on an easy route cut diagonally across and down the face.   The difficulty was to find this short cut in darkness and past experience of short cuts should have warned us against the doubtful attempt.   We judged our position on the ridge from an angle on the corner of a loch in Glen Sligachan, and then, at what we imagined must be the correct spot, struck sharply off the ridge on to the cliff.   A too innocent scree-run lured us down steepening rock into a chimney.   We scrambled down by torchlight over several pitches.   There was more scree at the base of the chimney, then blank slabs plunged in an ever-quickening fall to the black abyss of Glen Sligachan. On either hand were deep, inaccessible gullies.   We were now faced with the appalling prospect of climbing several hundred feet back to the ridge, or of stopping where we were till daylight.   Had there been the slightest weakening in Donaldson I should willingly have bivouacked, for the night was good.   But his spirit was indomitable and the vote was cast for retreat.

We rested for a few minutes and ate some glucose.   The light from our tent a mile or so up Glen Sligachan gleamed brightly and tantalizingly through the night.   Roast chicken and eiderdown sleeping-bags waited for us there!   The thought was too much to bear.   We rose, and somehow reclimbed those weary leagues to the ridge.   Thereafter we literally staggered downhill to the south, stopping every five minutes to rest.   A further blow fell upon us when we ran into a cordon of slabs, only to fetch up against yet another when the first had been avoided with difficulty.   We stopped involuntarily.   Donaldson confessed that unless we reached easier ground at once he would be unable to keep going.   I myself felt likewise and we could hardly stand erect without swaying.   We did not reach easy ground at once; yet we did keep going.   If the spirit is willing the flesh can be driven, weak or not.

We had lost the normal route off the end of the ridge, but we broke through the ring of slabs at last and gained slopes of heather and bracken. Even these seemed relentless, jolting, jarring, jerking our feet and bodies on the everlasting downhill climb. Donaldson, nevertheless, had sufficient inward command to make nice calculations and subtle deductions concerning the nearest whereabouts of the path in Glen Sligachan. For a flashing moment I was glad we had come down that ridge. It was a heartening discovery, of present value and future comfort on mountains, that Donaldson knows no limits; he will go till he drops.

There came a time when the slope grew level under our feet, followed later by a second of intense relief when the narrow line of the path materialized—a miracle, in the white glare of the torch. We finished our last tablets of glucose, then tramped, so it seemed, mile upon endless mile along the stony highway, our bodies aching under the strain of maintaining an upright posture. The dull gleam of Loch an Creitheach dropped behind us and the moorland was broken in turn by the waters of Loch an Athain. We left the path and rounded the head of the loch. The cheerful light of our tent shone but a hundred yards away. We reached it at one a.m. and our day was done.

The roast chicken was demolished with remarkable speed, but with less enthusiasm than one might imagine. Sleep, not food, was what we sought most eagerly; nor could all the hastily devoured fowl in the world have stemmed the tide that shortly engulfed Donaldson and me.

The next day was warm and sunny. We slept till noon; then the midges found us—insolent, rapacious midges. They bit us into wakefulness (a remarkable feat), they bit us on to breakfast, they bit us into the laughing brown loch, and then, when we came out, they bit us all over. At four o'clock we struck camp, and fleeing up the glen, came down like ravenous wolves on Sligachan. We dined there when the bats were about in the cool of evening. That was a meal we shall not forget. But we remember it well less for intrinsic merit than as marking

THE HEBRIDES FROM THE CUILLIN

the end of the longest and grandest day's rock-climbing that we shall ever carry out in Scotland—or elsewhere in the world. One was left only with the recollection of pure colour, form, and movement. Not an ache remained, not an effort lived. Here, if you like, was the Greek catharsis. So much so, that we opened a bottle of champagne—and toasted the scree-slopes of Garsbheinn, the foxes of Coruisk, and the long, easy ridge of Blaven.

[NOTE. The first traverse of the Cuillin ridge plus Blaven was made by I. G. Charleson and W. E. Forde in June 1939.]

17 *New Year on Ben Nevis*

HOGMANAY ON THE PLATEAU

THERE IS MORE THAN one way of observing the New
Year in Scotland, and it may be that the devout pub-crawler
alone knows true wisdom. Wherever the truth may lie,
R. G. Donaldson, G. R. B. McCarter, and I, in a fit of ascetic
resolve on Hogmanay, severed all ties with the triumphs of
1939 civilization in order to mortify our flesh on the icy summit
of Ben Nevis.

On 30th December we met in a black frost at Bridge of
Orchy. There we decided to pitch a tent on the Nevis plateau.
A preliminary reference to the Scottish Mountaineering Club
guide revealed that winter hurricanes on Nevis could reach a
velocity of a hundred and fifty miles per hour. It seemed too
much to hope that we should enjoy the privilege of such an
experience; but in midwinter all things are possible on Nevis.
Our imaginations leapt to the conception that our tent with ourselves inside might be uprooted at midnight and hurled through
Cimmerian darkness to the two-thousand-foot contour in the
Allt a' Mhuilinn. Therefore, we planned to countersink our
tent in the snow-cap by excavating a two-foot pit and building
a two-foot wall above. As insulation from the snow we pro-
cured light sponge-rubber mats (not a success), four single
sleeping-bags, and one double bag. Our tent was a high-
altitude model, weighing ten pounds, with sewn-in ground-sheet.

We proceeded to Fort William, and at noon on the last day
of the year sallied forth from Achintee. Our rucksacks weighed
thirty-five pounds each. We followed the path for two thousand
feet, and thenceforward snow lay heavily. The sun shone from
a cloudless sky and tempered the freezing air to a choice crisp-
ness, so that we could walk slowly and breathe deeply, drinking

168

the cool air as the thirsty climber drinks his beer.   After three
and a half hours we arrived on the summit plateau, where the
great snow-fields were surfaced with an icy crust, the whole
awash with the fire of sunset until we seemed encompassed by
seas of live flame, as though not only Nevis but every summit of
Scotland had reverted to red-hot lava.   The sky had become a
riot of all colour from palest green to scarlet.   The beauty was
agonizing, yet there was no feature describable.   We watched,
hardly breathing, until the colours began to fade.   We felt
dazed, as though the eyes of the soul had been blinded by too
great a wonder.

'I 'd rather be here,' said Donaldson slowly, 'than have done
the best rock-climb on Nevis.'

He meant so much more than that—but what more, or what
less, could one say?

The weather was now so settled that we abandoned our plan
of excavating a pit, and without more delay pitched our tent
south of the Observatory ruins, whose walls projected six feet
from the snow.   Therefore the snow-cap must have been six
feet thick.   From the door of the tent the snow-slope dipped
sharply to Glen Nevis, so that we could look straight across
the twisted spine of the Mamores to Glencoe, past the Blackmount and the hills of Crianlarich, until the eye came to rest on
the dim outline of Ben Lomond, twenty-one miles south.

The cold was now intense.   There was not a breath of wind.
With three of us there was no tent-space for rucksacks, so we
left them beside the Observatory and took into the tent only
food and sleeping-bags.   Before tying up the door I took one
last look out.   The horizons were everywhere dull and dark
with night, but far out to the west there lingered one long, thin,
and blood-red streak.

Both the doors and ventilators had been completely sealed, so
that after preparing a meal we found it warm enough inside to
sleep with only one bag.   But we paid dearly for this comfort
later in the night.   The temperature in the tent was too high
in relation to the extreme cold outside, with the result that

condensation of body moisture reached enormous proportions. The sponge-rubber mats on which we lay gave poor insulation; water-vapour condensed in such volume on the groundsheet that our sleeping-bags were soaked right through. We roused ourselves toward midnight and drank in the New Year from a communal mug filled with 'Mummery's blood.' The moon was up by this time; we could see it shining through the tent fabric. We put on our boots and went out to the open snow-fields—out into such a splendour of moonlight as one sees but rarely in a lifetime.

I took my axe and wandered alone toward the North-east buttress. My shadow moved thin and black along the glistening snow-crust, which crunched quietly underfoot. For twenty miles around me the world was a storm-sea frozen, inundated by a pure, even light, the heavenly grace outpoured to earth. The sky was crowded, shining with stars that were steady and did not twinkle; and four thousand feet below in the depths of the Spean valley, wrapping the foot-hills in a light transparent vapour, hung a fine white mist, which the moonbeams pierced.

I cannot believe that any human could look long and alone upon that pale-faced night and not be stirred by awe—stirred if with naught else by despair at his insufficiency, by the sternness of the trials that must lie ahead before it be possible for his mind to contain the true beauty; by awareness that for such attainment no sacrifice could be too much. And should thought be confused, none the less he will know that Masefield was right, and that beauty, the intangible, can take a man by the throat.

Donaldson and McCarter joined me. From the top of North-east buttress we admired the rock scenery of the cliffs, then separated and prowled about the plateau in silent delight. After a while each went to the summit cairn, returned to the tent, and slept uncomfortably until eight-thirty a.m.

The darkness was noticeably lessening when McCarter opened up the tent to get snow for breakfast. He looked out and gave a shout of astonishment. 'Another damned dawn,' I thought.

THE SUMMIT OF
BEN NEVIS

The Carn Mor Dearg
Arête occupies the
middle ground, with
the Allt a' Mhuillin
glen beyond

But sleepiness vanished and cold was forgotten when I saw the sight for myself. Across the entire length of the east horizon, from farthest north to south, ran a broad crimson bar, fading to orange in its upper fringe, then melting into pale-blue sky, which darkened and deepened toward the zenith and became navy-blue in the west, where night still hung over the frost-bound land. Very long, very thin, unsubstantial streamers of cloud hung about the sky, and these were caught and fired by great beams of light which radiated from a central point in the crimson bar. The whole made a perfect geometrical pattern like a vast cobweb, of which the threads were jets of orange and pink flame suspended across the vault of the sky.

The mountains of Wester Ross, incredibly wild and icy, dominated the north. They looked like the original Alpine range of ten thousand feet from which they are reputedly descended. Now the most aged mountains in Europe, and but the stumps of their former selves, they still display their old nobility in the sharp lines of ridge and peak. Farther east the Cairngorms bulged against the sky in huge rolling domes, like 'frosted cities of infinite sleep.' But the absorbing subtleties of this northern panorama were soon swamped by the stirring crudities of the eastern skyscape, where like a cannon-ball white-hot from the forge the sun came flashing, streaming, blasting up in a glory of blinding light; higher, higher, until we could no longer with level eye look squarely into its face. The colours vanished from the sky, which became an even blue; the icy sparkle of the snow-peaks changed to a growing glare.

Gardyloo Gully

After breakfast we sped south-east to the Carn Mor Dearg arête, and thence toward Coire Leis, down steep snow-slopes. The too icy surface forbade a glissade and instead we were embroiled in several hundred feet of rapid step-cutting. The descent went with a fine plunging swing, for a one-armed slash burst the crust.

At ten-thirty a.m. we surveyed the long array of cliffs from the Allt a' Mhuilinn. Hardly a rock showed through the snow plaster. I was sure that none of the great ridges would go in the six hours of daylight left to us. Perhaps not in double that time. Yet we felt incumbent upon us, since we were first-footing the cliffs, the pleasant duty of climbing a route worthy of the occasion. My eye travelled up Observatory gully, a broad snow corridor between Tower ridge and Observatory buttress, until fifteen hundred feet overhead the gully was split by the unclimbed Gardyloo buttress. The right fork was Tower gully; the narrow left fork Gardyloo gully, an excellent climb, very severe in summer, which might now be anything from difficult to impossible. 'That,' said I to the others, 'is the very climb for us. We can get down to-day if it won't go.'

We crossed the Allt a' Mhuillin and climbed for an hour up Observatory gully. The snow there was soft and powdery, and we frequently went in up to the knees. Whenever we passed the tilting snow-field that slants toward Tower gully, the angle of the slope greatly steepened and we entered the deep slit of Gardyloo. Thus far we had been able to kick our foot-hold with ease, but henceforward every step had to be cut with pick or adze. We stopped to rope up, and being honoured with the lead, I placed Donaldson second and McCarter third.

While we were roping I noticed that the wind was loosening snow on the sunlit upper buttresses, and intermittent trickles of powder were tumbling over the walls and hissing in serpentine streams down the centre of the gully. Before I had run out a rope's length the stream grew to a cascade, and the hiss to an insistent swish. The angle of the slope rose to sixty degrees and the snow gave place to an unusual type of snow-ice—dark grey, indeed most often black, yet without the clearness of pure ice. It was gluey. My pick stuck after horizontal strokes. However, I could slice it vertically with a strong blow of the axe and the crunch that sped from shaft to hand was like that of slicing dried clay with a spade. But the delight of working such excellent material was spoiled by eddying clouds of powder,

GARDYLOO GULLY, BEN NEVIS

which caught by down-draughts of wind, filled the gully from wall to wall with a whirl of spiculae, whitened us from head to foot, iced the neck and stung the cheek-bone, infiltrated through every crack in our harness, and at times so blinded me that I could see neither Donaldson twenty feet below nor the slope three feet before my face.   My axe-shaft became as slippery as an eel and each step cut was a Pyrrhic victory, for each was promptly swamped by spouting powder and had to be hunted for and cleaned out afresh by my followers.   With thought dwelling on defeat I made the steps capacious, but the worse conditions became the more stubborn I grew, and swore that if we turned back now it should be for nothing less than a technical impossibility.

After a savage struggle of two hours we suddenly won clear of the blinding dust and found ourselves in calm air beneath two great boulders bridging the gully.   The slope eased to forty degrees under the arch, but immediately beyond was a thirty-five-foot chimney and cave, draped in clear ice from top to bottom.   The lower chimney was vertical, but only ten feet high; the cave above was narrow, its floor sloping and glassy, its entrance pillared by a tall icicle, one foot thick, and its left wall, by which any route must go, curtained in shining blue folds.   I have never seen a nobler ice-pitch on Nevis, but we admired it with dismay.   Donaldson was the first to break the silence.   'Perhaps we'd better go down,' he said.   'We may not have time to get up, but there's still time to get out.'

Did I feel unequal to the task his words were designed to give me a good excuse to withdraw; but in my heart I knew that a pitch so well iced should be climbable.   With that sinking in the pit of my stomach, which I am more used to associate with the last ice-pitch of Crowberry gully, I said I'd try.   Thereupon I took a grip of myself, and once any climber does that the rest is sheer enjoyment.

I set to work on deeply fluted ice on the lower chimney. Although very difficult it fell in ten minutes, whereas the more technically severe cave was destined to consume considerably

more than an hour. The ice was exceptionally hard. At the
first few blows of the axe it merely changed colour from bleak
grey to white. Then the chips came out. I hewed a stance in
the cave's floor, and resting my back on the right wall, faced
left and spent five minutes thinking what to do next. The
broad tactics were plain: Traverse the blue curtain until clear
of the roof and then force a route up the open wall of the gully.
The detail, that is the siting of individual holds among the folds
of the curtain and round the pillar, was highly complicated—
so much so that later Donaldson had acute difficulty in locating
my trail, for the combination key, so to speak, was known only
to myself.

At first I despaired at the great amount of cutting to be packed
into the hour or so available, but the prospect brightened when
at last I reached the pillar. I wrapped an arm round it, and
leaning over the gully, carved half a dozen holds round the
corner. Then I swung round the pillar to the outer wall. Its
face bore an even layer of ice, inches thick. I worked my way
up, wrists and arm-muscles red-hot with the one-handed swing
and cut, the familiar ice-spray exploding in my face at each
blow of the pick. On this upper wall I had to fashion the holds
so that I might raise my legs with the knees turned sideways to
avoid their jamming on bulges. At four p.m. I passed beyond
the roof and thirty feet above found anchorage in firm snow.

After thus spending nearly one and a half hours on the last
seventy feet, I was shameless enough to urge the others to hurry.
For the sun had set half an hour ago, the light was failing, and
there was still a cornice to negotiate. I could now have kicked
myself for lack of foresight in not cutting down a portion of the
cornice during our stay on the summit. There is record of one
determined party, who, failing to tunnel such a cornice before
nightfall, retired to Fort William and returned next day to finish
the climb. Such a heroic course was now closed to us. Despite
exhortations, forty-five minutes raced past before my companions were able to join me, each arriving with exclamations
of amazement at the involutions of the ice.

Donaldson now took the lead and cut the last fifty feet to the cornice. The overhang was twelve feet thick, but our luck rose superior to our deserts, for there was a less than vertical passage on the side nearest Gardyloo buttress. At five o'clock, five hours from the foot of the gully, we clambered on to the summit.

Between us we travelled over a thousand miles to reach Nevis at the New Year; we carried one hundred and fifteen pounds of equipment through a vertical height of four thousand four hundred feet; we spent an uncomfortable night on the snow-cap; our car was frozen when we returned to Achintee. For all this work and unpleasantness we have, say the Philistines, nothing to show except one gully climb. Nothing to clink in our pockets, so to speak. Nothing but a memory. A memory of the wide, silent snow-fields crimsoned by the rioting sky, and of frozen hills under the slow moon. These have remained with us.

NOTE. The time required for a winter ascent of Gardyloo gully varies greatly. As a general rule, longer time will be taken in December and January than at Easter: the less the snow the harder the climbing. In April 1937, after heavy blizzard, I climbed the whole gully in one hour. Both the arch and the cave were then obliterated.

18 *High Camping in Winter*

O UR PURCHASE of a high altitude tent had proved on Ben Nevis to be the best investment that Donaldson and I ever made. The first month returned dividends of several thousand per cent. But our preliminary experiment, a week prior to New Year, was somewhat disastrous, and even on Nevis the foremost problem of camping on Scottish snow mountains with very light equipment, namely, reconciling avoidance of water condensation with reasonable warmth, remained unsolved. Therefore, I think that our experiences upon first encountering such problems, and in finding a correct solution, may interest mountaineers and campers.

Our purpose in procuring a high altitude tent was threefold. We intended to employ it in winter in the Cairngorms, at whose heart a base camp would save a daily walk of eighteen miles or four and a half hours' time. The Cairngorm bothies were dark hovels and their site was fixed, whereas a tent was cheerful and its mobility gave greater freedom. Secondly, we proposed to indulge more often in the delights of moonlight ridge-walking. But where one is obliged to return valleywards for sleep after a moonlight night, his descent, rest, and reascent usually involve a loss of time that debars the mountaineer from a good route next day. That limitation could be removed by a tent on a summit or high corrie. Lastly, and less practically, there is a pleasure in camping on mountains inexplicable to the unbeliever, but which will be at once apparent to any one of imagination.

For our safety no less than our comfort it was essential that we should have a tent able to withstand the most violent of Cairngorm blizzards. In fact, nothing less than a high altitude tent would meet our requirements, and from Messrs. Burns of Manchester I obtained the ideal article.

The tent was made of reinforced cambric, fawn-coloured, with sewn-in groundsheet, and at each end a circular sleeve-door and ventilator. A ventilator in use could either hang outside like a small wind-sock or be drawn inside—a point that proved of great importance. The poles were bamboo and the tent-pegs aluminium, broad-bladed for snow. Around the outside ran a broad canvas skirt, on which snow or boulders could be piled up and the tent anchored independently of pegs. The guys were of stout rope. The tent's total weight was ten pounds, and the size four feet high by seven feet long by four and a half feet broad. It was testified that the tent had withstood hurricanes of a hundred m.p.h. in the Himalayas. The price was six pounds ten shillings.

In honour to unknown craftsmen, I feel bound to say that not only was the fabric flawless and the whole beautifully made, but that to come suddenly on to a mountain plateau, and there to see its lonely splash of fawn between silver snow and blue sky, was in itself enough to lift up a man's heart.

However, I never have taken and never will take any article of mountaineering equipment on trust. Before using the tent on Nevis, Donaldson and I agreed to a trial camp on the summit of Clachlet (three thousand six hundred feet), between the Blackmount and Glencoe. Were the moon favourable we might accomplish the famous winter ridge-walk from Sron na Creise to Stob Ghabhar. This very first experiment revealed one appalling weakness, no fault of the manufacturers and easily remedied later, which gave us one of the most shocking nights we have ever spent on a hill.

We arrived at Kingshouse Inn on Christmas Eve and received a royal welcome from Mrs. Malloch, who very pardonably believed that we had come to stay the week-end. Thoughtlessly, we said nothing of our intentions, and after enjoying an excellent dinner our embarrassment was considerable on hearing her announce, in the charming accent of the western isles, that our bedroom was ready for us. Mrs. Malloch, moreover, is of commanding presence and one of the great characters of the

Scottish highlands, and my heart quailed as I gulped out my confession. Donaldson, whose eye I vainly sought for moral support, was convulsed with suppressed laughter as he watched the very different expressions of myself and our hostess—Mrs. Malloch, head high and hand on hip, incredulous; and myself, apologetic and very conscious that every word I uttered must sound to her like the most youthful folly. I have no doubt that the latter saved us. Mrs. Malloch is accustomed to young mountaineers; but she let me see by a subtle expression of eye that she had thought more highly of me than this. She flung up her hands in horror.

'A tent on a mountain-top!' she exclaimed. 'Who ever heard the like? And this Christmas Eve with snow on the hills, whatever, and maybe more to come! My, but *you*'re not frightened!'

Being at heart genial and grand of manner she had mercy on us and allowed the matter to rest there. But she was soon to taste the sweets of revenge, and in after days, whenever any of my friends called at Kingshouse, she would recall that night with the opening words, 'There's Mr. Murray now—*he*'s not frightened! . . .' adding with shattering inconsequence at the end of the tale—'and these breeches of his, all torn and patched, why, they must be nailed up on my wall as a trophy one day!'

We left Kingshouse at nine p.m. and went one mile down Glen Etive. It is not generally known that Argyll can boast a funicular railway, of modified type perhaps, spanning the river Etive below Clachlet. The contraption is a wooden box, suspended on wheels from two wire ropes. The river was fast-flowing and broad, and the box, needless to say, on the far side. I threw off my heavy rucksack and made an enthralling traverse of the swaying wire, which at night one might classify as 'exposed but moderately difficult.' I returned in the box and Donaldson stepped in with both rucksacks. The total load was then about thirty stone and the wire considerably sagged, giving us a downhill run to mid stream, whence the box refused the uphill gradient. It began to look as though we must camp overnight in mid air. But eventually, by tremendous straining at the wire, we managed to haul the squealing truck to the landing-stage.

During the two hours' ascent by the western corrie the sky grew ever more cloudy and the moon nebulous. The air was unexpectedly mild. At midnight we arrived at the summit and pitched the tent on the snow-field near the cairn. The snow was a foot deep and soft, but when stamped down gripped the tent-pegs like concrete. In any event, the weight of snow banked on the outer skirt held all secure. The moon was now obliterated and the clouds rolled thickly overhead. Our hopes of ridge-walking had to be abandoned and we withdrew inside the tent for supper.

After supper we unrolled our eiderdown sleeping-bags and placed underneath them two sponge-rubber mats, whose purpose was to insulate us from ground-cold and thus to prevent condensation of body moisture, which must result from a direct contact of our sleeping-bags with the groundsheet. I had anticipated the condensation problem by using whatever intelligence God had given me. And I was right. Unhappily I had not been given enough intelligence to foresee the solution. We rapidly discovered that whatever that solution might be it was certainly not sponge-rubber.

We had closed both doorways, but the wind was rising, and I tied up one of the ventilators. Then we wriggled into our sleeping-bags, and had almost fallen asleep when the wind began fiercely clutching at the cambric, which aroused us sufficiently to notice that the sponge-rubber was already, within two hours, damp with condensed water, which was beginning to penetrate the eiderdown. However, there was nothing we could do now, and we were beginning to doze again when the rain came down in sheets. Within a few minutes we felt a fine spray of water on our faces. I thought it must be coming through the open ventilator, which I promptly closed. But to our dismay, a few more seconds sufficed to show that the spray came from the roof. The incredible truth at last dawned upon us. Our tent was snow-proof in a hurricane at twenty thousand feet, but was not rain-proof in a half gale at three thousand six hundred feet. In fact, it had not been intended for use at altitudes where rain was possible.

Donaldson and I lay back and laughed weakly—very weakly. We had been well and truly caught out, and nothing remained but to take our punishment as it came. The wind was fairly howling outside, and each time it seized and shook the cambric a shower of half-atomized rain fell on us. Within an hour the tent was swimming in water, which could not escape off the ground-sheet; our sleeping-bags were drenched and their wretched occupants soaked to the skin. The rubber mats were now worse than useless, simply sopping up water and passing it on to us. In the end they were submerged.

The remainder of the night was indescribable, but any one may sample the same experience in his own house. Let him step fully clothed into a cold bath at two a.m. in midwinter, and recline there with a cold shower playing overhead until eight a.m. He will then know, like Donaldson and me, what it means to be grateful for the dawn. At eight-thirty a.m. we struck camp, a process of which it might be more truly said that we weighed anchor.

When we returned to Kingshouse Inn Mrs. Malloch's eye gleamed rather brightly; but she said nothing. Not just then. She waited until we had done justice to a hot meal, and fortified by tall mugs, 'with beaded bubbles winking at the brim,' were arm-chaired before a blazing fire. Then some other mountaineers arrived and, for the first but by no means the last time, we heard those introductory words: 'Now, there's Mr. Murray and Mr. Donaldson—*they*'re not frightened! . . .' Mrs. Malloch on top form is matchless: she soon had us helpless with mirth. It is remarkable how a few hours can change the bleakest misery into matter for jest.

A week later came our New Year camp on Ben Nevis. That was one of the greatest of our mountain days. Our practical experience there was that of camping on snow in an exceptionally low temperature, around sixteen degrees centigrade. There were three of us inside, and by sealing up the tent we kept warm during the night. The result was the choicest kind of fug, which is not in itself a bad thing. But our breath and body moisture condensed in such volume that our sleeping-bags were literally soaked. The amount of water exhaled by the lungs and exuded by the skin during one night is extraordinary. I had never understood how great until I saw that moisture condense on the groundsheet in pools. The sponge-rubber was again a failure, but so far I had had no time to find any alternative.

However, we were now completely converted to the frequent use of a tent on winter mountains—provided we could stop condensation and yet keep warm. It was a double problem of which one half could at any time be solved; for whenever we opened one of the doors the groundsheet starred with ice, the cambric hoared, the condensation at once ceased; but although we were fully clothed inside eiderdown bags the intense cold robbed us of sleep. The choice then before us was to spend a dry night frozen or a damp night warm. We hesitatingly chose the latter. It is interesting to note that recent Greenland expeditions found exactly the same problem and chose likewise; one of their nightly discomforts being permanently wet sleeping-bags. None the less, I remained convinced that all such discomfort could be overcome by experience.

We were determined to solve the problem, but Donaldson had to leave Scotland shortly after New Year. The great frost slackened for a space and intensified. In town the very buildings stiffened with cold; in Glencoe the night temperature dropped on the 20th to fifteen degrees centigrade. Meantime, I had been lucky enough to enlist Douglas Laidlaw, with whom I decided to place a tent on the crest of the Aonach Eagach ridge in Glencoe. It had always been one of my ambitions to make a moonlight traverse of the ridge in winter. This we could do and still have ample time to settle the vexed question of water versus frost.

We sat down to a council of war several days in advance, and decided that our new tactics must be comprehensive. Firstly, a more effective insulation than sponge-rubber must be found,

G

and the material must be very light—an inflatable mattress was out of the question on the score of weight and bulk, as was everything else I could think of. Laidlaw supplied the right answer from his greater experience. It was a very simple one —a sandwich of brown paper and tar. The sheets were light, easily folded in a rucksack, but were they effective? I was sceptical.

Secondly, the tent *must* be properly aired by the full opening of one or both ventilators according to the wind and cold without; for the lower the outside temperature the more fresh air was required (within limits), and the higher the wind the less the opening of ventilation sleeves. With condensation thus eliminated, but no more, by fine adjustment of ventilation, the problem boiled down to the simpler question of keeping warm: to counteract the admission of freezing air within the tent a single sleeping-bag was not enough. Therefore, I bought a larger sleeping-bag, which could be pulled over my ordinary bag, or be used as a mattress, or be occupied by us both. Experiment would soon decide which was best.

Thirdly, for the size of tent three men were too many, the condensation from their bodies too heavy to be avoided save by opening one of the doors. That not being practicable, for no man in his senses will tolerate being frozen needlessly, then more than two should not be admitted.

We arrived in Glencoe at ten p.m. of 21st January. On our way northward there had been every promise of a bright moon, but when I brought my car to rest under the east end of the Aonach Eagach the sky was again clouded. A moonlight climb is truly the chanciest of all mountaineering propositions. Deep snow lay to the roadway and the glen was rigid with windless cold. When I drained the car's radiator the hot water froze upon the instant of touching the ground. Therefore the degree of cold that must prevail three thousand feet up on the summit of Am Bodach, where we intended to place the tent, was a matter for the most satisfactory conjecture. Could we keep dry and warm this night we could conclusively say that we had cut the claws of one more mountain lion.   But I was not optimistic. Despite Ben Nevis, Clachlet took a bit of living down.

At twelve-thirty a.m. we reached the summit of Am Bodach. Upon the northern rocks, which were clad in hard snow, we found a little way under the cairn a ledge just large enough to accommodate the floor-space of the tent, which we pitched broadside to the ridge, with the guy-ropes shooting out at strange angles to rock-spikes and boulders.   From this site we had an unobstructed view to the moor of Rannoch, where the sun would rise, to the crest of the Aonach Eagach, which we should traverse, and to the north, where all the mountains of Lochaber stood before us.

The moonlight was locally strong, but by reason of the cloud-film visibility had fallen from upward of twenty miles to barely five.   In such conditions a moonlight traverse offered no charms to rival those of daylight, and we postponed our climbing plans to the morrow.   We retired to the tent and sealed the doors. Although enormously strong at the reinforced corners, the fabric of the roof was sufficiently fine to allow ample light inside, and in this respect held great advantage over most high altitude tents, which are perforce distressingly coffin-like.   In cloud-diffused moonlight we lit a candle inside for the sake of cheerfulness, and not as essential lighting.

We brewed tea, had supper, and went to bed.   We began the night with one open ventilator.   Condensation showed signs of winning.   Therefore we opened both ventilators and discovered that by leaving one sleeve outside and drawing one sleeve inside, fixed parallel to the roof, a current of air across the roof could be induced and yet no draught fall to our own level. The cambric quickly whitened and condensation on the ground-sheet stopped; yet the decrease in temperature was not remarkable.   The final test was at hand.   Could we now keep warm and sleep comfortably?   For the first time it began to seem certain that we could.

Unlike the sponge-rubber, the tar sandwich was astonishingly effective.   It gave us excellent insulation against ground-cold, provided that two layers of down sleeping-bag interposed between one's body and the paper. In other words, inside my two bags I could now rest in comfort—not too warm, but feeling no cold that could interfere with sound sleep.

We tried other arrangements, which gave the following results. By using the large bag as a mattress, one has good insulation against ground-cold but too little against air-cold to permit true sleep as distinct from dozing. By using ordinary bags as mattresses and both sleeping inside the large bag the greatest warmth was developed and sleep easy.

Our problem of high camping with light equipment was thus solved. But there must be borne in mind this fact, that condensation and cold are overcome at low temperatures not by one method, but by four, which are complementary:

The ventilation current must be confined to the roof area. There must be effective insulation from ground-cold. The tent must not be overcrowded. There must be effective protection from air-cold. This last means that each man must either have two sleeping-bags or else have one as a mattress and both share a third double bag. The former is preferable for greater comfort; the latter, since it involves three bags instead of four, for economy in equipment. But the double bag is less desirable for a long-term camp. For a short camp it is tolerable; there is no room for childish sensitivity on a mountain-top. Each party must make its own choice. Lastly, these measures apply to severe cold and not in mild weather. They break down where the weather is so foul as to prevent ventilation.

After we had settled down we slept so well that dawn failed to waken us and we were roused only when the first blaze of sunrise shone through the frosted roof. We looked out to find the sky clear and blue and the sunrise splendid as from Nevis at New Year. We dressed quickly—simply a matter of pulling on boots and windproof jackets—and made breakfast. A small tin of milk had frozen solid overnight and we had to carve the contents with a knife and spill the splinters into our tea; otherwise our breakfast was not inferior to that of most highland hotels.

At nine-thirty a.m. we seized our axes and rope and stepped up to the summit of Am Bodach. There was no wind. Down on the moor of Rannoch and in all the valleys of Lochaber a thick ground-mist lay motionless all day. The Aonach Eagach ran one and a half miles westward, its south flank forming the north wall of Glencoe, its narrow and rocky edge blinding white in the sunshine. We made a sharp descent on snow-smothered rocks and walked past the crags of the Chancellor until the crest dipped to a col, whence we ascended the main peak of the ridge, Meall Dearg. Thenceforward the ridge became more slender and craggy, and we had repeatedly to ply our ice-axes in short spells of step-cutting. At the narrowest stretch we came to a *gendarme*, whose glazed rock forced us to rope up and move singly. Immediately beyond we cut hand- and foothold up an icy wall to a higher continuation of the ridge, where double cornices, projecting on the left over Glencoe and on the right toward Kinlochleven, made the safeguard of a rope still more imperative. Between the two overhangs we trod where we hoped the ridge might be, and our divinations were happily correct.

In three hours from the tent we came to Sgor nam Fiannaidh, which marks the western end of the Aonach Eagach, although the ridge continues to the Pap of Glencoe. We lazed inertly in a rocky corner and sunned ourselves while we lunched. Beyond the pointed Mamores the North-east buttress of Nevis was particularly clear and icy. We hoped it was not going to waste and that some lucky men were climbing there! Above all, the flowing line of the summit plateau drew my eye, dispensing time and again a pang of nostalgia.

At one-thirty p.m. we set off eastward, regained our tent in two hours, and had packed up by sunset. Then we heaved on our rucksacks and returned to the crest.

The sun had sunk into a dense haze, which screened Ardgour and Morven in bright orange. There was little of the variety of colour that usually distinguishes a west highland sunset in winter, but the effect upon the white flank of the Aonach Eagach was unique. I had in the past criticized mountaineers who print snow photographs in sepia. Who, I asked, ever saw brown snow—who ever heard of it? Certainly nobody I had ever met. Crimson, pink, gold, silver, blue, orange, and violet snow are common enough in Scotland. But never brown. Yet before our astonished eyes the orange north wall of Glencoe darkened, until for miles to the west its snows were rich chocolate.

When twilight had turned all to monochrome we set off downward. Later the moon rose, and when I turned to look for the last time at the ridge above, flung a phantom sheaf down to a frozen tower. Facing us across the glen, the vast corrie under Stob Coire nan Lochan was in cold, pale-blue shadow; then the many peaks of Bidean nam Bian lit up one by one, and burned. The whole majestic cluster scintillated like a candelabra. In sheer height, silent aloofness, beauty of form, it filled me with that despairing awe that comes to us all occasionally. Merely to have seen that beauty for a few minutes, to have felt as I felt then, seemed worth any sacrifice and hardship.

Our plan for a moonlight traverse had been mistimed by twenty-four hours. But we were well content. We had made high winter camps a pleasure in themselves, quite apart from any opportunities they offer for mountaineering, by the removal of the worst discomforts, and had therefore given ourselves incentive for their frequent enjoyment.

That dire penalities may lie in store for the inexperienced I have shown at my own expense. But knowledge comes quickly and makes one free as the mountain wind. One gains nothing worth having on mountains without paying for it; beyond the snowline minor hardships will always be met in a small tent, and the sooner a man is trained to rise above them the better. In the end they are far outweighed by the joys of dwelling for a space on snow-fields close to the sky, where the dawn and sunset come like armadas in slow and solemn grace, and the very air has a beauty, which we call purity.

19 *Raven's Gully and Crypt Route*

THE NORTH BUTTRESS of the Buachaille Etive Mor is cleft asunder from the Cuneiform buttress by a straight gash of four hundred feet. Since the mountain first uprose from the hardening earth, or more likely from recent times, in the seventy thousand years after the fourth Ice Age when its towers were hewn by the chisels of time, the recess of that fierce stroke has bred the cloud and later the raven, and to these remained sacred until our own day.

The inviolate state of the sanctuary was acknowledged by the Scottish Mountaineering Club when they most appropriately named it Raven's gully. Attempts at penetration failed. At last, in June 1937, J. B. Nimlin led a party up the gully in nine hours. During the next two years, several attempts to repeat the ascent were repulsed—twice violently repulsed, when expert rock-climbers from England fell from the overhang at the fourth pitch, the angle of which allowed to each leader a fall of twenty-five feet clear of obstructing rock. And since the rope held, neither suffered injury. Around the gully there closed once more an aura of impregnability. One might say that the raven perched upon the fretted crags, and like Poe's bird of omen, croaked its 'Nevermore.'

In June 1939 I began to feel that a visit to my friend the raven was long overdue. To call on her soon after the breeding season seemed mannerly; in fact I had no choice. So long as the rock had been wet I had determined not to set foot on the fourth pitch. I could afford no handicap where better men than I had failed; but by 12th June not a drop of rain had fallen in Glencoe for a fortnight. That same evening I arrived at Kingshouse with MacAlpine and W. G. Marskell.

A cloudless morning followed—one of those light-hearted mornings peculiar to spring, windless yet fresh, when colours shine with a brightness of fairyland. We drove first to Lagangarbh, on the Glencoe road, and walked thence across the moor to Buachaille. Two thousand feet up on the north face, Raven's gully looked an absolutely perpendicular slash, as black as midnight. That closer acquaintance would dispel those illusions we knew; but many an otherwise willing climbing party must have been turned away by that gape of gloom. It is an unfortunate and misleading effect of distance—an effect that lessens the closer one approaches up the boulder-strewn slopes of heather, until at last one enters harbour between the towering flank of North buttress on one's left and the lower tongue of Cuneiform buttress on one's right, and finds, before one's upturned face, a gully clearly lit, enticing.

We roped up and were almost tempted astray by an obviously possible line for a new route up the slabby wall of North buttress: an ascent of which has since been made. We gave it a moment's consideration, but my heart was set on Raven's gully and would turn to no other lure. Like all good gullies it rose in steps, approximately ten in number, all of which were not as yet visible. Rarely elsewhere have I seen such a vista of overhangs crowded within so short a distance. The gully bristles. As it cut back into the rock so the flanking walls, pearly-grey on North buttress, sea-grey on Cuneiform, projected further and rose higher, gaining wildness of outline as the gully grew in splendour of height.

However, if we had come visiting we were not as yet admitted to the entrance hall. The gully started straight away with a ten-foot overhang, discomfiting as the stare of a barred door. The raven, it seemed, was not 'at home.' Moreover, despite the fine weather the rock was wet. Since we had all exchanged boots for rubbers I avoided the damp rock by climbing on to Cuneiform buttress, and from there gate-crashed by a traverse into the gully's interior.

A red pitch of fifteen feet rose in front. I was glad to observe it was only vertical. One must be grateful for these tender touches in Raven's gully. We relished a strenuous climb up its right corner and strolled across a level scree-floor to the most notorious tier, from which recent predecessors had retired in haste.

The gully was here twelve feet wide and rose in a step thirty feet high. Recessed midway up the face was a low-roofed cave, from which the upper half of the step overhung the gully floor. Misguidedly I began to study the rock and to speculate. Such a place grows worse, and the pale cast of one's thought more appropriate to Elsinore than Glencoe, the more one looks. Action was demanded unembarrassed by reflection. I climbed up to the cave.

To avoid the overhang there was but one possible route—up the dull red wall of the North buttress. From the floor of the cave one might traverse out over the gully on a yard-arm of rock. I edged out to its tip and looked up the wall. That was a dismal surprise if ever I had one. The wall was bare of holds. I returned to the cave and considered tactics, which began to crystallize round an excellent spike in the cave's back. My companions would have to work their passage. They both joined me and I asked Marskell, who was middle man, to go out to the end of the yard-arm; MacAlpine, who was last, to sit in the back of the cave and tie himself to a spike—to which he also tied Marskell and then gave me the safer belay around his own waist.

The grouping of the party made a simple tableau of man's progress through the ages: with Marskell balancing on his spar as the Java ape-man; MacAlpine squatting on his rock floor as the Neanderthal cave-man; and myself as *homo sapiens* about to ascend over their shoulders to the higher life. I thought the fancy appropriate, but my friends were blind to these similes. Every one sees the world in his own way.

I traversed out beside Marskell and climbed up his back until I stood on his shoulders. His poise over the gully was by no means too secure, but he maintained a Dunn-like immovability,

* G

which tempted me to linger longer than I ought. By my right side a snout of the overhang jutted downward, leaving a widish crack between snout and wall. I tried to avoid the constriction of the crack by climbing a few feet up the face, hoping thereafter to traverse to the top of the pitch. That was an error of judgment for which I met condign reward. The sole foothold lay well to my left, the only handhold a thin score to my right. My body thus lay on a slant across the wall, and the moment I tried to move higher my legs swung under the overhang. I found myself forcibly doubled round the snout; a mortifying moment for one with only a shirt between stomach and rock. Being helpless to move, I was obliged to come down.

To Marskell and MacAlpine my venture on the wall had appeared much more precarious than to myself; as a man driving a fast car is more at ease than those who sit behind. When I returned to the cave they were doubtful whether a second attempt should be made, but were loyal when I determined to try again. For although the first attack had been foiled the reconnaissance had been successful. I knew now exactly how to climb that fourth pitch.

Marskell again trod the yard-arm and again I went to his shoulder. I stepped on to his head and transferred straight into the crack. With a most bitter struggle I somehow forced my way up by counterpress and friction. I again found the finger-tip score, but this time came directly underneath it, and by its aid wrenched a further inch or two. When nothing more in this way could be done I stretched up my right arm and my grasping fingers closed on a magnificent notch above the bulge. With a violent pull on one arm I dragged myself up. More holds appeared. The roof of the overhang fell back. I was up. That I believe to be the hardest fifteen feet of rock in Glencoe—as nearly unclimbable as anything I have yet ascended.

A sharp incline of running scree rose from the sloping edge of the overhang. It looked highly dangerous. I shouted to Marskell to take shelter. Whenever I set foot on the scree a shower of stones slipped over the edge and flashed like hail before the crouching cave-dwellers. I climbed ten feet up the gully but could find no belay, therefore I settled myself ankle-deep in the delicately poised scree and informed Marskell that I could hold, but not pull without dislodging both myself and the gully bed. The problem was therefore how to pull up the last man to offset his lack of the initial 'shoulder.'

We solved the nasty problem by bringing the last man up second. He sent up an end of his spare rope on the slack of my own rope, and thus protected, climbed up with his ever safe and steady deliberation. Marskell was now left below, tied to both myself and MacAlpine. In addition I sent down my own end of rope as a handrail. Then MacAlpine pulled, I pulled, and Marskell pulled, all quite gently. By good fortune Marskell has a special aptitude for high-speed climbing, and whether a pitch be hard or easy makes singularly, one might even say startlingly, little difference. In five minutes he was by my side, pale from effort, and breathing hard. We rested awhile from our exertions.

Without more ado we went up a short way until the scree ran into the tall cave of yet another overhang, a more courteous sentinel than we had met hitherto; for it leaned to the right half of the gully, granting access to the left half by way of a strenuous chimney. We went back and knee up its smooth walls, worked outward to a chockstone, and thence up a very steep groove. Still higher we arrived at the most satisfying rock of the climb —a twenty-five-foot wall, which I need hardly say was vertical. It was bestarred with minute holds, curiously arrayed, reminding me of the Tennis Court wall of Scafell. Save that the latter is difficult and this severe, the two share the same technical charm.

Thenceforward the gully narrowed, and high above was spanned by a fallen crag. We climbed a broad uproll of brown rock, and passing under the great arch came at last to the true heart of the gully, the inmost sanctuary where the overhanging wall of the Cuneiform and the loftier tower of the North buttress achieve their climax of might. Before us the gully forked: on the left, rising in a sunlit shelf high on the North buttress wall;

on the right, extending long and straight, flagged with loose stone, a twilight aisle into a vast cavern.

I swithered at the cross-roads for a few minutes. But I was filled that day with a single-minded determination to climb Raven's gully. Such fits come over me from time to time. As I had turned from a new route below, so now I turned from the distant cavern, which threatened a cul-de-sac. I climbed an exposed rib on to the lower end of the shelf, where the gully fell from our feet with unusual steepness. We continued by Nimlin's route.

For some days thereafter I never regretted a decision more. Had I only borne right for a few hundred feet, along that brown aisle and beyond the architrave, what wonder might I not have found? A grotto, like the glimmering nave of some old Gothic abbey? Or merely a dripping hole? Most likely of all, if I can judge of rock formation, a subterranean chimney to the top of Cuneiform buttress, like those within the bowels of the Church Door buttress and Bhasteir tooth. I lost that opportunity of exploration; with a quite unconscious wisdom I threw it away. It remains an aspiration: 'a possession,' says Stevenson, 'as solid as a landed estate.' Thus no less than heretofore Raven's gully entrances me with that siren song of the Unknown. Assuredly I shall go again.

The shelf rose convexly for a hundred and fifty feet. We moved slowly on and up, the members of the party still climbing only one at a time, until we looked far over the ponderous crag, which bridged the lower gully, to the desolation of the moors east of Mamore. At length I arrived on a platform where the shelf ended at a last short wall. Immediately above lay the trough between the two buttress-tops. I sat down and sunned myself in a sheltered corner, while one by one the others came to me. I could see straight down the plunging gully and felt disappointed at seeing no sign of the raven; but her shyness was pardonable. Then I heard her croak.

Thus pacified, I turned to the wall and forced my way up a crack. At one p.m., two and a half hours after entering the gully, we made our exit at the top. We were seven hours earlier than I had any right to expect, but we made the ascent under ideal conditions and I was encouraged from behind by a powerful party, on a day when each one of us suddenly struck top form. The climb was very severe. Provided there be good ice at pitch four, it is my firm opinion that Raven's gully will provide a thrice-royal route in winter.

A sudden accession of good form is a pleasant and usual experience for a leader, but sudden loss of form on a hard rock-climb is one of the most frightening things that can happen to him. The experience is rare and has assailed me but twice. The circumstances that give rise to it are well demonstrated by my first visit to the Crypt route on the Church Door buttress of Bidean nam Bian.

Upon the north face of the buttress an arch two hundred feet high overhangs the screes. The normal route goes by a flake to the right of the arch, then up and across the roof to Raeburn's chimney, by which one gains access to the upper buttress. Now this arch was pierced by two holes, and it had long seemed to me that a direct route might be made by climbing straight up the wall under the arch and going through one of the holes on to the roof. Therefore, on 5th June 1938 I persuaded Marskell and MacAlpine to go with me to Bidean nam Bian. None of us was aware that this route had already been climbed by an English party and entitled 'Crypt route.'

We went to the buttress, which is situated in the northern corrie directly under the summit, on a day of careering mist. The crags emerged like a great castle on a promontory, clothed in silvery purple light and backed by storm-cloud. Starting from a snow-gully below the arch, we climbed seventy feet up a chimney, then penetrated by a stepped corridor into the bowels of the buttress. We came to a dark chamber at the end of the passage and thought we could go no further. I groped my way round the left wall and discovered a shaft boring upward through solid rock.   We forced our way through and arrived in a second and much darker chamber, which a flaring match revealed as not unlike the king's tomb in the heart of the Great Pyramid, but smaller.

Again I thought we could go no further, until above me on my left the last flicker of the match revealed another hole.   This led to a third rock chamber.   A faint streak of light betrayed a final tunnel, which must surely take us to the open air.   The tunnel was so small and tortuous that I spent almost half an hour struggling on my stomach; to gain admittance I had to take off my rucksack and push it in front of me, greatly wondering what surprise would come next.   Had Dunn been with us our climb would there and then have failed, for his broad shoulders would never have fitted into the aperture.   I myself fitted rather too nicely, and only by the most strenuous propulsion of forearms and boots could I wriggle forward.   I should say that this route is the safest in Scotland, for though much effort is required to get up, it is equally difficult to fall down.

Since the rucksack in front blocked the light I could not see where I was going, but knew that our route had now spiralled inside the buttress so that we must be facing Glencoe.   Suddenly I found my head and shoulders projecting from a window in the face of the cliff.   I looked directly down to the snow-gully and outward across the corrie, now dismally curtained in sleet, from which I was protected by the arch close overhead.   It was good from this shelter to see the clouds wildly driving around the crags.   Reluctantly, I pulled myself out of the hole and found foothold on a slab, where I waited for Marskell.   He had a hard struggle—in fact he was obliged to go back and remove his clothes before he finally wormed through the tunnel. Thereafter I climbed open slabs to the lower hole in the arch, where I found an easy way to the roof.

Our only remaining task was to cross the arch and go up Raeburn's chimney, which is difficult and slightly exposed.   I had climbed it often before without finding trouble.   But three causes now combined to throw me quite off form.   Firstly, we had been climbing constricted chimneys in the safest of rock-climbs; therefore the change to more exposed rock was sudden and unwelcome. Secondly, we had come to try what we thought was a new route—the issue had been much in doubt and our arrival on the arch a triumph; therefore I felt that the climb was finished, and with success came reaction. Thirdly, I waited for thirty minutes in paralysing cold for the others to reach the arch.

The psychological result was complete loss of confidence. I traversed the arch and uneasily mounted a slab to the foot of the chimney. With every movement that followed I felt a dreadful qualm in the pit of my stomach, and not since I was led up my first rock-climb had I been at such a loss what to do next or so dominated by a strange environment. Half-way up I found myself, for the first time in my life, pounded—unable to move either up or down. Time passed. I could do nothing but watch flakes of sleet alight and melt on the wet rock before my nose. My fingers lost all sensation. At last it became evident that should I stay where I was a moment longer I must fall. Whereupon I rallied my strength of will and forced on myself one more movement. At once the invisible fetters fell away and I climbed perfectly. Curiously enough, Marskell saw nothing alarming in my climbing save that I had been unconscionably slow; but the escape had been narrow and I was unhappy even on the moderate rocks above the chimney.

When a mountaineer sees two or more of the above forces combine against him he should keep a sharp look out and pull himself together. The danger lies in his being caught unawares, but he will have no trouble if he be mentally prepared. Loss of form is not usually a sudden thing, and a good party in top form has to reckon with only one subjective danger—carelessness on easy ground. That more than anything will bring a climber to disaster; but nowadays mountaineers are so well warned of easy rocks of descent that they automatically increase in watchfulness when they come to them. In consequence, I have been in less trouble on mountains than in valleys. But I learned a salutary lesson in Glen Falloch.

I had climbed that October day on Buachaille with Mackenzie and T. D. Mackinnon. On our way home we visited the falls of Falloch, which were in full spate and a sight well worth seeing. Above the topmost fall was a long and narrow gorge, through which the congested waters dashed foaming to leap with a thunderous roar to a rock cauldron. At one point the gorge was narrow enough to challenge one's sporting instinct. Was a leap possible? We measured it up with the eye. It would have to be a standing jump from spray-drenched rock.

'Easy!' scoffed Mackenzie, and with one bound was across.

One by one we jumped safely. The gut was narrower than it looked. We had been too impressed by the fury of the water. Thus, I was just a trifle less careful in making the return jump; my foot slipped off the wet rock and down I went into the gorge. I struck my head against one of the walls and was already half-stunned when I hit the water. My body was seized, whirled round, shot along the gut and hurled twenty feet down to the cauldron.

I came to the surface with bursting lungs, but was pinned under the fall and gulped in more water than air. Each time I strove to swim out a powerful up-current threw back my body like a twig. I tried to each side in vain, and everywhere that current tossed me back, until I grew dazed by the pounding of the fall and my breath was battered from my body more effectively than by iron bars. Within five minutes (I had really no conception of time), my violent struggles to swim out became a more desperate struggle to keep afloat, for the weight of my clothes dragged me down and the surface was churned so high that I could not breathe without swallowing great draughts of water. My struggles grew weaker, then stopped through sheer exhaustion. Immediately I went under.

Meanwhile, Mackenzie and Mackinnon were helplessly watching from the edge. They could not reach me, for the rock wall was high and undercut all round. For any one to plunge into that boiling cauldron was a madness likely to result in the drowning of two men instead of one. Notwithstanding—when

Mackinnon saw me go under he could contain himself no longer, and forgetting even to remove his hat, dived in. I came up again to see him striking out hard for the fall, but powerful swimmer though he was, he could not get near me. The current spun him round and cast him up on a shoal at the low end of the cauldron. A most noble effort.

When I saw that no help was possible I truly thought that my last minute had come, but nevertheless made a last fight. I think that that is one of the most shocking moments in a man's life, when he knows that his life is lost but is not yet resigned to death. He has a feeling of despair not pleasant to look back upon. A man in that state is capable of superhuman exertions, and although 'exhausted' I tapped hitherto unsuspected reserves of energy. But the forces against me were too great; for the last time my struggle weakened; then I surrendered, and sank.

My past life did not flash before my eyes. Save for one thing of which I cannot write, I thought only that I had chosen a foolish way of ending my life, which might have been expended to a worthier end on mountains, where one seeks beauty, than in horseplay at a waterfall. The instant I was reconciled the peace of complete detachment came upon my mind. I discovered for myself, once and for all, that in approaching death there is nothing to fear. It is pleasant. Like the release from prison to freedom—a little strange at first.

A few minutes later Mackinnon and Mackenzie were pulling me ashore at the low end of the cauldron. I had gone to the bottom, been driven sideways by an undercurrent, and then propelled to the surface beyond the grip of the great back-eddy. Thereupon I drifted by the side of the cauldron down to the shallows.

For half an hour I lay on the bank and vomited water while Mackenzie thumped my back. By the time they had stripped and dried me I was sufficiently alive to resent the fuss. But seven days afterwards I was still too exhausted to rock-climb. The only serious result was the loss of Mackinnon's hat, a stylish and expensive model, newly purchased, which he would not allow me to replace. Like a true Scotsman he blamed only himself for not having had the presence of mind to take it off!

Who will wonder that I feel more at home on hills than in low country? The higher the safer. We should all remember that Edward Whymper fell off a platform at Birkenhead after lecturing on the Matterhorn.

20 *Crowberry Gully in Winter*

A T THE END OF JANUARY 1941 I received orders to
join the Middle East forces in Egypt. The occasion clearly
called for one long last climb on the Buachaille Etive Mor.
I had already made seventy-nine ascents by one route or another,
and each had but strengthened my conviction that Buachaille
was the most splendid of earthly mountains. I was destined
not to see it again for four years, and therefore can never be
sufficiently grateful to R. G. Donaldson, a true friend, who cut
his own work at Cambridge and came north to climb with me.
We selected Crowberry gully as the best winter route in Glencoe, and one that would give us all that we bargained for and
more. In this hope we were shortly to be confirmed by events.
Crowberry gully rarely yields so early in the season.

We drove up to Kingshouse Inn at two o'clock in the morning
of 1st February. A quilt of new snow covered the ground, the
sky was heavy-burdened, and large flakes fell twisting through
the beam of the car's head-lamp. After our long drive through
snowstorms on Rannoch moor, the old inn looked a true outpost
of civilization. Nor, despite the unearthly hour and the profit-
less trouble we had caused her in past years, did Mrs. Malloch
fail us. A fire, hot tea, food, and beds—all were waiting for
us—even a gift of that strange substance, more precious in war
than blood—Pool petrol.

Five hours later we wakened to a perfect morning. At nine
o'clock we went down to Coupal bridge. While we plodded
over the snow-clogged heather the sun rose clear over Rannoch
moor. A cloud-flock hovered overhead, but was fast disappearing before we reached the iced boulders of the lower
slopes. Towering high in front, so that we stopped with our

heads well back to look, the walls and slabs of Buachaille, muffled in new snow, dazzled our eyes where the sun struck. The mountain looked like a fortress of ice, its summit diamond cut deep into a royal blue sky.

It was this last that held us there. It was not alone the confusion of snow-turret and bastions, nor even the ridges racing up and up, drawing in to the white blaze where the last rocks leaped against the blue; not grace of design, nor colour, nor height—none of these things alone—that charged our minds with wonder. These beauties were indeed endless, but were brought to unity and fulfilled in that austere and remote line dividing snow from sky. It was the signature of all things. It held us spellbound. It is hard to know why, until we know that it is the most simple things that most deeply impress a man. Until we know that we shall not hope to know the true beauty. Up there, nothing stirred. Not even 'the sigh that silence heaves'; only a breathless stillness. A bright light. A pureness of beauty above all that eye can see, or ear hear, or it can enter into the heart of man to conceive. One may say nothing of it that is not somehow false or misleading. For the truth that can be spoken is not the truth. Yet on the heights of truth one never climbs in vain.

We continued slowly uphill, delayed from time to time by short ice-falls. While cutting a step below the main cliffs I struck a powerful backhand blow with my axe and snapped the shaft near the head. We had now but one axe between us for such big game as Crowberry gully, and the question arose whether we should go on. I had another very short axe for cutting on ice-walls. This could stop a slip on hard snow but had no value as a belay. However, I recollected that the big pitches in Crowberry gully spring from shallow caves, where the second man can find stances to give the leader body-belays. The leader, therefore, would carry the large axe and all should be well. I did not like this arrangement, but the reasons for retiring so soon were not good enough. We continued upward.

At eleven a.m. we traversed into Crowberry gully. It began

invitingly. The angle was low and the slope wide. We were still in sunshine, and a bend in the gully hid the verticalities above. But a climber is no more satisfied with snow than a farmer with weather. An inch or two of new snow lay on old hard snow, and the top layer kept slipping on the lower. We floundered inelegantly, trying to avoid step-cutting so early in the day on so easy a slope, until at last exasperation overcame ingrained laziness. We are unsophisticated enough to find step-cutting a joyous art. But one grows impatient if time be scarce.

An introductory pitch of snow-clad rock, then a long and concave slope, led to the first bend, whence we had our first view of the climb as a whole. It appeared as a thousand-foot shaft, splitting deeply an enormous expanse of snow-plastered cliffs. To its right lay the North buttress, to its left the Crowberry ridge. Between these close walls the gully soared tier upon icy tier to the gentle curve of a far-away snow ridge, where one wisp of cloud idled.

The gully quickly steepened to the first shallow cave. From here to its end Crowberry gully rises in a glorious crescendo of difficulty, each pitch in winter being noticeably harder than the preceding one. The crux, and the final cave pitch that immediately follows, share the honours in severity. This mounting difficulty has disadvantages. Certainly it tunes one up for the final onslaught, but if either crux or cave pitch is unclimbable one is defeated late in the day with all the gully to climb down again. I have never seen any belays on the gully-walls for roping down. Therefore it is not difficult to get oneself benighted.

From now on each of us led alternate pitches. Donaldson started off. The first three obstacles all involved the same glazed slabs and snow; each was separated from the others by one or two hundred feet of hard snow surfaced with new, in which every step had to be cut with the adze; none was exposed but each ran true to form, the long groove of pitch two and the overhang of pitch three being respectively more difficult than its predecessor. On this last pitch Donaldson had a stiff struggle.

Half-crouched below the overhang of frozen snow, to which he clung with one hand while leaning out at an alarming angle over the down-race of the gully, he scraped and picked at the frosted flank of the North buttress in prolonged and repeated efforts to find or fashion hand- and toehold. He won his way in the end. But these pitches consumed much time. It was three-thirty p.m. before we reached Thin Crack chimney, a feature of the gully in summer. Here we paused and considered.

In front lay three notable pitches. We could see them framed between giant white walls. Three hours of daylight remained, if one counted late twilight. Yet the last two pitches might themselves take one and a half hours each for the leader alone; this excluded Thin Crack chimney, a very hard thirty feet when the chimney was blocked with snow, as it was to-day, and the climber was forced on to icy slabs to its right. Our decision was that unless we were over the crux by four-thirty p.m. we must turn back.

We lost no time. In thirty minutes the Thin Crack was behind us and we drew to a standstill in Crowberry junction. At this crux in the climb Crowberry gully branches. The left fork is a chimney shooting up to Crowberry Tower gap—it had not yet been climbed. The right fork, beginning as a broad belt of slabs which have never been climbed in summer, runs up to the climax of the cave pitch and debouches on the open brow of the mountain a hundred and fifty feet below the cairn. Between these two forks stands an unclimbed buttress. Amidst this welter of unclimbed rock the summer route winds its tortuous way, twenty feet up the unclimbed chimney, then across the unclimbed buttress into the right fork above the slabs. This route is not difficult, but in winter had never proved possible. Then one relies on a good coat of ice over the slabs of the right fork. The work there is severe, even exposed, and requires a hundred-foot run-out. To-day there was no ice on the slabs. Their only coat was thick powdery snow. We had, after all, come too early in the season to find ice in good quantity. Such was the cheerless situation.

I reflected with pleasure that this was Donaldson's turn to lead, but I tried the slabs myself out of curiosity. They were impossible. From past experience of Crowberry junction I thought that our only hope of finding a route was in forcing a way up the angle between the central buttress and right fork. For such a hazardous task some simple rope mechanics were essential. To this end I repaired to a snowy stance about twenty feet up in the depths of the left fork. The chimney was hereabouts arched by a square crag, over which, after several abortive efforts, I cast an end of rope to which Donaldson tied himself. Then I anchored myself to a thick pillar of clear ice. The position thus was that if Donaldson came off on the first fifteen feet he would not fall, but would merely suffer a harmlessly sensational swing across the gully. In face of this improvised gallows Donaldson remained as unperturbed as an aristocrat on the scaffold. If the rocks were climbable at all he would get up. I was sure of it. Yet he did not get up. He made ten feet, after which not all his tenacious ingenuity could get him higher. We both came down to the junction and changed places on the rope.

I tried to force the passage where Donaldson had failed but could find no adequate hold. The rope came to me at too wide an angle to be of assistance, but I thought that there were possibilities of readjusting the rope to allow a more direct pull. Meantime, my arms and wrists ached with hanging to minute holds and I prepared to climb down. At this instant a small powder-snow avalanche, discharged from the North buttress at a great height above, came trundling down the gully, poured over my head, and swamped the rocks around. Large quantities of freezing powder shot down my neck and formed a waist-belt of liquid horror. This discomfort was quickly forgotten, for the small holds by which I had ascended thus far were obliterated, and try as I would I could not find them again with my feet. Handhold was too sketchy to allow of leaning out to prospect. I realized that I should be bound to come off, and warned Donaldson accordingly. Nevertheless, I contrived to climb down a few feet before the rock and I parted company. I swung across the gully, feeling like a parachutist, and keenly aware of the thinness of climbing-rope. A few seconds later I came to rest on the gully-bed, and after unroping joined Donaldson above.

The time was four-forty p.m. By previous agreement we should now have turned in our tracks and hastened down to avoid benightment. We agreed that the game was almost up —but not quite up. The sterility of pessimism had not yet descended upon us, whilst the fertility of optimism suggested, first, an attempt at the summer route, and if that failed, then a readjustment of the rope over the chockstone to afford a more direct pull on the corner route. We had only to think of the difficulties below to be fortified in these decisions.

I set to work on the summer route by traversing 'back and foot' to the outer edge of the chimney. But I failed to start the traverse across the buttress. The rock was slabby, thinly iced, and engulfed in powder-snow. However, I changed for the better the rope running over the chockstone and made my slow way back to Donaldson. A third attempt on the corner route was now our only hope, but I had to confess to Donaldson that I was temporarily too muscle-weary to try. He then climbed down to the junction and again took the lead.

Once he was launched on the rocks I could not see what was happening, and a long period of suspense followed. Like myself, Donaldson is not communicative on a climb. Twice I was enjoined to hold the rope tight, from which I gathered that he was luxuriating in more than moral support. The rope moved no more than a few inches in twenty minutes. I passed the time by scrutinizing the retaining walls below with an eye to a traverse out of the gully. In all the wide acres of rock on the North buttress I could detect not a single line of escape. The Crowberry ridge through almost all its length was overhanging, and in any event an escape there would be one from the frying-pan into the fire.

My eye wandered back to the rope: little movements were to

be seen that indicated something alive at the far end of it.   Then, gradually, still inch by inch, the rope snaked—upward!   I could hardly contain myself.   The tempo of rope-movement steadily quickened, often going out a foot at a time, until a hundred feet had scuttered over the snow-encrusted chockstone.   A faint call of 'Come on!' floated down to me.   To any future climber, belayed after sunset to a pillar of ice in the left fork of Crowberry gully, I guarantee that these hackneyed words 'Come on!' will stir his spirit like a flourish of trumpets.

I reached Donaldson at five-thirty p.m.   A little more cutting, a little more kicking of steps, and we arrived below the final cave pitch.   Its appearance shocked us.   Having come so far, and toiled so hard, we were in no mood for spectacular severities. But the cave arched forty feet overhead, thrust down at us a tusk of red rock, and looked impregnable.   Our natural reaction after the crux, combined with a grey twilight, lent a degree or two, as it were, to the verticality of the flanking walls.   Donaldson settled in his frost-lined cave and gave me a belay, while I used the failing light to search out a weak spot on the North buttress side, where a layer of black ice spread over the rock like tar.   It is unlikely that I could have solved the problem of starting at all but for two lucky chances.   At a height of four feet, and again at ten feet, a clump of frozen snow adhered to *verglas*.   Both occurred where there was no other vestige of hold.   Either might break away without warning, but each was sufficiently low down for the risk to be taken safely.   When put to the test, both clumps held and did not break until later.

After reaching the second clump I could at first see no way of getting higher.   The ice was still too thin to use save as a last resort.   The protruding bones of rock were glazed and badly spaced.   For a moment or two I leant my back against the tusk and allowed my gaze to wander downward.   I gained rest and lasting memories at the same time.   Beneath my heels Crowberry gully plunged in a grey cataract, and far below disappeared in a sea of darkness, which slowly and surely seeped up the gully like a flowing tide.   The sheeted walls and snow-banked ledges of the North buttress had long ceased to sparkle, and looked unspeakably bleak.   I know nothing more merciless than frost-bound cliffs at dusk.   After the setting of the sun, grimness is their keynote and their hymn hostility.

Donaldson by this time was making anxious inquiries about conditions ahead, to which I replied with the usual non-committal noises.   I managed to move up a foot, then, unexpectedly, another foot.   The ice became thicker.   There followed three-quarters of an hour of continuous cutting—a race with ebbing light.   The angle was too high, and therefore balance too delicate, to permit any weight behind these axe-blows.   I had to peck away, using one hand from the wrist, trying to hew holds wherever allowed by rock bulges and brittle ice, which cropped up, with a kind of inevitability, always in the wrong place. This was one of those pitches that wring from a climber, when he is half-way up, a hasty declaration that never again will he set foot on iced rocks, and when he is up, a solemn oath that never in all his life will he forsake them.   And so it turned out. I reached the top with aching muscles and a joyful heart.

I had to cut some further distance up shallow snow before finding sufficient depth to sink half my axe-shaft for a belay. Donaldson's position was now an unenviable one.   The extra cutting had discharged rivulets of chips over all the holds carved so laboriously.   It was becoming too dark to see details of rock or ice for delicate climbing movements.   However, I shouted down, 'I'm up!' and after the conventional interval, 'Come on!'   Donaldson, frozen stiff with his long wait while night closed round, and uncertain of our prospects, welcomed the order with delighted liveliness; and that, with a tight rope and his own great skill, carried him up the pitch within fifteen minutes.   He gave a remarkable exhibition of resolute climbing.

Our only anxiety now was the bad state of the snow in the last stretch of gully—powdery stuff lying on old granular snow at a high angle.   We continued to move one at a time from axe-belays.   A small awkward pitch of ten feet caused trouble;

beyond was a hundred feet of plodding to the snow-ridge where the gully ended.

We stepped on to the open mountain-side at seven-fifteen p.m., and came face to face with a cloud-racked, starry sky. The ring of low crags under the summit, the ground beneath our feet, and all the rocks around were buried deep in fog crystals. Although night had fallen, yet up there so close to the sky there was not true darkness. A mysterious twilight, like that of an old chapel at vespers, pervaded these highest slopes of Buachaille. We stood at the everlasting gates, and as so often happens at the close of a great climb, a profound stillness came upon my mind, and paradoxically, the silence was song and the diversity of things vanished. The mountains and the world and I were one. But that was not all: a strange and powerful feeling that something as yet unknown was almost within my grasp, was trembling into vision, stayed with me until we reached the cairn, where it passed away.

We went down to Glen Etive for the last time, and I fear we went sadly. The moon shone fitfully through ragged brown clouds.

21

Cairngorm Blizzard

ONE DAY IN MAY I fled the noise and tumult of cities for the peace and quiet, as I thought, of the Cairngorms; and thus once again there was demonstrated the truth of those oracular words of La Fontaine:

> On rencontre sa destinée
> Souvent par des chemins qu'on prend pour l'éviter.

Had I only known, when I arrived at Aviemore that afternoon, what in fact lay in store for me on the morrow, I should have thought twice before stirring from the Great North Road. Doubtless I should have stirred none the less. Men prize most highly what they win hardly.

I had come alone to indulge in a little hill-walking. It is good for a climber to go off by himself from time to time; a practice greatly to be encouraged—it sharpens up his mountain-craft; his feeling for the hill scene is heightened and his eye for detail quickened—but a practice to be discouraged in the Cairngorms in spring or winter: hills that command my respect more than any other range in Scotland. Moreover, when I looked south to their distant swell, it was manifest that I should be lucky to see anything save a compass-dial. A pall of cloud hung over the mountains, its underside lurid from the reflected glare of the snow plateaux.

My plans were accordingly modest, until an evening stroll by the shores of Loch Balladern introduced me to a fair-haired youth of quiet eye and upright bearing, who stood dripping before me on the shingle after a swim in the loch. While he dressed he told me his name was Mortimer. I liked him on the instant, and with no more ado asked him to climb with me next day. He welcomed the idea and I shared a meal in his tent by the loch-side. We laid plans for the morrow. We should go nine miles to the head of Glen Einich, five more to the

Devil's Point, then northward to Braeriach we should enjoy a five-mile walk at a height of four thousand feet—a total round of thirty-one miles.

Now that I had a friend with me the wicked look of the weather already offered consolation. A course of compass-work is never amiss; for the one way efficiently to handle map and compass is by practice, and the Cairngorms are said to be the best training-ground in Europe. I suggest that such an opinion puts the cart before the horse; one had better train elsewhere and leave to the Cairngorms the final test. That their heart lies ten mountainous miles from human aid has been realized too late by many an ill-equipped climbing party; for the range is sterner in foul weather than may be found anywhere at a like latitude, and a Cairngorm blizzard can be the last word in natural savagery.

However, we were particularly well supplied with food and clothing. We assembled this gear in the tent, and added to the pile a coil of Alpine rope, which in the end came near to saving our lives.

Next morning we were up at six a.m. and away at seven. The first stage of our journey went by twilit tracks through the forest of Rothiemurchus. There had been high wind and rain during the night and we marched to stirring music, 'The sea in the pine-tops murmuring.' The branches still dripped and swayed, and the fallen drops gemmed the tangle of undergrowth, from which arose a moist breath, so fragrant that to this day I can recapture the emotion it aroused. I can well understand the sentiment of that Scots soldier in Iraq, who, according to John Buchan, described his camp site as 'twa miles on the Rothiemurchus side o' Baghdad.' At the furthest fringe of the forest we crossed a barred gate in a deer fence, where a battered notice-board warns the free Briton that he is liable to be shot. There was an ugly sky behind us.

From now onward we began to lose touch with the human world. We had reached a no man's land, where the outpost of the Cairngorms, Carn Eilrig, and the last pines of the broad Spey valley, confront each other like rival sentinels on a frontier.

The furthest tree dropped behind and our track drove its lonely scratch over a wilderness of heath and stone toward the dim recess of Glen Einich. Meantime, the growing commotion of the sky forced itself on our notice. The whole north-western horizon was congested with gathering storm-clouds. They had flung out slate-grey skirmishers, which even now were racing in squadrons overhead, throwing themselves athwart the mountain bulwarks. Down in Glen Einich there was no more than a spit of rain, cold and ominous.

Seven miles out, at the lower bothy, we took shelter and asked ourselves seriously whether it were worth while going on. There seemed a promise of big developments in the sky; but the day was too young to be termed hopeless, and if need were we could descend from Cairn Toul and cut the second part of our programme. Good reasons, no doubt, for going on—but the truth is that human nature is happily perverse, and the delight of wrestling a fall with the elements an exhilarating prospect.

We covered the next two miles to the upper bothy in record time; for the rain gave place to hail, which came down harder each moment. This ramshackle hut of blackened wood is perhaps the most famous refuge in the Cairngorms. A haven where many a storm-tossed climber has been thankful to ride out a blizzard. We found the inside to be damp, gloomy, and indescribably dirty. Despite such minor drawbacks we derived a thrill of snugness from the devil's tattoo of the hail. Everything pointed to this being our last chance to eat in comfort, and we settled down to second breakfast. The time was nine a.m. Then my eye was caught by an array of carvings on the wall. On looking closer I was surprised and delighted to find the engraved names of several mountaineering friends. The bothy was so lonely, so deeply buried in the mountain fastness, and therefore my finding of these old names so unexpected, that for a minute my imagination ran away with me. 'All the wistful past waked in one glance,' and I could fancy that friendly voices and the laughter of former days still echoed through the hut.[1]

---

[1] The upper bothy has recently been destroyed.

THE BRAERIACH PLATEAU

SCALE IN MILES

0 ¼ ½ ¾ 1 2

Murray's and Mortimer's Route - - -

The hail slackened and went off, but shuddering planks indicated a strengthening wind. I thought the sign excellent, for my opinion was that with the wind rising so fast the clouds would ride high before noon. Thus encouraged, I set to work. I applied a protractor to the one-inch Ordnance Survey map and took every bearing and distance we were likely to need on the hills. I noted these on a piece of stray cardboard, which I pushed inside my glove. The map could thus be dispensed with during the remainder of the day.

When we sallied out at ten-thirty the glen was lively with breeze and bluster, every top cloud-engulfed. We had a five-mile climb before us to Devil's Point, but the first half mile took us south by the shores of Loch Einich. A most dismal scene. Beyond the far bank the hoared precipice of Sgurr Dubh stared down through veils of shifting mist—suddenly loomed, lingered, and slowly faded in a regular rhythmic cycle. High on the cliff a darker gash repeatedly remained behind when the face had vanished, destitute of visible support, like the grin of the Cheshire cat. We steered south-east into a corrie, at the back of which steep snow-slopes gave access to the summit plateau. As one might expect, the wind was rising as we gained height, but as yet this was more an assistance than otherwise. Our progress was unexpectedly speedy. The wind pushed us uphill, and near the top we could lean right back on it and allow ourselves to be carried forward. We found the plateau heavily covered in snow, soft drifts alternating with case-hardened patches. The tendency of the wind to push us too far south had to be constantly corrected by compass.

After an hour had gone by there arose the dangerous feeling that most of us experience sooner or later on mountains—a feeling tantamount to an absolute conviction that our compass was wrong, quite wrong, that the true course lay much more to the south. It is easy to yield, dreadfully easy to compromise, but any man who does either is set for a nasty surprise at the end of his journey. We held by the compass, and at one o'clock drew close to Devil's Point, where the wind was exceeding gale force in short gusts, some of which must have approached a hundred miles per hour. We had to crawl on hands and knees over the last twenty yards to the cairn, for we were unwilling to be picked up and hurled down the Lairig Ghru face. For a moment we were tempted—the first of the day's three great temptations—to find a route down to the Corrour bothy in the Lairig Ghru. But this seemed too gross a betrayal of our day's expedition and we let the idea go—reluctantly, for the wind was bitter.

After we topped Devil's Point we began the real work of the day, our six-mile journey northward. That we might have to spend more than five hours on it was not at this stage credible, and all went well on the first mile and a half to Cairn Toul. On our right hand, the parallel rift of the Lairig Ghru, just visible as a blur of gloom, was a sure guide in case of need. But the wind was now against us. Although no snow was falling, twisting snow-devils were racing across the surface of the plateau and hurling handfuls of powder and spiculae into our faces. Often these gusts were too violent to bear and we had to turn our backs and wait for them to slacken.

We were thankful now that our bearings were ready beforehand, for in such a gale map-work would have been highly troublesome. A compass check on direction was occasionally essential, less on account of mist, which had cleared a little since Devil's Point, than of clouds of flying drift. On top of this major irritation came the minor difficulty of breathing. The wind literally flung our breath back between our teeth. To avoid its impact on the mouth we had to go head down to it.

In half an hour these terrific gusts eased off and became infrequent. We had easy walking for a while, and when we came to steeper slopes the wind was much less violent, although the height was now three thousand five hundred feet. At the end of an hour we began to feel the intoxication of filling our lungs with Britain's purest air, the supreme property of these high-level plateaux. To that was added the zest of fighting a wind that was no longer implacable, that was yielding with no worse

H

than a stout resistance. One had the pleasing sense of being detached from one's own body. One drove it over the plateau as though wielding a weapon in battle. One had the mastery and exulted. When one halted the feeling was different; then one dwelt in the body as though in a tent for a brief bivouac, the real self or soul being no more confused with the body than the camper with the canvas and pole. On a wind-swept plateau we may drink the living waters of freedom and learn of our heritage.

When we started on the last rise to Cairn Toul there came a wider clearance than usual. Suddenly Mortimer gripped my arm and pointed uphill through the mist chasm.

'Look!' he exclaimed. 'Two men crossing to Glen Einich.'

Upon looking up the slope I was duly surprised to see two climbers a long way ahead of us. And we had thought ourselves early on the mountain, and considering the weather, almost brazen! I watched them traverse a full fifty feet from east to west across the snow-slope, one about ten yards in front of the other. I hailed them, but the wind tore my voice in the wrong direction. We advanced and saw them halt, apparently to wait for us. At a hundred yards' range they turned out to be two black boulders. So great was out astonishment that we failed even to laugh at ourselves. It was a perfect illustration of the eye's absolute need of some framework before it can distinguish a moving object from a stationary.

We had found the long plod to Cairn Toul arduous, but had little to complain of, for the snow underfoot had been pounded into hard sheets. When we passed four thousand feet the clouds were rapidly receding before our uphill advance, and we arrived at the cairn with a sense of enlarging sky and broadening vistas. The day showed every sign of turning out exactly as we had hoped, a strong shouting day—fierce but harmless.

Leaning sideways to the breeze we were lucky enough to get a superb view of the eastern Cairngorms. Here and there a hail shower trailed like crystal tapestry over their rolling domes. For the most part they stood clear, in truth 'palaces of death

THE TREES OF THE MOUNTAINS

and frost.' The cloud ceiling continued to rise, fast-pacing as ever, until the giant back of our plateau lay bare. Its outflung limbs stretched far toward Inverey and Rothiemurchus, Cairn Toul brooding over the one and Braeriach the other. Between lay leagues of snow.

The sense of our minuteness on these empty wastes became acute. I felt a tiny speck swallowed up in an environment incomprehensibly great, like the flicker of earthly life amid the uncountable galaxies. Here we knew what it meant to be alone, yet to feel distant kinship with the gods. One might imagine that the human spirit would be cowed by the inhuman majesty of the scene; but this need not be so. Although he be alone, many a man will find the contrary to be true. Whatever there may be of greatness in a man's mind will grow and go out in sympathy with the greatness of the mountain world: whatever is little will shrink. So that where one man is intimidated another is ennobled.

There is, too, something in the plateaux that makes appeal to man's restless heart, an appeal that seems to be felt by people of all countries. For I found it again in the course of twelve months' travelling in the deserts of Syria, Iraq, Egypt, and Libya. There I discovered the same bold sweep of horizon and sky, the bare and boundless distance, the wind and desolation. The same simplicity. Despite all barrenness and hardship, the deserts stir deep instincts of the human mind, the impulse to rove and explore, the love of quest that betrays the yearning of the race. These powerfully urge us across the mountain plateaux and the lonely summits.

Our correct prophecy of the cloud clearance had immensely pleased us; and as erring humans will, we began to assume our judgment infallible. Uttering our grave opinions like a bench of law lords, we declared that the wind, though moderating, would keep the tops clear all day; we could safely press on with part two of our programme. Yet be it noted, the cloud ceiling remained close overhead. At three p.m. we started north-west by the brink of the cliffs to Angel's Peak.

Then, most surprisingly, before we had gone any distance, the wind died away. An uneasy silence fell. At the gentle slopes of the col we stopped and watched a great change overtaking the sky. In every direction, as far as eye could see, stretched an unbroken mass of dark storm-clouds, rapidly pressing down upon the mountains like a leaden canopy. White flakes were beginning to wander high overhead. We hurried into action again. Ten minutes later we were enveloped in dense mist.

This calm prevailed through the journey from Cairn Toul to Angel's Peak. We were just underneath the top when as suddenly as the wind had died it returned. It came from a point more to the west, loud and shrill, buffeting the west flank and spinning streamers of snow around us. The light turned an ugly yellow and then darkened to iron grey. Down in the lowlands, the stories of the Grey Man who is alleged to haunt the neighbouring summit of Ben Macdhui is a fit subject for derision. In threatening storm it is less incredible, and when I suddenly saw a great grey shadow loom through the murk, a blurred figure taller by far than human form, I confess that for one moment I was startled out of my wits. Then my Grey Man materialized as Mortimer on the cairn above me.

The renewal of the wind persuaded us that although the cloud could not be broken up, at least foul weather might again be staved off until sunset. If so we had time in hand, and since our bodies had been hard punched by the weather we sheltered for thirty minutes on the lee-side of the peak, where we pulled on all reserve clothing, ate food, and checked our bearings to Braeriach.

We were determined henceforth not to try to follow the line of the cliffs, but to keep well clear of them. I know of one party of four climbers who in thick weather gaily walked over the edge of the north corrie of Cairngorm. They were properly tied on a short rope, but when the leader dropped through the cornice the second man was caught napping and was plucked like a straw into the void. The others promptly followed.

THE
BRAERIACH
PLATEAU

Most luckily they missed the rocks and struck steeply inclined snow, which glanced them downward for several hundred feet. By a miracle, not one of them suffered fatal injury. Therefore, to preclude chance of a similar fate, we made our route on three bearings—half-mile west to the head of the Garrachoire, a cliff-ringed corrie deeply breaching the plateau, then one and a quarter miles north to the north top, point 4,036, and lastly three-quarter mile easterly to the summit.

At four p.m. we set off. If the sky monsters had scowled on our trespass before, it was not until now that they roused themselves in good earnest. It became obvious that a thick snow-storm must at any moment close down on us. The flakes came faster and faster, at first fat and whirling, then driving and vicious, applying an icy lash to the cheek. We had gone half-way to the Garrachoire when a blizzard came down like the wrath of God.

More intensely than on Cairn Toul we now felt much alone— a feeling that did not so much intimidate as rally one's inner resources; for the fact that civilization might as well be a hundred miles away for all the difference it could make in emergency, lent the mountain fury an inspiring quality unknown on more accessible ranges. The rough hair of our woollen balaclavas was shortly a mass of icicles, especially around the mouth. The wind-proof cloth of our breeches went stiff as a board and our chests were encased in breastplates of white armour; even our eyebrows and lashes were iced, and we felt thankful we had no moustaches.

To add to these discomforts we began to have trouble in navigation. Our compasses especially caused us vexation of mind, being unreadable on the move and hard to read at the halt, against the battering of the wind. At the head of the Garrachoire, and despite my compass having a floating dial, I seemed to spend hours (they were probably minutes) helplessly watching its gyrations. The visibility had fallen to almost nil, and for twenty minutes thereafter we could not see beyond our boots. Below, above, on all sides, was the impalpable writhing whiteness, which left the eye nothing to focus on, nothing to which one could relate one's own body. The result was that our sense of balance was quite upset. We had the sensation of floating rather than walking, an illusion repeatedly shattered as the heel jarred into invisible depressions or the toe stubbed on hummocks. At the moments when visibility improved we had great difficulty in distinguishing large objects far off from small ones a few yards away. The compass by itself was thus well-nigh useless.

We met the situation by Mortimer's halting in front, when I took bearings on his figure, or in his general direction when he disappeared. Then I went forward on the correct line and passed him by thirty paces. He, meantime, had rejoined the proper line and was sighting on my own figure. We thus advanced one at a time. The system was slow but the alternative was aimless wandering.

We passed what we hoped was the south top, and were henceforth moving above four thousand feet and exposed to the full wind force. To give the eye a focusing point the first man threw snowballs in front, but they were not satisfactory and occasionally we found a rucksack better. When cast ahead it could be seen as a darker blur through the whiteness. On the other hand we had to be careful not to lose it, for when we had recourse to this device the plateau was seething. The noise deafened us. Added to the pulsing blast of the storm on the mountain flanks, now louder in one place and now lower in another, was the fierce instant *swish* of loose powder sweeping across the snow-fields, rising in pitch by hoarse shocks, then diminishing to its *swish—swish—swish*.

In these conditions, and wading through a snow morass, we found accurate compass-work excessively trying. There was sore temptation to skimp the task and take a chance—say to take bearings only once in five minutes—but we stuck to our wearisome routine determinedly. At what he thought was close to the second top Mortimer stopped and shouted in my ear:

'Back to Garrachoire—wind behind us—down to Corrour.'

That was the third and last of the day's temptations. The Corrour bothy lay low in the Lairig Ghru. We could rest there until the following morning, for we had food enough for two days.

Such a move was alluring, for the wind was not merely violent but unconscionably cold. I wore a woollen vest, a flannel shirt, and four sweaters beneath a windproof Grenfell jacket, and still felt frozen. The wind pierced my balaclava, which had to be reinforced with a scarf. My hands were numb under two layers of heavy woollen mits. And Mortimer, who delayed putting on his second pair of gloves until too late, suffered later from frost-bite.

We very nearly took the lure, for the uproar of the storm seemed to hammer all thought out of our heads, and only by an effort of will could we bring our brains to reason. Presently, however, sanity prevailed and we saw the situation in its true light. We were experiencing not a winter blizzard but a spring blizzard, which would last only a day. To stampede down to Corrour would be childish. The true Cairngorm blizzard blowing for several days from the south-east was a very different matter; even then the bothy could be more a trap than a refuge; for down there, surrounded by high mountains and hourly deepening snow, with increasing cold and a dwindling food supply, we might simply be weakened and then caught by a second and killing storm. That had happened to Baird and Barrie—and to others. It is best to fight a battle when one's vigour is unimpaired.

We pressed on and had travelled one hour forty minutes from Angel's Peak when we began to feel anxious about the north top. For the last mile from the south top I had been counting my paces to avoid overshooting the mark, point 4,036, which we assumed to be only an undulation on the rolling plateau. Mortimer in addition had kept a time check, reckoning our speed at a little more than a mile an hour. In view of our staggering and broken progress we had disturbing doubts of these calculations, without which we should yet have been lost. When we had gone the correct distance there was no sign of any top.   Visibility was thirty feet.   We went further, returned, went off at right angles.   No use.   It was suggested that we separate and search independently, but the proposal was vetoed. Our search for the top might develop into a more anxious search for each other.   There was nothing for it but to bestow full confidence on our own estimates.   There being no top in sight anywhere around, we agreed to assume that we stood on it.

Our final bearing was now three-quarters of a mile easterly. A small northerly error in angle subtended thus far would lose us the summit.   Therefore to avoid landing in trouble by passing it to the north, we decided to bear south of it to the broad target of the eastern precipice, from which we could follow a sure line to the cairn.   We left the north top at five-forty p.m. Fifteen minutes later we stopped to rope up; in thirty minutes I reckoned we were very close to the cliffs.   They must be less than a hundred yards away.

I happened to be in front just then, and it became my chief duty not to fall through a snow cornice.   Therefore I began to sound any doubtful step with my axe-spike.   Whenever Mortimer saw what I was about, he stopped me and said that his hands had become too dead to hold a rope in emergency.   I had already guessed that and was not alarmed, for I could trust myself to find a cornice when I came to it, but to ease his mind we switched the rope and I went to the rear.   At first he was able to continue without probing, then visibility shrank to a few feet as great waves of wind strove to sweep us off the plateau.   As though prospecting for crevasses on an upper glacier, he now thrust in his spike before each step.   Five minutes later I saw him stop and retire a pace.   He turned to me with a yell and a flourish of his axe.   He had found the cliffs, and as it happened, saw the lip from a distance of three feet.   We turned north to the summit.

As daylight ebbed the snow-fields were pervaded by an unutterable gloom, like the grey twilight of interstellar space. We wasted no time at the cairn, which we reached at six-fifteen p.m.   A storm by day in the Cairngorms is a hard experience.

A storm by night would have killed us. Rarely have I been more exhausted and numbed with cold, which now gripped not only the extremities but the whole body. Our one anxiety was to get off the mountain. The snow had stopped falling before we turned down the long east ridge to the bealach, but the fury of the wind had no whit abated and the whole world for us was a raging chaos of wheeling and scudding drift. That anywhere on earth there could be such cheerful comfort as a hot bath, an old arm-chair before a fire, or better by far, urns of steaming tea, seemed but the golden fantasy of some Miltonic Eden. We felt the gross illusion that here were the only realities of a mechanistic universe—bleak rocks, bitter wind, snow, and withering cold.

We had gone five hundred feet down the ridge when its east flank fell back sufficiently to allow an easy route to the Lairig. The edge was heavily corniced. I smashed the overhang with an axe and cut a foothold or two on the wall below. Five minutes later we went careering down the snow slope. Our blood spun to the swoop of standing glissades, but the surface was rough and we suddenly reverted to the vulgar sitting position, which gave an increase in speed and a decrease in pleasure, for our boots sprayed an icy back-wash into our faces. In a gratifyingly short space of time we were sitting on a boulder in the Lairig Ghru. We rested only long enough to untie the rope, then climbed to the top of the pass. The time was seven-thirty p.m.

That nine-mile descent to the Spey!—it went on for ever, down—down—down everlastingly into depths of increasing darkness. When we reached Rothiemurchus it was with something of wonder, a weary surprise rather than thankfulness. Down here the wind merely snuffled round the boulders, but a rousing blast, discharged at judicious intervals, served to jog the memories of three hours ago. Already the wild turmoil far above our heads seemed infinitely remote; and the Braeriach plateau, like some lost continent of the skies, but a legend of a bygone age.

* H

22   *The Evidence of Things Not Seen*

THE MOON WAS NEW-RISEN.   It balanced like a yellow
apple on the black barb of Schiehallion.   The flood of its
mellow light poured far across the moor of Rannoch.   Driving
north from Bridge of Orchy I was obliged, for the first time of
my life, to wear sun-glasses at night.   I can truthfully say that
in three years divided between Asia, Africa, and Italy, each
famed in story for its bright nights, I have seen but one com-
parable to this that I shared with Douglas Laidlaw in December
1939.

Our intention was to climb the Buachaille Etive Mor by its
eastern cliff and we had chanced on the ideal conditions.   By
the time we reached Kingshouse the moon had swept the sky
clear; neither cloud stemmed nor star survived the torrent.   At
a quarter-mile's distance the inn appeared to float upon the
moor, 'whiter than new snow on a raven's back,' and the tops
of the pines were silver-tipped.

After an hour's delay we went down to Coupal bridge in
Glen Etive, whence we crossed the moor to Buachaille.   I had
imagined I knew this mountain under every whim of the elements, yet here was something more than new: for though we
may not postulate absolute beauty of things material, the
Buachaille was less clogged with the pollutions of mortality
than is normally granted to an earthly form.   Therefore let
us speak of the unspeakable, for there is no speech so profitable.
The east face was washed by intense light, so searching that no
shade was cast by ridge or buttress.   All detail merged in the
vastness of one arrowy wall, pale as shadowed milk, impregnably

erect. At the remote apex, a white crest broke like spume on
the high seas of infinity:

> So shalt thou see and hear
> The lovely shapes and sounds intelligible
> Of that eternal language which thy God
> Utters, who from eternity doth teach
> Himself in all, and all things in Himself.

But I lacked the quick vision of Coleridge. To my unaccus-
tomed eyes the scene at first bore an appearance of unreality;
yet the more I gazed, the more surely I knew that I saw not an
illusion greater than is usual, but truth made manifest: as though
our everyday world had been a dull image in the crystal mirror
of Shalott, only here woven on the magic loom by an artist,
one of true intuition, who rejecting inessential things had
selected in masterly economy those precious to the truth, thus
throwing into high relief the hitherto obscured beauty that
underlies the world. Unlike the Lady of Shalott, I failed to
break the spell and gaze straight upon the ultimate reality;
yet the hills that night were big with it; its signs unmistakable.

It is this that Goethe calls 'the open secret.' It is this that
mountaineers style 'the mystery of hills.' Put more broadly, it
is the mystery of the universe, of which the forms of man or
mountain may be likened to veils that reveal its being yet mask
its very essence. Ask Nature what she does and we are
answered, as Faust was answered:

> So at the roaring loom of Time I ply
> And weave for God the garment that ye see Him by.

If the answer be taken to heart our understanding of mountains
is broadened and deepened toward the understanding of all
things created; but the point of its last line strikes home only
when applied to oneself.

Our destination was the base of D gully buttress, where we
arrived at eleven o'clock. We swarmed up the first few hundred
feet, and roped where the plinth narrows for the upward drive.
All around the rocks were stark, scrubbed clean as the decks of

a battleship, the shade of palest ash.   Near at hand they sparkled with a coarse crystalline glitter, never seen by day.   It is affirmed by Chesterton that one is sometimes uplifted as though by trumpet-call not so much by the beauty of Nature as by her generous and defiant ugliness.   'Has the poet,' he inquires, 'for whom Nature means only roses and lilies, ever heard a pig grunting?   It is a noise that does a man good.'   This paradox rejoices the true rock-climber.   He is no mountaineer who can look upon the ugly face of those age-gaunt crags, and fail to feel their rough honesty go straight to his heart, there to kindle sympathy to a flame of delight.   In their mere proximity there is happiness.   A contentment of the same kind, if less high, as that where the friendship of two men ripens until the delight of simple companionship removes the need of speech.

We met no rock-work that posed a problem greater than that of daytime.   But the cold, steadily growing since sunset, gripped the world in frost, which we countered by wearing gloves as far as the one severe pitch of the ridge.   Bare hands and numbed fingers were then the order of the night.

The remainder of the ridge took shape as an attenuated staircase.   Half-way up the weather changed abruptly.   An icy wind whipped out of the north, and a great cloud mass, which must have been piling up unseen to the north-west, suddenly tumbled over the summit.   With one mighty roll it engulfed us.   Snow began to fall, at first idly, with a soft crepitation, then fast and silently.   The wind rose.

The light above the buttress was still surprisingly good, so we traversed northward on to the crest of Crowberry ridge. With mist writhing about us and snow shrouding the rocks, we flitted up the Tower like phantoms in a phantom world.   On top of the Tower the wind died and the snow stopped.   The fog hung dense and still.   Well, I thought, we had enjoyed a splendid night-climb, but we must now forgo all hope of a still finer prize.   However, we had come for the mountain, not for the rock-climb alone, so down we went to the Tower gap and up the lofty brow to the cairn.   The mist at the summit

BIDEAN NAM BIAN

Westward from the summit of Buachaille Etive Mor

was bright and pearly. It seemed to be thinning, and our dead hopes stirred in the first pangs of resurrection. Perhaps . . .? Who knows . . .?

We sat down to it.

Just a quarter of an hour: then the clouds began to stir uneasily, rent by deep internal stress. Caverns, vast as mountain corries, swirled open and closed. Yet not a breath of wind touched my cheek. The effect was tantamount to the supernatural: I understood as not hitherto what strange emotion quickened the Ancient Mariner when his sails filled and no breeze blew. The caverns widened—deepened—the mist sank to the Tower and the clear moon burst from a clear sky.

The cloud bank was now stabilized at three thousand feet, its spread fleece flowing to every horizon save the south. We looked out upon the glimmering surge as though from 'magic casements, opening on the foam of perilous seas, in faery lands forlorn.' Through the swell of the tumbling billows projected the iceberg islands of Argyll and Lochaber. As the Corellian devil observed, hard frost, like hard times, brings noble work into prominence. And this blanketing of intervening country, combined with the dazzle of their frozen snows, drew all the peaks unnaturally close in a fantastic optical illusion. Nevis looked but a stone's throw, and Bidean nam Bian a practicable leap.

Within an hour the cloud-sea broke up. When the preliminary boilings and heavings had subsided, the surface caved into maelstrom, spraying up streamers of shining mist, which shrivelled to tenuous wraiths, and like the ghost in *Hamlet* 'shrank in haste away.' On every hand the entire mass then dispersed and swiftly rose far above our heads. The final state was a high ceiling of widely deployed cumulus, still as becalmed galleons. But the Mamore and Nevis peaks retained their own bank, and seen now in correct perspective, looked for all the world like a flashing necklace, flung down carelessly on a cottonwool pad. Nor had we ever realized what teeming waters spatter the moor of Rannoch, until we saw these hosts of white

eyes upturned, calmly looking to the moon.   Like them we
waited:

> With heart as calm as lakes that sleep
> In frosty moonlight glistening,
> Or mountain rivers, where they creep
> Along a channel smooth and deep
> To their own far-off murmurs listening.

That was our heart's desire—to wait, to wait for we knew not
what.   Nor did our instinct err.   For we had yet to learn that
from this inner stillness, which lifts the mind far beyond the
imperfect offices of prayer and praise, comes the great flight of
the spirit: and its apprehension of glory and beauty eternal.

But the wings do not grow of their own accord.

Toward four o'clock in the morning we returned to Glen
Etive.   Our most sanguine expectations had been met; our
eyes feasted and our hearts elated.   We had set out in search
of adventure; and we had found beauty.   Thus we had found
them both in their fuller sense; for in the architecture of hill
and sky, as in great art and music, there is an everlasting harmony with which our own being had this night been made one.
What more may we fairly ask of mountains?   None the less,
I came down from the summit filled with the acute awareness
of an imminent revelation lost; a shadow that stalked at my side
ever more openly among the hills.   Something underlying the
world as we saw it had been withheld.   The very skies had
trembled with presentiment of the last reality; and we had not
been worthy.

Those fairest forms of the mountain way—are they all that is
spread out for us to read on the high places of the earth?   Something in that night cried out to us, not low, nor faltering, but
clear, true, urgent—that this was not all: that not half the
wonder had pierced the clouds of our blindness; that the world
was full of a divine splendour, which must be sought within
oneself before it might be found without: that our task was to
see and know.   From the deeps of the earth to the uttermost
star above the whole creation had throbbed with a full and new

life; its music one song of honour to the beautiful; its word, 'Holy, holy, holy, Lord God of hosts, heaven and earth are full of thy glory. . . .' And we knew, as surely as men know anything on earth, that the implacable hunter had drawn close. Turn where we would, there was nothing anywhere but He. One's ear caught the ringing of His footstep; and one's eye, 'gleams like the flashing of a shield.'

> At last I heard a voice upon the slope
> Cry to the summit, 'Is there any hope?'
> To which an answer peal'd from that high land,
> But in a tongue no man could understand;
> And on the glimmering limit, far withdrawn,
> God made Himself an awful rose of dawn.

23

Rocks and
Realities

I HAVE ALWAYS FELT that Leslie Stephen's celebrated shaft missed its mark when he identified as 'the one point of superiority' of Scottish mountains their leagues of heather. There are two hundred and seventy-six mountains in Scotland. To any one who sees them at all seasons, their unique virtue becomes that wedding of rock and water portrayed to such perfection down the western seaboard from Cape Wrath to Arran; less perfectly but still notably among the rivers and lochs of the central and east highlands. In heather there is much to admire; of its season I have no good to say. The climax arrives in August, of all months in the year the most noxious to Scottish mountaineers, when the great midge plague has stricken the valleys and every hill is oppressed by a sultry atmosphere. That season, thank God, is brief! The Atlantic and the lochs, on the other hand, are with us at all times, of all mountain settings the most brilliant, matched in none of the twenty foreign lands I have seen for myself, and the true point of distinction.

The varied charms of water make deep and universal appeal. And they are common to all hill country. Whether it be water storming in frolic under a highland bridge, or at peace in brown rock - pools, or an evening tide - rip ablaze with sun-start, or morning hills in a still tarn, the endless forms of contrast are met in the valleys. One need not climb to see them.

But if not more subtly, yet still more greatly moving is the sweep of sea and loch that greets a man treading a western mountain-top. His wider view I hold more noble than the valley scene. It is the setting of Scottish hills amid broad or winding waters that gives rise to a particular form of beauty which I have given up all hope of seeing equalled.

However, it is by our physical presence on the cliffs and ridges, by the exploration of their gullies no less than by wandering the plateau and wooing the waters, that we come fully to know these mountains and win the high reward of intimacy. To him that hath shall be given, always it is thus; through the very steps that a man takes by reason of his love of hills, there is added to him the joys of a sport.

Thus it is of vital consequence to note that though mountaineering abounds in healthy adventure, it implies to a mountaineer much more than sport. If he is a young beginner, as I was, or not much given to thinking, he has not the slightest idea what that 'more' is. He cannot imagine what has happened to him. He feels only a great hunger to know mountains wholly, in their every aspect; he is urged from within by some overpowering need, which in its earliest stages, when he is walking the hills for the first time, can make him truly sick with the mountain fever. For mountains can be at first all life to him. He is driven to explore every part of them, in their every mood, and in doing that he schools himself in the technique of climbing: which is undoubtedly a sport. Moreover, that sport is packed with fun, excitement, skill, and the sternest kinds of test, the most soothing rest of body and contentment of mind. Who will blame a fallible man if he lose sight of the further goal, or falsely identify it with the sport? He may even be so led astray as to contract a disease, whose symptoms are a man's 'peak-bagging' with an eye to records, or his making new routes with an eye to his reputation. The instinct to explore is here perverted.

Of what real benefit is the original, overmastering desire? To what good end is it directed? By what way do we get there?

It is no adequate answer to say that we get there by mountaineering. If a traveller should ask us the way to Cape Wrath, he is little wiser if we reply: 'By travelling.' Yet, however much like a traveller to the unknown, a mountaineer in his early days is given, at least once, a sure indication of the way. For his journey's end is like a magnetic pole to which instinct is a sensitive compass needle.

That first blind instinct to know mountains wholly is, I think, both good and true. But the most obvious implication is most apt to be missed: that a man has need of a catholic taste if he would arrive at his end. Here analogy breaks down. For the ways are not one but many, and I hope clearly to show that all should be followed. On moor and plateau and upon summer rocks the ways are widely known. Therefore, as a first step, I wish to shed more light on the snow and ice way on the cliffs —it is grievous that the best mountaineering in Scotland should be greatly neglected. I shall be practical. Thereafter we may arrive as it were upon a promontory, from which we may see the ways and the end and find our questions answered.

I cannot claim to know mountains better at one season than another. However, I have not disguised the truth that I prefer winter to summer mountaineering; for it is in winter that the Scottish hills excel. No one who has seen the skyward thrust of a snow peak, girdled by its early morning cloud wisp and flushed with the low sun, will dispute with me. Follow a long ridge of encrusted rock to its sunset tower, tread the summit at moon-rise; and you will agree that without that intense experience your life would have been a poorer thing. Such an ascent calls for a technical skill and knowledge more considerable than that demanded by summer rock-work.

To the art of rock-climbing there is added, firstly, the judgment and treatment of snow and ice. As a general rule Scottish snow is surprisingly coherent and not much given to avalanche —one may often ascend soft snow massed upon the crags at angles that would be dangerous in the Alps. One's greatest difficulty is then persuading the snow to support the foot; there is rarely danger of the mass sliding. When the danger is present an experienced mountaineer is protected by an instinctive feeling for the state of the mountain, but that is of no comfort

LOCH HOURN

to the beginner. What every one must avoid like the plague is very wet snow or very dry powder lying in bulk upon ice or slabs. I know of one man who has lively recollection of climbing the Castle buttress of Nevis and finding the upper slabs heavily covered with powder bearing a wind-slab crust. How innocently silken, how inviting it appeared to the unsuspicious eye! He threw a boulder on to the middle surface. For three seconds there was silence. Then he heard the ugliest sound that a mountaineer can hear, a noise like the cutting of cardboard with heavy scissors—and a crack opened across the snow sheet. But crack or no crack, one retires.

A more usual danger is the collapse in spring thaw of water-logged cornices, whose bombardment, with stones intermingled, once routed me from Coire Ardair in April. I was attempting a first ascent of the Centre Post with Dunn and MacAlpine. The day was warm, yet the snow of the gully seemed firm enough. But whatever its appearance of safety we *felt* the mountain to be thoroughly dangerous; every cliff has an atmosphere of its own, and that of Coire Ardair had this day passed out of sympathy with us. Such was our unease that after climbing the first hundred feet without difficulty we unanimously agreed to withdraw. We were later walking down the corrie when the cliffs seemed to tumble like a pack of cards. We had to take to our heels and fly for our lives.

The cornice menace especially applies to Nevis, whose summit lies close to the level of perpetual snow, and where cornices may attain a thickness of forty feet. But they are infrequently higher than ten feet at the gully exits. The conditions under which they collapse are unmistakable. The mountain drips. And under such conditions I once saw two Welshmen dance upon the cornice of Tower gully in June. The mist was dense, and they were inclined to resent my remonstrances, until they discovered that the drop below was not ten feet but upward of two thousand. The fall of cornices is not necessarily delayed till spring. As a general rule they are safe while frost prevails, but are always liable to collapse in whole or part after heavy

snowfalls.   They become overweighted, have not time to con-
solidate and freeze, and down they come.   Several accidents
have been caused by climbers going to the gullies too promptly
after blizzard.

In theory, it is a straightforward matter to pass judgment on
doubtful ice.   Either it is too thin or too brittle or it is not.
In practice, there is sometimes acute difficulty in deciding
whether the danger signal has appeared.   In a groove below
the crest of Crowberry ridge, for example, I suffered a minute's
agony of doubt at the base of a thirty-foot wall of brittle ice.
Ten feet underneath, Mackenzie belayed me with an ice-pick
driven into a four-inch tongue of snow-ice, and close behind
him the groove bent over the chasm of Crowberry gully.
I resolved the doubt, and went up with a safety margin as fine
as one can justifiably accept.   This situation is unusual, but
that problem is not; each man must judge for himself, and the
moment he feels unable to give a verdict he is defeated.   He
must acknowledge defeat and go down.

In these several incidents we may find a simple guide to action
after judgment.   Prudence is not a goddess, to be worshipped
—least of all in youth: or sea and air would yet be unnavigated,
no man ever have shared his last crust, or climbed a mountain.
But there are times when we must pay her tribute, when to do
otherwise is stupidity.   It is the greater honour to a mountaineer if he retire rather than overreach his skill or his day's
form, or presume upon the forbearance of a mountain in bad order.

In the treatment of high-angle ice, technique varies according
to the quality of the ice; upon that I touched lightly in de-
scribing S C gully.   Elaboration of the problem can serve no
purpose; one can learn to cope with iced rock in only one
school.   The delight of such climbing springs both from exercise of muscular skill and deliberate engineering of the route,
a craft that gives satisfaction to mind and body alike, that
strengthens mental energy and self-reliance—craft exercised both
in detail on gully pitches and in greater scale over the breadth
of a snow-bound ridge or buttress.   Upon these, the best

THE MOUNTAINS
South Cuillin

winter route may follow a line of least resistance very different from the best summer route.   Errors in the art of route selection have led not a few parties into benightment or near escape therefrom, even upon climbs well known in summer.   I have described such an error and escape of my own on the North buttress of Buachaille, which as winter rocks go is not hard, and the moral of which is that in winter a mountaineer has much greater need of an alert intelligence, especially where no difficulty is anticipated.

There is further added to summer rock-work the winter merit that no route is the same twice.   The accumulation and condition of snow and ice vary enormously from month to month. The most remarkable change I have seen was the transformation of Garrick's shelf between my first visit, when the rocks were swamped in soft snow, and my second three months later, after blizzard, thaws, and frosts, when the shelf was a mass of clear ice five hundred and fifty feet long.   Likewise, on our second visit to the Deep-cut chimney of Stob Coire nam Beith, we encountered an ice ribbon of two hundred feet.   The change from snow had occurred within three weeks.   Conversely, a short severe gully may by heavy snowfalls become in a few days an easy and straightforward snow slope.   I have seen such a fate overtake Gardyloo gully, normally a very hard climb. In short, one can state no rule about the effect of snow and ice on rock.   Impossible summer rocks may become climbable; moderate rock unclimbable: a week later the reverse may hold good.

Each winter ascent thus affords to the mountaineer a pleasure fully equal to the rare ascent of a new route in summer.   He sets out in the morning to explore unknown difficulties, amidst scenery more splendid than in summertime, and ever new; he is awakened by suspense quickly to see and long to remember a score of details, hitherto unregarded, of beauty near and afar; his is the joy of a hard-fought climb, and when doubt of the issue is at last removed, the elation of winning the only true victory—one that cannot be taken for granted.

Suspense lends keen interest to the shortest route, but is there naturally of short duration, and if need be retirement is simple. On the long gullies and ridges, say between six hundred and two thousand feet, in which Scotland abounds, doubt of the issue raises serious consideration of time. Let a mountaineer have as much experience as you please; he will be able to form a general estimate of snow and ice conditions, but he cannot foresee their detail at the various points of a long route. He cannot say that a fifty-foot groove, a thousand feet above, is lined with frozen snow and not brittle ice, that the slabs beyond it are coated in snow-ice and not thin glaze. Therefore, upon what he finds but could not foresee may in extreme case depend success or defeat, or whether his climb take five hours or fifteen. And on winter days there are only eight to twelve hours of daylight.

Consequently, where a man frequents long hard routes he is sooner or later bound to complete one or two of them in darkness. In that event he has nothing to fear; should he be unfortunate enough to lack moonlight he has nevertheless a competent party, electric torches, and spare batteries. Without these no winter ascent of rock should be ventured.

By means of torches a strong party can climb by night well-nigh anywhere—provided the line of the route be known. That applies less to summer rock than to snow and ice, upon which torchlight is adequate as sunlight. The snow shines brightly, every detail of an ice-pitch stands clear, and one can no more make a mistake than in broad day. Climbing in a gully by this method is particularly simple, elsewhere it is slower. Yet these facts are not widely appreciated. It is to be borne in mind that a torch is of no avail for route selection on the indefinite rock of a difficult buttress. The route may indeed be very hard, but must be well known or clearly defined.

Only twice have I been obliged to complete climbs by torch-light. The moon has favoured me. I have more frequently begun climbs by torchlight, when sun or moon were laggard in rising. Need of a torch at the day's end is often avoidable by an early start; one hour lost in the morning, which never seems important at the time, can most readily lead to the loss of several hours in darkness. But not all the precepts of the Stoics have ever got a man out of bed sooner than his nature inclined him. One makes pious resolutions. Always one will improve next time. But in fact, only the certainty of a good climb does the trick.

These latter sentences do not apply to the Alps, where snow conditions greatly worsen in the afternoon.

If a younger climber with hopes set on winter ascents should read some of the routes I have described, he may be visited by qualms on the score of danger. My very last wish is to discourage him. From what I know of his breed there is little risk. I can assure him that some of the climbs were handpicked for description because the prevailing conditions were unusually difficult; that there is no need to go straight to the hardest routes and every need to start on the easier. The ability to cope with advanced winter climbing derives simply from training and practice. Undoubtedly it has sometimes every appearance of danger, which I regard as an unmixed blessing, for danger is a good teacher, and as Hazlitt says, 'makes apt scholars.' It is that which at first we cannot do which in the end is done to perfection. We improve by constant practice.

In Scotland there are easy snow gullies by the hundred. When, and not until, a climber can conduct himself safely both on summer rock and on straightforward snow like that of the centre gully of Beinn Laoigh, or many of the Nevis gullies, he can hardly do better than visit such snow-covered rocks as the Curved ridge and the North buttress of Buachaille, the crags of Stob Coire nam Beith and the Aonach Eagach ridge. In almost any high corrie he will find a well-iced crag or boulder, upon which he can first practise, as I did, cutting holds in ice.

He will find the work fascinating and not so hard as he thought; he will speedily learn how to space his holds, and that he must never impatiently outstrip his handhold, leaving himself on foothold only—the frequent and fatal error of the novice.   Then let him go with a good party to the upper couloir of Stob Ghabhar in the Blackmount.   He will, between January and April, find an ice-pitch there, which may vary in size from ten to thirty feet, and can watch his leader cut ice for anything from twenty minutes to one and a half hours.   It is a very good gully, but too short to rank as a first-class winter ascent. On no account must he neglect practice in the arts of roping down and climbing down.   With such experience behind him he could well be led up the big climbs by a strong party.

Where the members of a climbing team have followed such a course of training, it is difficult to see that any element of danger peculiar to winter climbing need arise.   Danger is a relative conception—relative to the strength of the party, to its skill and judgment.   Crowberry ridge, for example, is never dangerous in winter.   But a weak or careless party might commit suicide by going to it when a strong one would be safe as though strolling in a public park, and that whether it meet success or defeat.   As with snow and ice, so with the grass and loose stones of summer rocks; in themselves they cannot be considered dangerous: one may say only that one party has the skill to deal with them, and that another has not.

The real or objective dangers on home mountains are rare. A falling stone may come at any man—Nevis is again the prime culprit.   No judgment can forecast the date of collapse of a Cuillin overhang.   It has been there for fifty thousand years, perhaps, and who shall say it will fall to-day at two-fifteen p.m.? Yet, one collapsed within a minute of my passing over it.   The fall of a cornice is sometimes unexpected, but the cornice that sags over a gully in thaw is not truly an objective danger, inasmuch as it is avoidable by any one with eyes in his head.

Therefore, if any climb be free from falling stones and snow, to describe it as 'dangerous' is to make an unmeaning noise. One may say that a named route would be dangerous for a named party, but that is a very different thing.   My conclusion is that for a well-trained climber acting within his powers, which is simply common sense, there is little danger in Scottish mountaineering.

Everywhere, however, there is the appearance of danger. He is indeed an unimaginative man who, upon the last pitch of Crowberry gully, can look a thousand feet down the snow-caked walls and not think what would happen if he let go. His finger, thereupon, tightens on its ice-notch, for there is no doubt that he loves life. Notwithstanding, he has come to one place where vigorous elasticity of nerve and precision of movement are required to preserve life. It is plain that if he love life he still more loves living—otherwise he would keep to a steam-heated room, eat to diet, and at measured intervals perform physical jerks to forestall the atrophy of his precious limbs. The joy of life will never be measured in terms of comfort and security, nor will the debased currency of the latter buy a true friend. Let us admit, therefore, that together with many another important element, seeming danger ensures that on mountains, more than elsewhere, life may be lived at the full.

Of all apparent dangers, there are none more boisterous and bracing than swift weather changes. The Scottish mountains afford a man ample opportunities of testing his body to the limits of endurance. In the Cairngorms high cloud can change in an hour to low cloud and a snow-laden hurricane. In Glencoe, Lochaber, Skye, and Wester Ross, I have seen changes little less violent occur in less than half the time. They often come at sunset, when mountaineers are nearing the top of a long route. If a party should then be beaten by glazed slabs, a rare misfortune so high, then each man will speedily discover of what stuff he and his comrades are made. If he is blessed with such companions as I have had, he is not likely to be disappointed.

When a leader turns down from the last impossible rocks, and hears the rising wind buffet on white-veiled cliffs, fast fading into night, and on looking down, watches his party again and again enveloped in clouds of drift-snow, torn from storm-swept ridges, he may feel, as I have, an instant's suspicion that the prospect is somewhat grim for hope.   An instant later, his rope reminds him that he is tied to men of high heart, that whatever the outcome, they, at least, will not falter.   And in that instant the battle is won.   Everything that is best in a man is called forth by faith in his companions, no less than by storm. For a fit youth is a fighter and a challenge stirs him.   He will shortly exult in the struggle.   And the course of later years will prove that rope 'the surest bond life yields of friendship.'

On the other hand, many a Scottish climb will turn out milder than a climber expected and disappoint him with an anti-climax.   Many a normally hard route may become astonishingly easy, or fall quickly.   Tower ridge has gone in sixteen hours and four and a half hours within the space of the same month. Still more instructive are my two winter climbs on Observatory ridge.   In 1937 we were occupied there for fourteen hours: the rock was smothered in powder-snow.   One year later we went up in six hours; the rock was encrusted with frozen snow. Now, on that second visit the ridge was of great difficulty. I shall ever remember a groove at three thousand five hundred feet that Mackenzie, the undauntable, was inclined to think not justifiable and which wrung startled exclamations even from Bell.   We moved quickly and saved eight hours' time by sole reason of the snow's firmness—especially after entering Zero gully.   Where previously we had had to excavate a foot of powder and for seven hours hew a clear ice-bed, we now met hardest snow.   By changing the lead as each man tired, we in turn cut fast and hard from the shoulder—one and a half hours to the plateau.

It is worthy of record that in the opinion of Bell, who has more than thrice my experience, that climb ranked with the best of his life.   On the several occasions I have tried to write of it, despair at its perfect beauty has consigned my effort to the waste-paper-basket.   The splendid opportunities provided by the Scottish rocks for winter mountaineering are known and used by a mere handful of Scottish climbers.   Once more we are brought to the need of a catholic taste.   Indeed, I can hardly pretend to myself that a man is a true mountaineer unless he knows his mountains winter and summer, on cliff and summit ridge, by day and night, in fair weather and foul. For until then he understands them incompletely; he is still in his novitiate, however expert a specialist.

Of these eight very different aspects and their permutations, it is in winter and by night that the mountains are most studiously avoided, despite that when the peaks are snow-capped and the moon full, visibility of twenty to twenty-five miles is by no means exceptional. Just think what that means. Choose, then, a clear and crackling winter's night; traverse the Aonach Eagach ridge in Glencoe, and you will find there an experience for which you would sacrifice most of your daylight climbs. Better still, if you are alone, as you should be sometimes, go up to the main ridge of the Mamores and walk the shining snow waves that link Stob Ban to the spire of Binnein Mor; only your boot-nails sound on the frozen snow-crust, so that when you stop to listen—and listen—you can hear an utter silence that no one has ever heard in company . . . you will know more of the world's song than may be set forth in books.

The snow specialist, the cragsman, and the hill-walker have chosen to devote themselves to one branch of mountaineering. But the beginner should avoid the trap into which they have fallen; for theirs is not the freedom of the hills, which can be earned only by a true mountaineer. To earn the freedom of mountains one must be able to climb on both rock and snow. Those who hold Bach to be the greatest composer do not for that reason refuse to hear Beethoven. Likewise, the hill-walker should not deny himself the pleasure of rock-climbing, nor the cragsman of snow-climbing. Should they do so, one of the best parts of the mountain world must remain to them unknown.

Rock-climbing is no esoteric sport, and skill is arrived at by simple practice. Difficulty is relative to skill. Thus, if he be accustomed both to difficult rock and the rhythm of long ridges, a climber will scramble on moderate rock with little output of either nervous or physical energy—then, indeed, he may claim the freedom of summer mountains: then there is open to him, by way of example, the greatest day in Scottish mountaineering, the traverse of the Cuillin main ridge. The most enchanting views of corrie and peak, loch and sky, sea and islands, change throughout that epic day with a rapidity unequalled on other ranges, so that again and again one catches beauty unawares. This infinite variety is made possible by the compactness of the twisting ridge, whose sharp edge, tossing in spires or dropping into clefts, acts as a natural curtain, constantly rising and falling to hide and reveal dramatic scenes on either hand; and to which it provides in itself a most noble foreground.

That day cannot be enjoyed by one not a rock-climber in hard training. For such to attempt the ridge is not entirely vain. But he will be robbed by bodily distress of mental reward. His achievement will be a feat. His lost opportunities, countless.

I seem to remember hearing, more than once, that mountaineering serves no useful purpose—and remember, too, rejoicing thereat. It does not increase our bank balances. On the moutains we know ourselves, and others for what we are; and, as Scott said of the Antarctic: 'Here the outward show is nothing, it is the inward purpose that counts. So the "gods" dwindle and the humble supplant them. Pretence is useless.' On mountains a man is brought face to face with his own strength and weaknesses, and these latter he may learn, if he wish, to correct; indeed he has little choice; he is compelled to internal honesty and self-discipline. His body is trained in subordination to the will; for there is no chisel more quick to shape character than storm, hunger, and hard work outfaced. In mountaineering, as in no other sport, his adventures are of the mind as much as of the body. The two go hand in hand. To the music of tinkling ice-chips and scrape of clinkers, and the silence of the summits, together they drive free and are tautened—are relaxed—find peace after toil. And when his mind is toughened he will come clearly to see that defeat is not

THE SUMMIT
The Inaccessible Pinnacle of Sgurr Dearg

failure: from the first he reaps wisdom, but the second he does not acknowledge.

Life is seen detachedly and in proper perspective from the mountain-tops. Whoever climbs cliffs to a summit cairn will find that the joys and sorrows of his everyday life have been left deep below in the valleys; they have not ventured with him to the foot of his mountain; they have been shed off like a husk; and he, the new man, may survey as from afar his daily round of thoughts, errors, resolves, and behaviour with the inward calm of a critic inspecting a stranger. And it is wonderful what a different complexion is then put upon affairs that he thought of consequence. The true is sifted from the untrue, the real from the unreal. In the quiet of this inner detachment his higher self is awakened; it rises above fatigue and discomfort to enjoy beauty, breaks the fetters that enslave it to bodily desires and environment, rules inwardly. Were a man to achieve little else in his life he would none the less, in achieving this, possess a pearl of great price—an undivided mind and the peace that is true freedom. For though we talk much these days of freedom, rare indeed is the man who bestows it on himself.

Even so, not until the threat of war in 1939 did I realize to the full what a wealth of friendship, care-free adventure and beauty the mountains had granted me on my own way, nor what knowledge of other men. Such discoveries came to me again with a strong sense of gratitude on the battle-fields of the Western Desert, and later, in the prison camps of Italy and Germany. Between the vertical crags of Scotland and the horizontal sands of Africa there might seem to be little relation. Yet the discipline I learned on the former applied with value to the latter. As an infantry officer in the shambles of defeat and the prolonged rearguard actions of June 1942, I found no call upon stamina equal to that demanded by Garrick's shelf in the winter of 1936, nor strain of suspense to match that of Observatory ridge in 1937.

But these latter considerations were not what I had in mind when I spoke of gratitude. In the worst days of war there shone most often before my eyes the clear vision of that evening on Nevis, when the snow plateaux sparkled red at sunset, and of Glencoe, when the frozen towers of Bidean burned in the moon.   In the last resort, it is the beauty of the mountain world in the inmost recesses that holds us spellbound, slaves till life ends.

In three years of squalor in overcrowded prison camps, where misery gnawed at men's fortitude, these stored memories heartened me like 'a light for memory to turn to when it wants a beam upon its face'; and youth, somewhat crushed in warfare, revived hope for the future from inexhaustible mountain springs.   That through mountains I have been given not only vivid memories but lasting joys and friendships more priceless than accumulations of gold is no idle theory invented in credulous days of comfort and security, but a sure knowledge won in adversity.

To what end may the mountain way lead?

Strictly, I am entitled to answer only for myself, but being an unexceptional man, I imagine that what I have found true should hold good for others.   Therefore it has been my endeavour to say by what many roads, at unexpected moments in mountain days, one may win fleeting glimpses of that beauty which all men who have known it have been compelled to call truth.   Such, for me, has become the end of mountaineering to which the sport is a means.

Is this an uninspiring or unlikely goal, do you think—is beauty too insubstantial to move a rational man?   Let him behold it but once and thenceforward he must ever seek for it— only in it, wherever it be on hill or low country, can be fulfilled his deepest need; for without beauty his spirit can no more live than his body without food.   Let him be starved of beauty and at once he declines from real being.   The most fleeting glimpse has the power of divine fire to cleanse and to temper; the more lasting, to fill him with this resolve: that henceforth he will take the only way by which he can hope to know its full splendour and to live in its presence.   Then must he become

SEA, HILL, AND CLOUD

practical: *then*, as on hills, he must give up dreams and clear for action. For his hope can be realized.

Mountains here discharge their highest service. A man of balanced intelligence will not make a religion of mountaineering; neither will he fail, by mountains, to be brought face to face with it. Wisdom standeth on the top of high places. From our promontory we look up to the cloud of unknowing that wraps the last height, and from its radiance we know the summit is in sunlight. The way and the goal are before us. To one of exploratory instinct action is irresistible, and he takes to himself the axe of single-mindedness and the compass of his love for beauty. His further ascent is severe, more adventurous than any physical one, dangerous if the route be lost, and the issue sometimes in doubt. In his every upward step is a joy surpassing all that mountains offer. Such a man has understood the schooling of life, and is destined to its fullness.

'I do not say unto you, "Believe this, for it is so," but "Do this." Little by little, as when a man climbs a mountain the earth unfolds beneath him, so for yourselves ye shall see and know, needing no testimony from another, no, not even from ancient scripture. . . . For the Kingdom of Heaven is within you.'

When I looked to the mountains of the future from behind barbed wire, I thought not only of ends but of the ways of striving, for the one adds lustre to the other; not only of solemn hours but of the familiar joys of mountaineering, for in these too there is beauty: dawdling under a blue sky up the crest of a sun-warmed ridge; the irrepressible gaiety of rope-mates, forcing wet slabs in mist and windy rain; stimulating doubts upon the blue ice-bulge in an unclimbed gully; the plunge into a shining tarn; the crackling fire in an inn after blizzard—the beauty of living and of life itself. Of all such days I thought, and before I knew what I was about, of these I found myself writing. In truth, I wrote with no dark design of enlightening others, but because I could not help myself. Bloodshed was forgotten awhile; once again I revelled in wholesome days, when the very air I breathed, in the company of Dunn, Mackenzie, and MacAlpine, of Bell and Donaldson, was that of rollicking adventure; when our mountaineering dreams were turbulent and our hearts high.

On a crisp winter's morning, the advance across Rannoch moor with trusted friends, to attack the snow-bound cliffs of Buachaille Etive Mor, until the axe-shaft, yellow in the sunshine, flashes to the frozen snow below some high gully—and many hours later the steel pick glints in moonlight as a weary arm hews the black ice, not so *very* far from the top; or four thousand feet up, on the north precipice of Nevis, fighting in a gale at dusk to cross the icy gash of Tower gap: *there* lies the true joy of battle, in exhilarating contest with the elements, upon mountains that may be won, yet never conquered; shared by companions who may be defeated, yet whose spirit I have never seen shaken:

> They have the secret of the rocks,
> And the oldest kind of song.

Index

I